IMAGES
of America

BATAVIA AND WILLIAMSBURG

ON THE COVER: In this 1949 photograph, Ralph Fuhr shows his young granddaughter Patricia the *Williamsburg Times* newspaper on the presses. Ralph served as the newspaper's owner and editor from 1920 until the 1960s, when his son D.J. sold it to Charles Danbury and Kermit Smith. (Photograph courtesy of Hazel Arnold.)

IMAGES
of America

BATAVIA AND WILLIAMSBURG

Linda Smith-Walker

ARCADIA
PUBLISHING

ISBN 978-0-7385-9365-4

Published by Arcadia Publishing
Charleston, South Carolina

Printed in the United States of America

Library of Congress Control Number: 2011941683

For all general information, please contact Arcadia Publishing:
Telephone 843-853-2070
Fax 843-853-0044
E-mail sales@arcadiapublishing.com
For customer service and orders:
Toll-Free 1-888-313-2665

Visit us on the Internet at www.arcadiapublishing.com

This book is dedicated to the people of Batavia and Williamsburg, especially Tim and Windy Ferree and Hazel Arnold, who were kind enough to share their photographs and stories; also to my fifth generation grandfather and Revolutionary War private Absalom Smith. After the surrender at Yorktown, he and his wife, Susan, along with their children left New Jersey and headed west to make their home in Williamsburg, Ohio.

—Linda Smith Walker, September 2011

Contents

ACKNOWLEDGMENTS

I am immensely grateful to Tim and Windy Ferree, who helped locate photographs and gather information to tell Williamsburg's story. After an initial source fell through, Tim said, "We'll help because we want you to know there are people in this town who are welcoming and who believe history should be accessible to everyone." Thank you for providing the photographs, the stories, the homemade soup, and the recipe for Comfrey herb tea. Most of all, thank you for your friendship. I am also grateful to the following people: Windy's mother, Hazel Arnold, a lifelong Williamsburg resident who opened her family photograph album, shared her stories, and provided the book's cover photograph; Ron Hill and the Clermont County Genealogical Society, for your permission to use photographs from your archives and for patiently answering all my questions; and Janet Booth for inviting me, a virtual stranger, into her beautiful home, sharing her love of history over a very tasty lunch, and inviting me to speak at the Williamsburg Rotary Club luncheon. Janet and her husband are the newest owners of the historic Underground Railroad home on Gay Street in Williamsburg. It couldn't have a more gracious caretaker, and I look forward to seeing its charm restored.

Thanks to Mark Jordan and Jean Hancock for providing photographs of the A.C. Jordan family, their store, and of Stamm's Garage; Daniel Bainum of the Williamsburg Fire Department for answering all my questions about the department's history and for providing the photograph of the 1935 pumper—it's a beauty; Steve Shinkle for opening up his Batavia store, Hayward House Antiques, after hours and allowing me to scan photographs from his private collection, and for lending me books on the history of Batavia; Molly Cribbet, assistant principal of Batavia Elementary School and daughter of the late Rosanne Hoberg, Batavia's historian, for providing access to her mother's cherished photographs; the Williamsburg Rotary Club for giving me the opportunity to share my enthusiasm for writing about their town; Leslie Jacobs, branch manager of Doris Wood Library in Batavia, for answering a lot of questions, helping me locate information, and showing me (more than once) how to use the microfilm machines; Clermont County Convention and Visitor's Bureau for providing historical information and pointing me in the right direction from the get-go.

Thanks also go to my daughter, Jenny Brock, and my sons, Nick and Matt Walker, for their enthusiasm and love, and to my friends and family, Tim Brock, Emma Walker, Kathy and Bruce Rossell, Chris Wachsmuth, Laurie Cox, Karen Hackman, Jenny Miller, Linda Alich, John and Mary Fajen, Debbie Hill, Diane Method, Stephanie Seals, Marcia Sargent, Lynne Ennis, and Colleen Graber. You are the best cheerleaders a girl could ask for.

Thank you to my editors, Sandy Shalton, Jim Kempert, and Jeff Ruetsche, and everyone else at Arcadia Publishing for accepting my book proposal, offering expert guidance, and giving me the opportunity to tell the stories of two towns very close to my heart.

Introduction

Often described as "Cincinnati's Historic Neighbors," the towns of Batavia and Williamsburg sit within eight miles of each other, both just a few miles from Cincinnati's eastern suburbs off US Route 32 in Clermont County, Ohio. They are small communities, places where flags still wave on Main Street and beautiful blooms spill a profusion of color in the gardens of historic homes. Many of today's town residents can proudly trace their family histories back to the founding fathers of the towns.

In 1796, Gen. William Lytle—who is often referred to as "the Father of Clermont County"—founded Williamsburg, the oldest town in the county. Lytle, a young surveyor from Lexington, Kentucky, quickly recognized the value of the land, which is described in Louis H. Everts's *History of Clermont County, Ohio* as a place "having soil that is fertile and possessing heavily wooded and fine belts of timber." The area offered the chance to begin a new, prosperous life in the Ohio country, and it was soon after the treaty ending Indian hostilities when settlers came by flatboat or wagon while leaving families and friends behind in New Jersey, Virginia, Kentucky, Pennsylvania, and other states.

Ezekiel and Phoebe Dimmitt were the first settlers to come to the beautiful Batavia valley in 1797. They lived there in relative isolation with Phoebe's brothers James and John Gest until 1806, when Charles Robinson, a native of Maryland, came to the area and decided to stay. Others soon followed, including George Ely, Robert Townsley, Richard Doughty, John Wageman, James Hulick, John Weaver Jr., John Slade, Henry Rust, Joseph Fairfield, Leban Brazier, William Brunaugh, and Daniel Duckwall. In 1814, George Ely and attorney David Bryan laid out the lots and streets that would soon become the village of Batavia.

Over the years, buildings in both towns have been razed, replaced, and rebuilt, but many original dwellings still remain. Stories are still told of long-ago events, such as Williamsburg's 11-year-old Lydia Osborne, whose Indian capture sparked a fruitless effort by a reported 1,000 searchers, including famed hunter Cornelius Washburn; and Batavia's George Ely, whose near mythical escape through icy river waters from a pack of wolves reads like a modern day adventure story. Like all places, Williamsburg and Batavia have experienced times of prosperity and periods of decline; however, community pride and respect for the past are qualities that still reside gracefully in these small Ohio towns. You'll recognize these qualities in the neatly painted picket fences, the lively banter at a town meeting, and in the careful tending of beautiful homes and the rich farmland that surrounds each place.

One

Settlers and Citizens

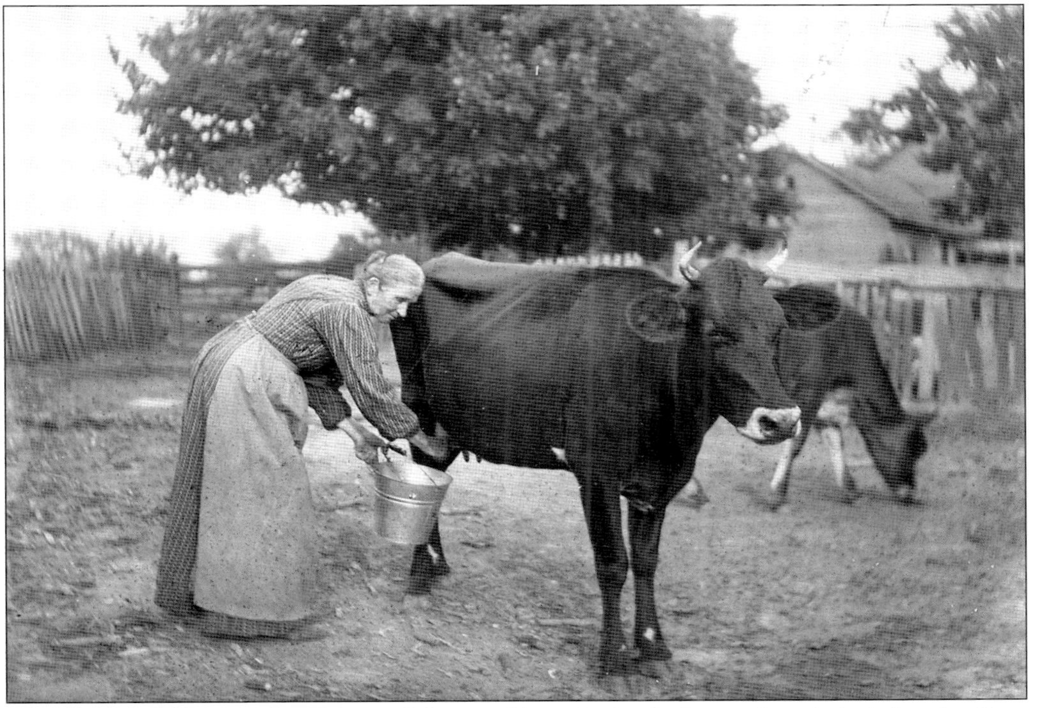

Immediately following the Treaty of Greenville with the Indians after their defeat by Gen. Anthony Wayne, the first settlements in Clermont County were established in 1795 and 1796. According to Everts's *History of Clermont County, Ohio*, "Cabins were put up in every direction and women, children, and goods tumbled into them in their haste to get a start in the new 'Ohio Eldorado.' " Women, like the one in this photograph, had lives filled with hard work from before dawn until long into the evening. "She made up the fires, awoke and dressed her children, made up the trundle bed, shoved it under the big bed, put on the tea kettle and mixed the Indian meal for the Johnny cakes and corn dodgers," writes Everts, and "After supper, she went to the pasture to milk the cows, then put the children to bed, and took again to the ever-busy spinning wheel, and then mended the children's clothes and darn stockings late into the night." (Photograph courtesy of Tim and Windy Ferree.)

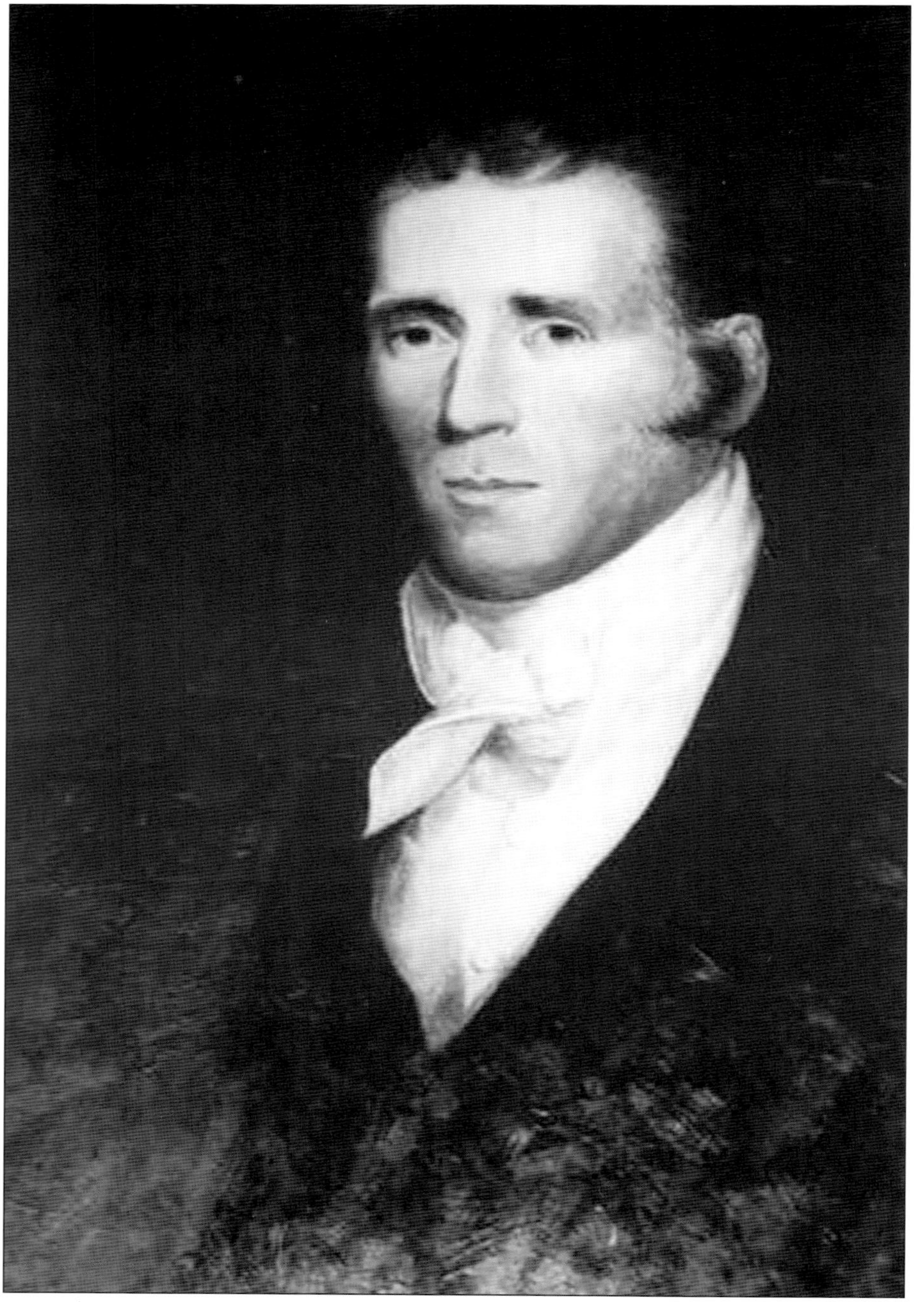

William Lytle Jr. is known as the "Father of Clermont County" for his many contributions to the formation and settlement of the area. In 1779, he came down the Ohio River by flatboat with his family, and by the age of 21, had several years of Indian fighting under his belt. By 1792, Lytle was a deputy surveyor whose work often brought him to Clermont County. In 1796, he laid out the plat for Lytlestown (later named Williamsburg) and reserved 600 acres immediately adjoining the town for a homestead, which he named Harmony Hill. (Photograph courtesy of Wiki Commons.)

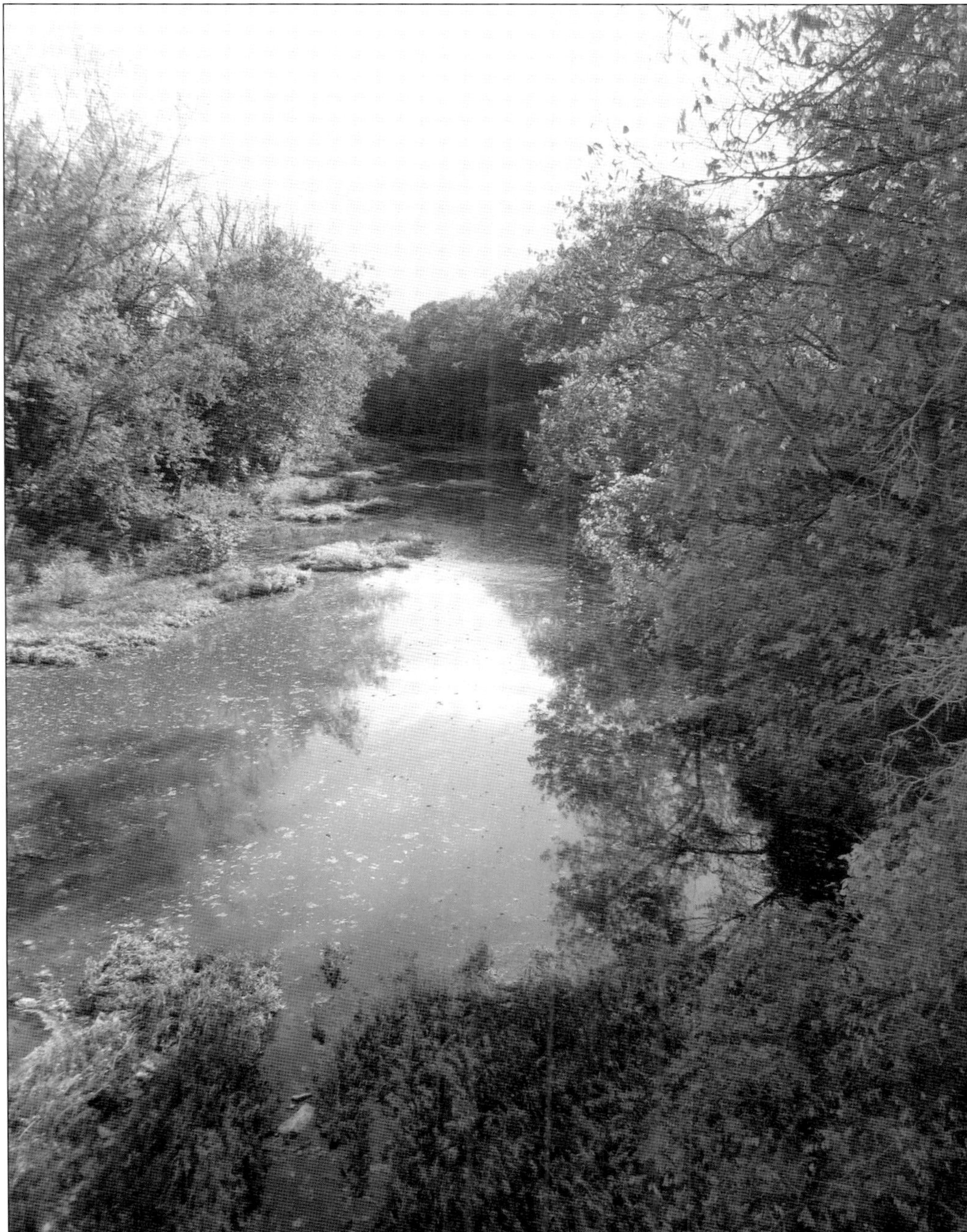

The East Fork is the main tributary of the Little Miami River, a nationally designated Wild and Scenic River. The East Fork begins near Hillsboro, Ohio, and flows through Williamsburg and Batavia before emptying into the Little Miami River. During the late 1750s, the Shawnee Indians established a settlement just north of Williamsburg, which functioned until 1793. In 1811, the site was a Wyandots village, the last Indian settlement in Clermont County. (Author photograph.)

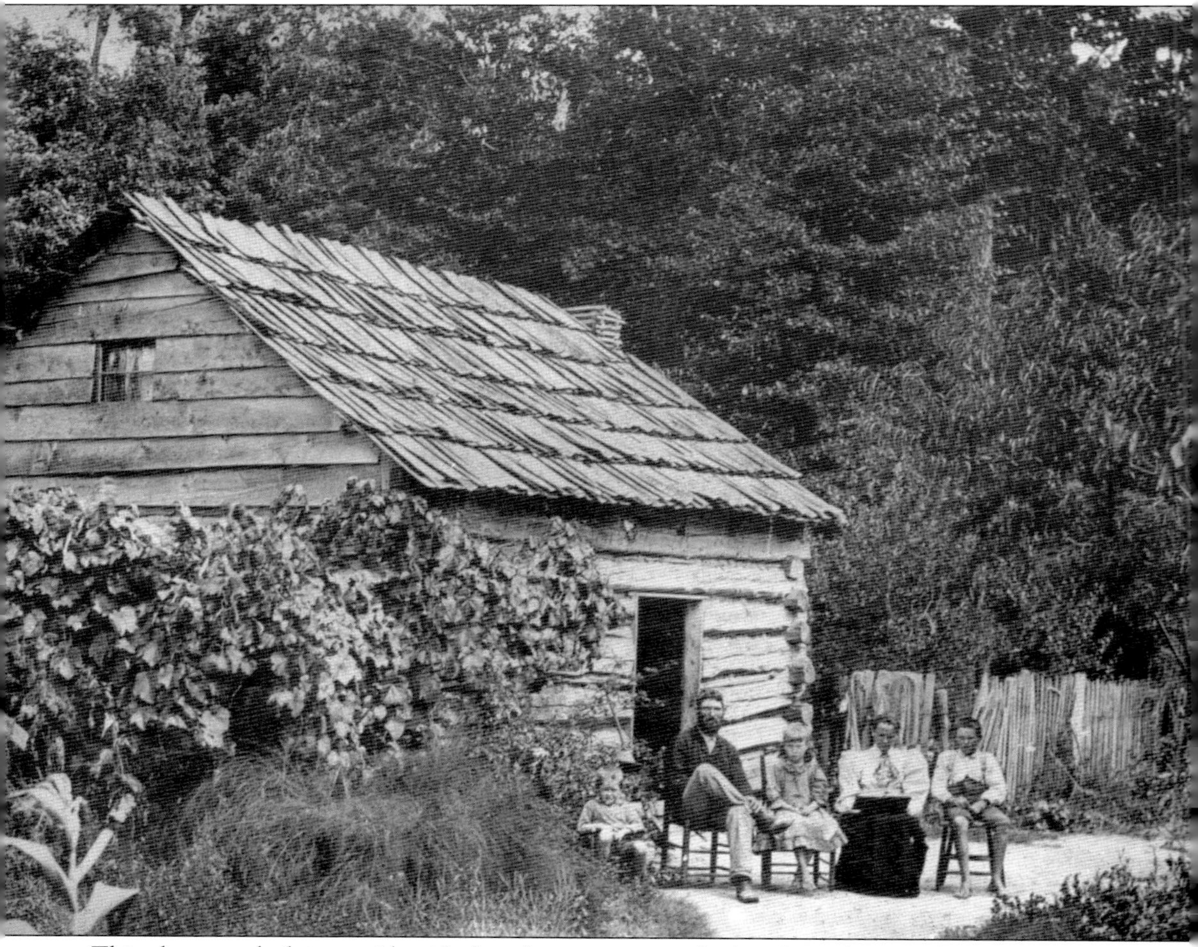

This photograph shows unidentified settlers sitting outside their log cabin in Clermont County. Immigration began between 1795 and 1796 mostly by way of Kentucky, where prospective settlers heard stories told by daring hunters, such as Simon Kenton and Cornelius Washburn, of the bountiful land beyond the Ohio River. While William Lytle was planning Williamsburg, Virginia-born Ezekiel Dimmitt came to the area that would become Batavia. He began clearing land, built a cabin, and returned to Kentucky where, on November 3, 1797, he married Phoebe Gest. He brought his new bride and her brothers James and John Gest back to Batavia, where they settled. (Photograph from the Sharp Collection, courtesy of the Clermont County Library.)

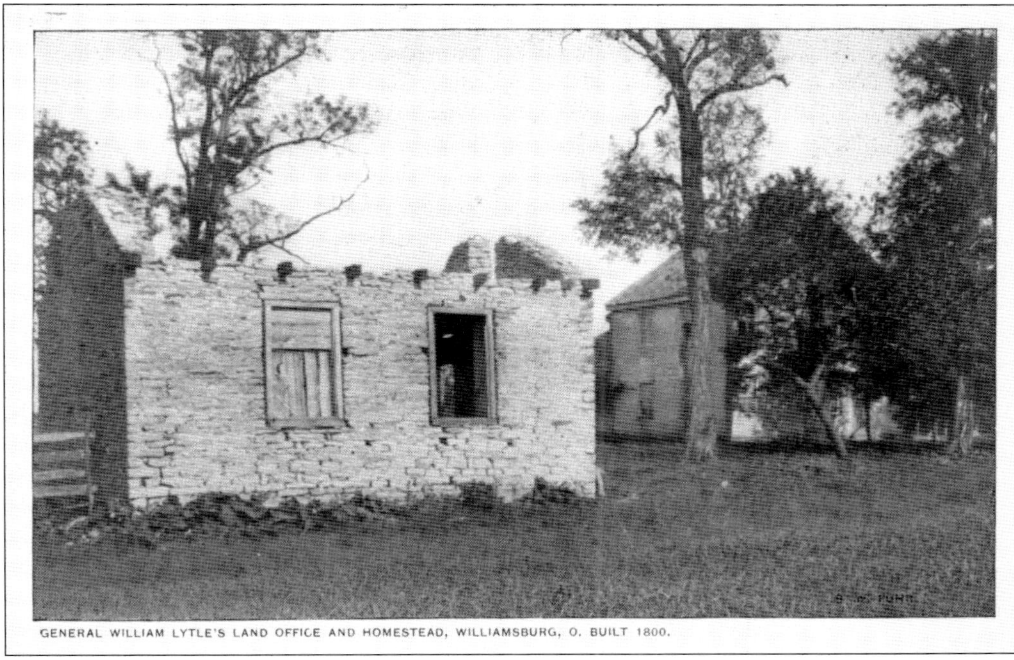

John Charles, the first stonemason in Clermont County, built Gen. William Lytle's land office in Williamsburg in 1800. His land office (pictured) stood on the 600-acre Lytle homestead known as Harmony Hill. In addition to the land office, Lytle established the only post office between Maysville, Kentucky, and Chillicothe, which was Ohio's state capital in 1803. (Photograph courtesy of Tim and Windy Ferree.)

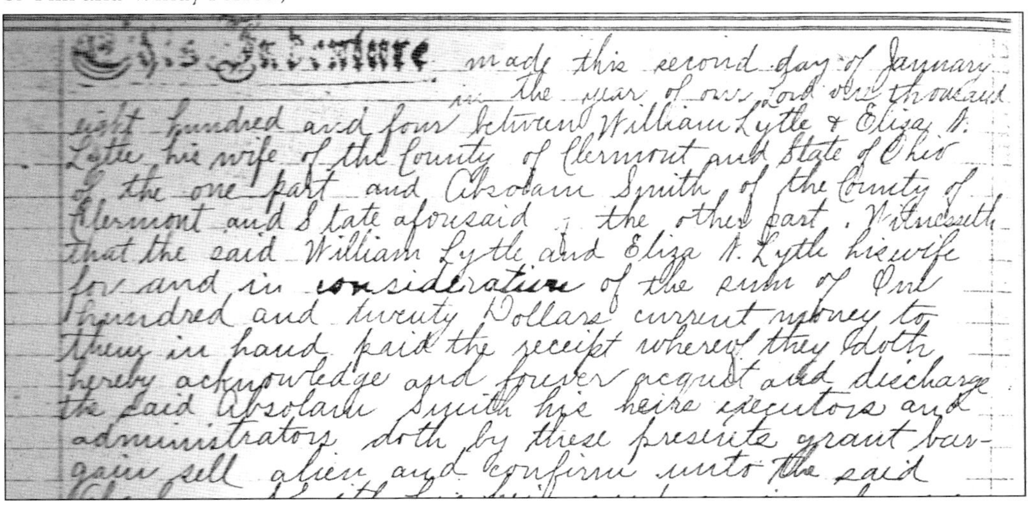

This Indenture made this second day of January in the year of our Lord one thousand eight hundred and four between William Lytle & Eliza A. Lytle his wife of the County of Clermont and State of Ohio of the one part and Absolam Smith of the County of Clermont and State aforesaid of the other part. Witnesseth that the said William Lytle and Eliza A. Lytle his wife for and in consideration of the sum of One hundred and twenty Dollars current money to them in hand paid the receipt whereof they doth hereby acknowledge and forever acquit and discharge the said Absolam Smith his heirs executors and administrators doth by these presents grant bargain sell alien and confirm unto the said

Revolutionary War veterans, such as Absalom Smith of Hunterdon County, New Jersey, saw an opportunity to start a new life in the Ohio country. This indenture, made on January 2, 1804, between Absalom and his wife, Susan, and William and Eliza Lytle details the sale of 50 acres of land "in the County of Clermont and on the waters of the East Fork of the Little Miami." Smith paid $125 for the land. Other Revolutionary War veterans who settled in Williamsburg include Maj. Hugh Maloy, Maj. John McKnight, Ramoth Bunton, Theodore Malott, Adam Snider, James Chambers, James Waits, Charles Waits, and Adam Bricker. (Author photograph.)

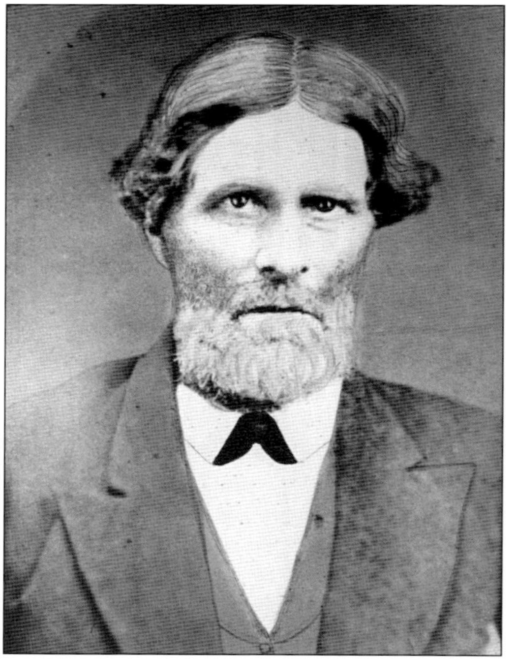

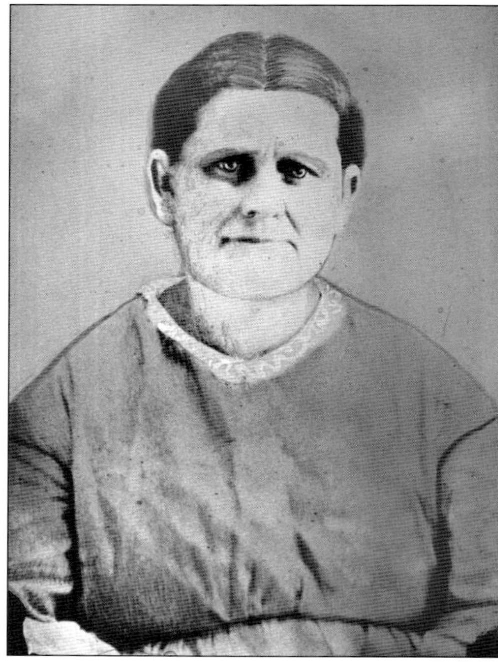

Joab, Absalom Smith's son, and Joab's wife, Hollander Malott, the daughter of Revolutionary War veteran and Williamsburg settler Theodore Malott, raised six children on their farm just outside of Williamsburg. Their son Melancthon (left) married Margaret Hill (right) on October 12, 1848. They raised 12 children, most of whom made their homes in the Williamsburg-Batavia area. (Author photographs.)

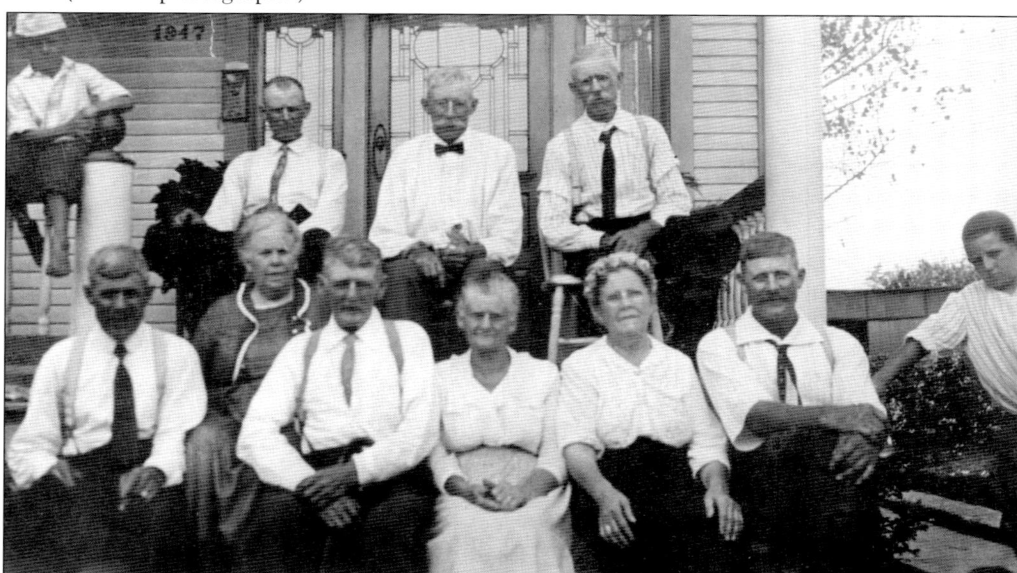

Melancthon and Margaret Hill Smith raised 12 children on their farm just outside of Williamsburg. In this photograph are, from left to right, (front row) David, Martha, Lorenzo, Margaret, Charlotte, and Joseph Smith; (back row) Melancthon "Lank," Richard Sherman, and William Smith; another daughter, Emma, died in 1883 at the age of 15. (Author photograph.)

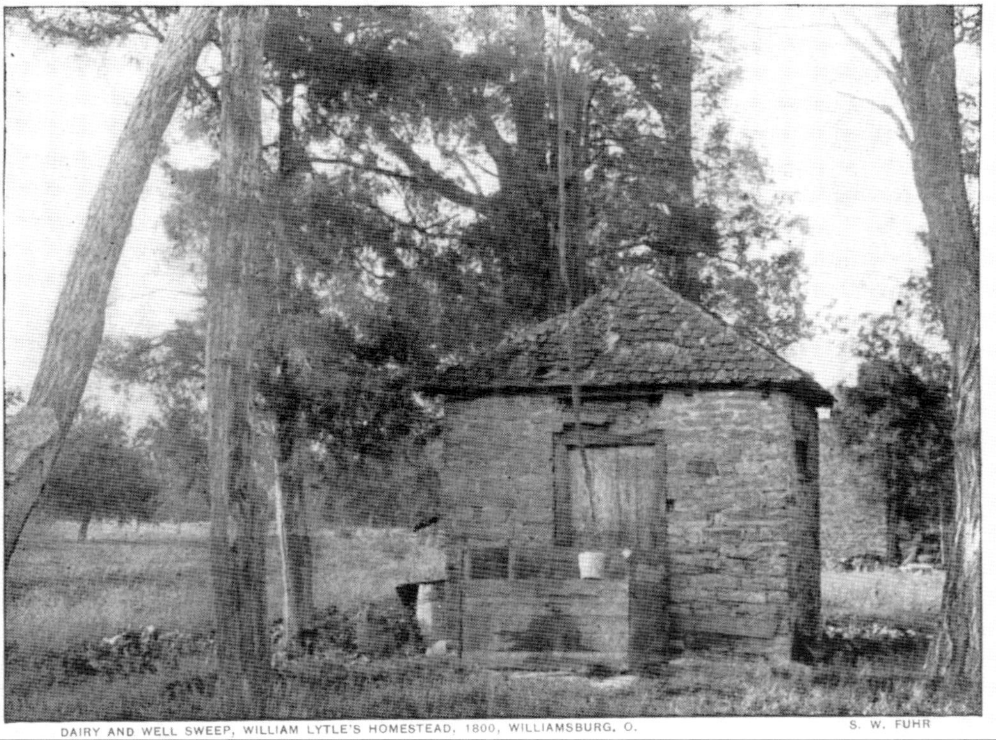

DAIRY AND WELL SWEEP, WILLIAM LYTLE'S HOMESTEAD, 1800, WILLIAMSBURG, O. S. W. FUHR

On February 28, 1798, William Lytle married Elizabeth Stall of Philadelphia—the woman whom he said was "the one to keep him at home." In 1800, he began construction of a home built of square hewn logs covered with clapboards and shingles on the 600 acres he reserved for himself in Williamsburg. The family lived there until 1809, when they moved to Cincinnati to take advantage of new business ventures and better education opportunities for their children. Lytle was very successful in business and became the first president of the University of Cincinnati. (Photograph courtesy of Tim and Windy Ferree.)

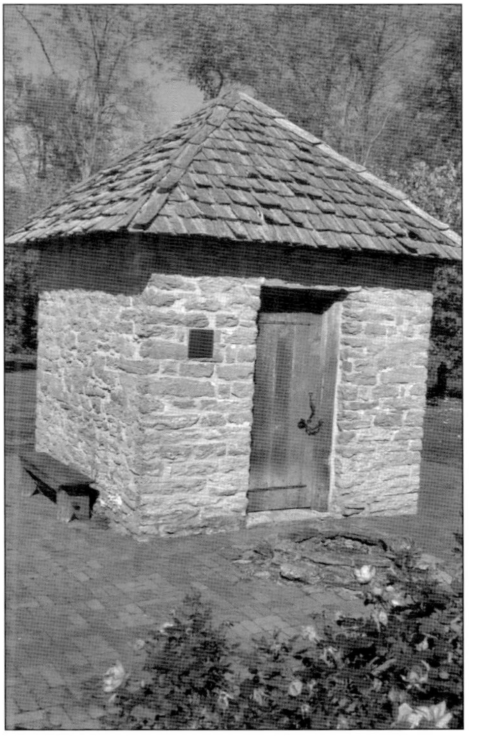

In 1802, John Charles was employed to build and finish a second story on the Lytle home. In the same year, he built this stone spring dairy house near a deep well that had been dug earlier on the property. The well was a popular feature for those who came to the land office, because in those days, deep wells were rare and a drink of fresh water was most welcome. Today, the only building remaining at Harmony Hill is the dairy house, which was renovated by the Harmony Hill Association. (Author photograph.)

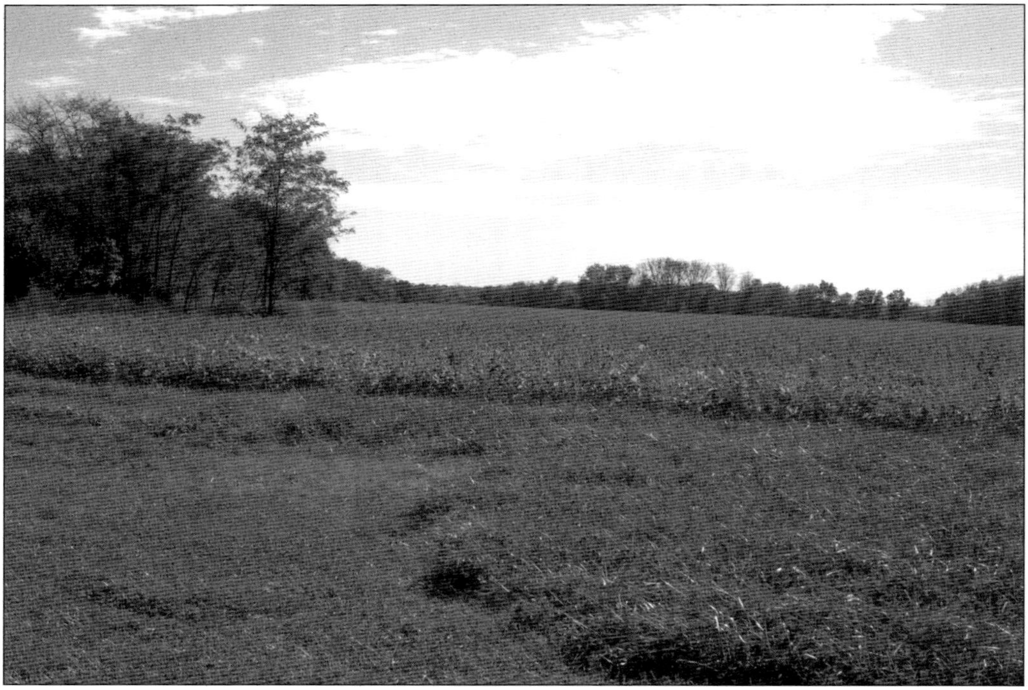

The fields that were part of the original William Lytle property are now leased to area farmers for growing crops of soy beans and corn. By the early 1800s, settlers coming to Williamsburg registered their claims to property at Lytle's land office. Neighbors from miles around brought their handspikes and skid poles to help with house-raising. According to Byron Williams's *History of Clermont and Brown Counties*, early cabin builders in Williamsburg had the advantage of finding logs already on the ground, because a tornado that had passed through a few years before had leveled so many trees, the area became known as "Falling Timber."

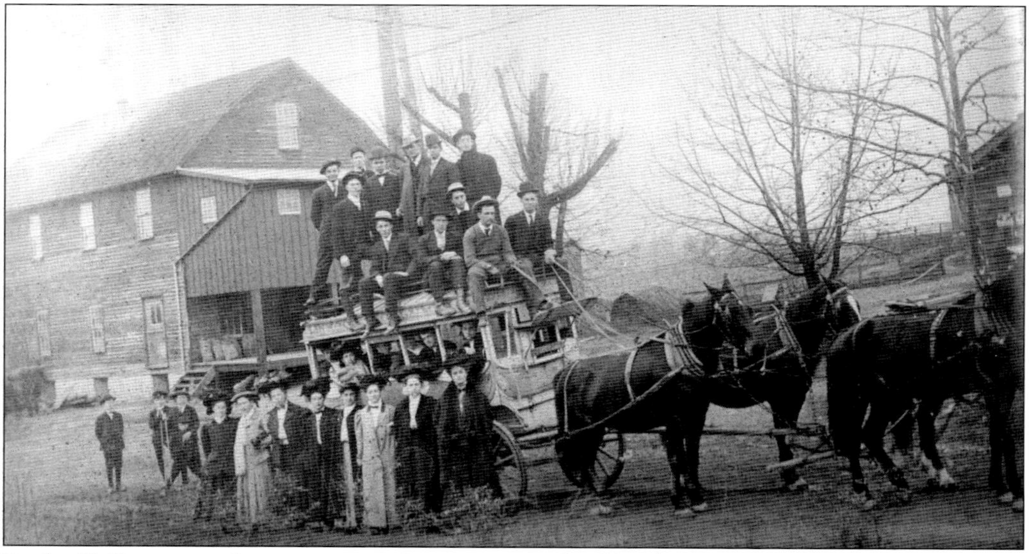

By the 1840s, men and women were taking stage coaches like this one from Cincinnati's Linwood-Columbia area to Clermont County towns such as Williamsburg and Batavia.

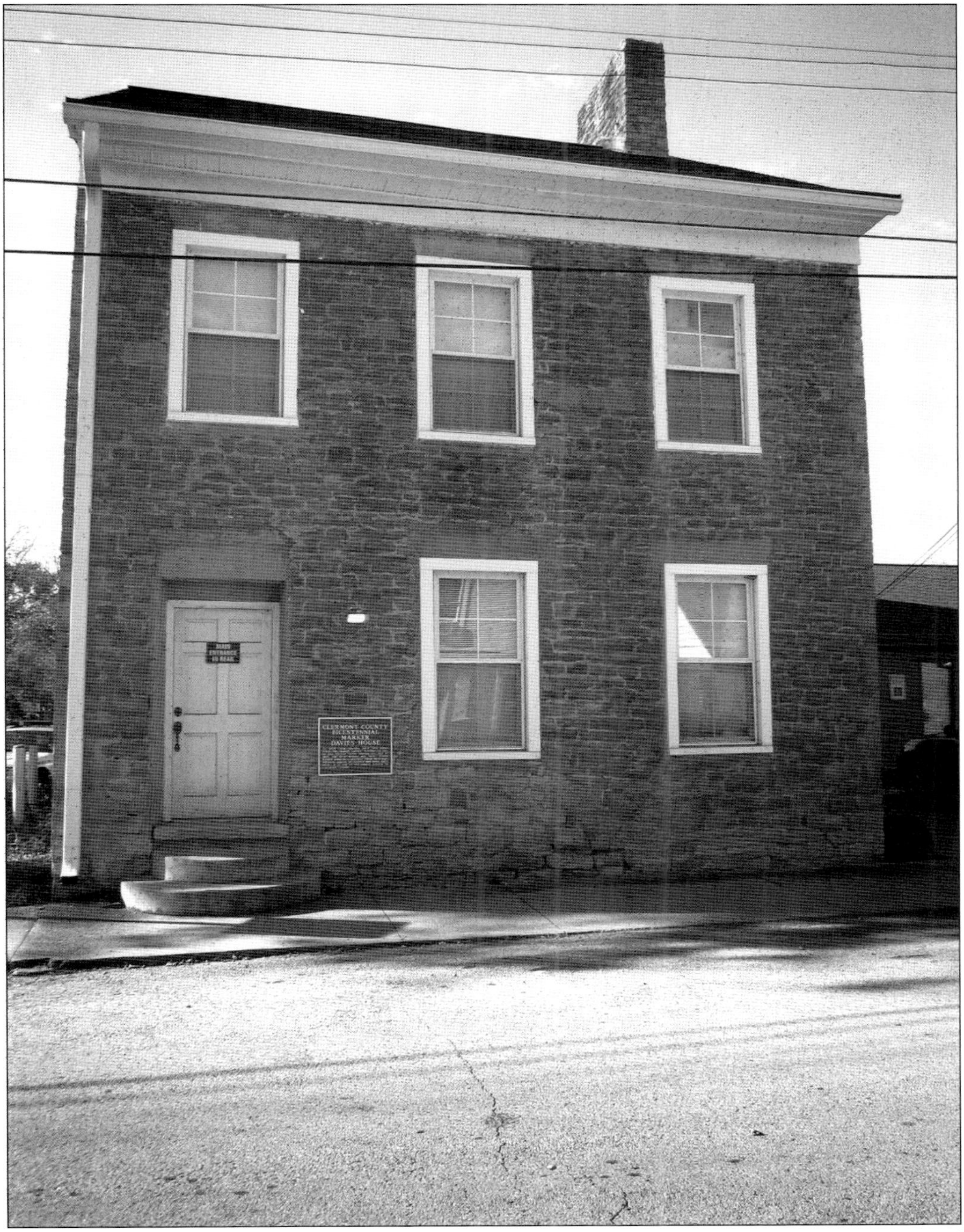

Col. Samuel Davis (or Davies) built this home in Williamsburg in 1805 with the assistance of John Charles, the first stonemason in Clermont County. The home served as a gathering place for Clermont's militia, and in 1833, the last of several military courts of inquiry were held in its parlor. Located on Front Street, it is now the headquarters of the Williamsburg Police Department. (Author photograph.)

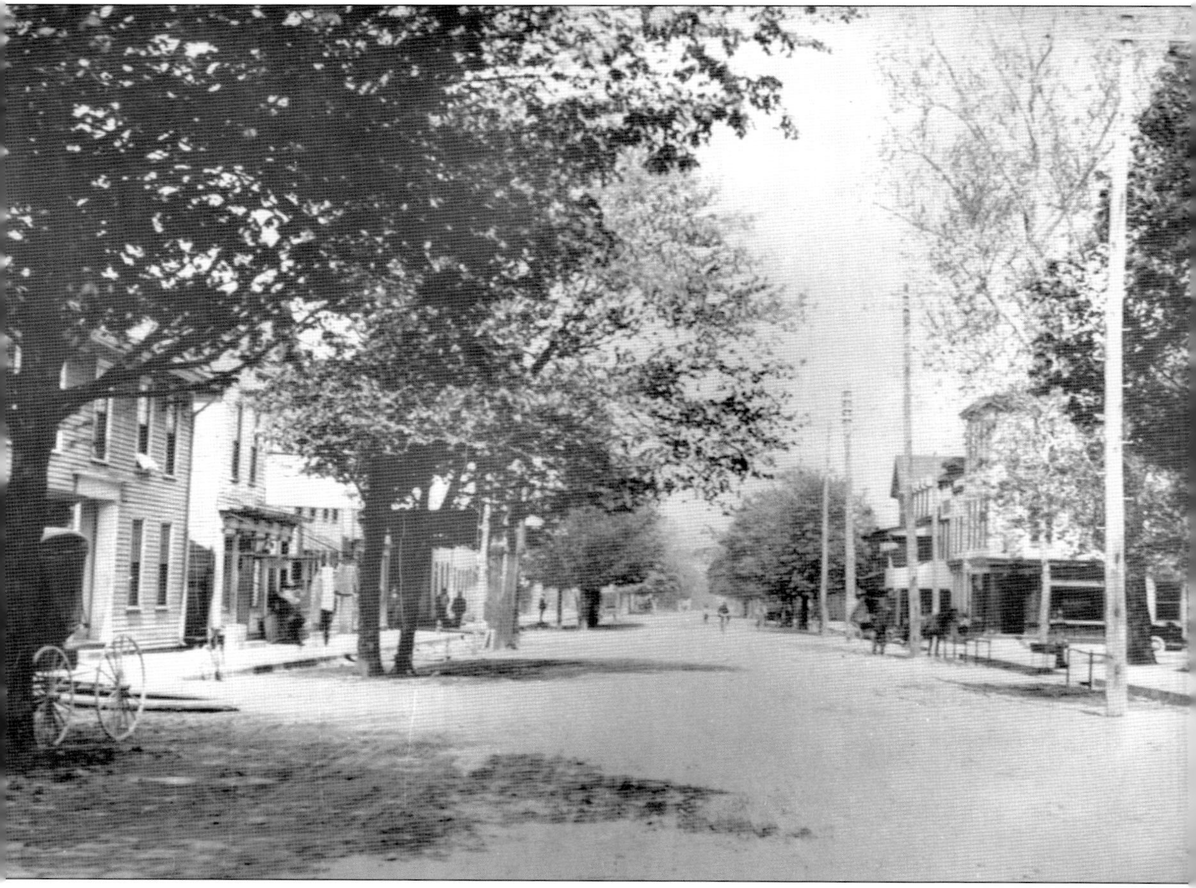

By the late 1800s, Batavia was a self-sufficient town with businesses offering every service its residents needed. This photograph shows Main Street during the days of the horse and buggy. (Photograph from the Sharp Collection, courtesy of the Clermont County Library.)

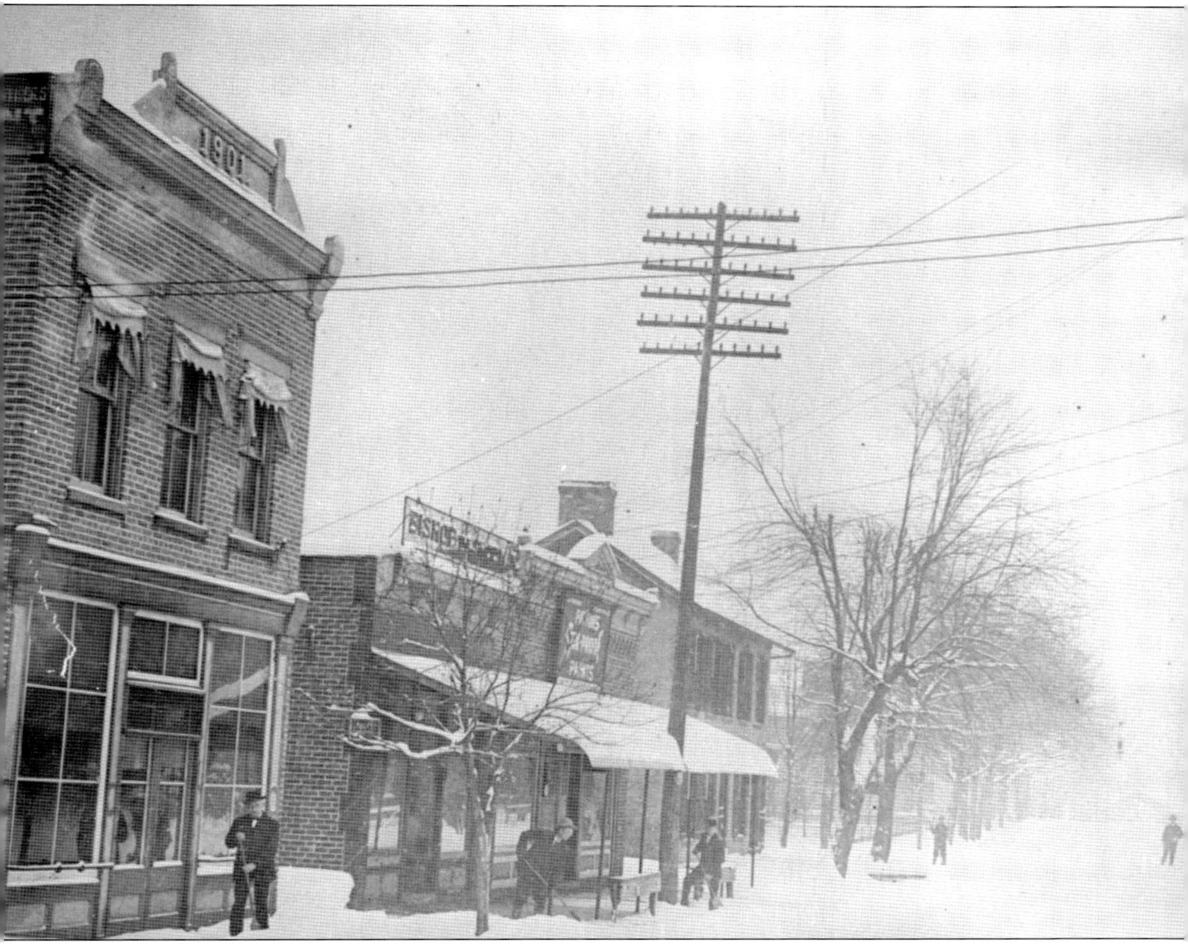

Williamsburg residents had a lot to contend with when 13 inches of snow fell in the area. This is a view of Main Street in 1910. The man on the left with shovel in hand is standing in front of the Kroger Grocery Store. The men in the center are in front of Elrod's Pharmacy, a business that served Williamsburg's residents from the late 1800s until its closing in 1958. (Photograph from the Sharp Collection, courtesy of the Clermont County Library.)

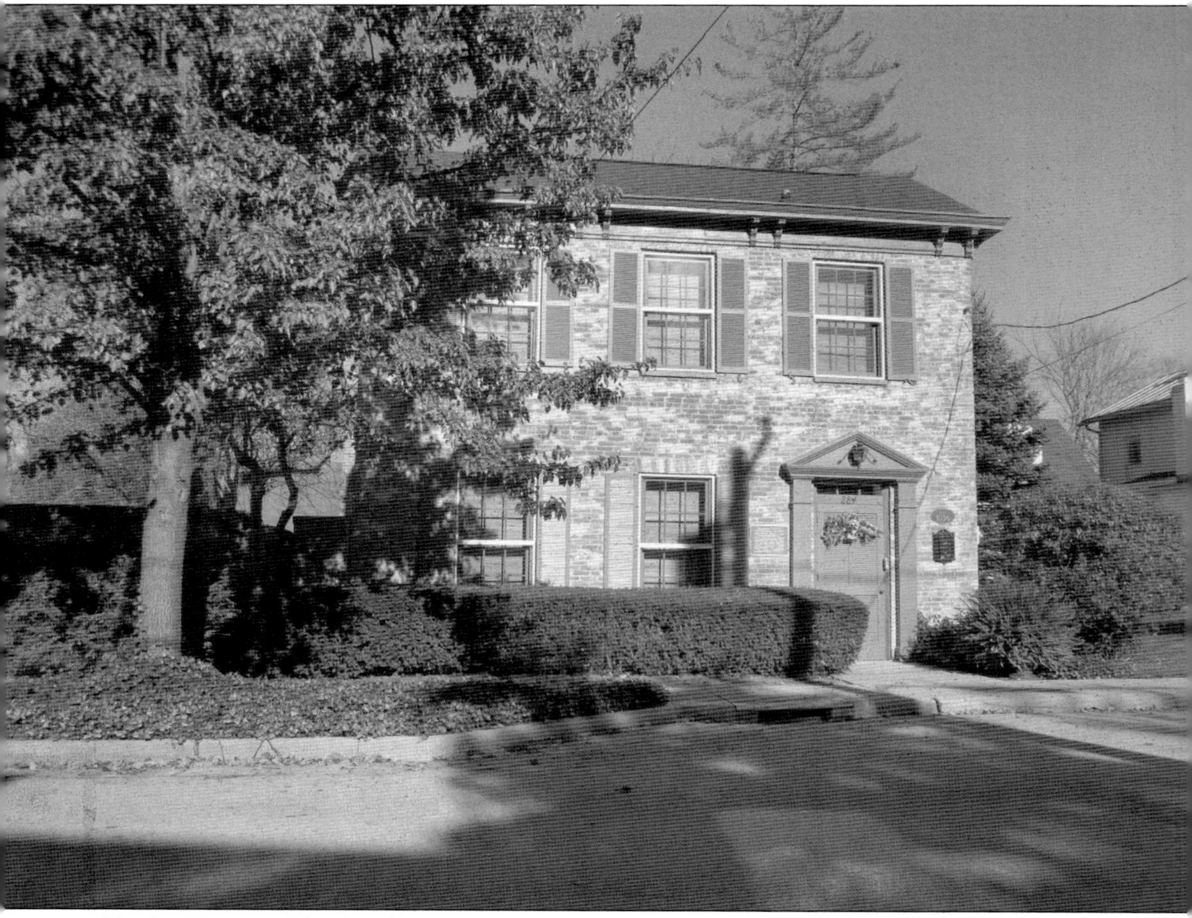

Charles Waits and his brother, James Waits, were Revolutionary War veterans who came from West Virginia to the Batavia-Williamsburg area in 1799. Charles owned a farm in the Whitaker Survey near Williamsburg and in 1836, he built this Federal-style home in Batavia with bricks fired on the site. Its 16-inch interior walls required stone foundations for support. The house still stands on North Street in an area that used to be called "Judges Corner." (Author photograph.)

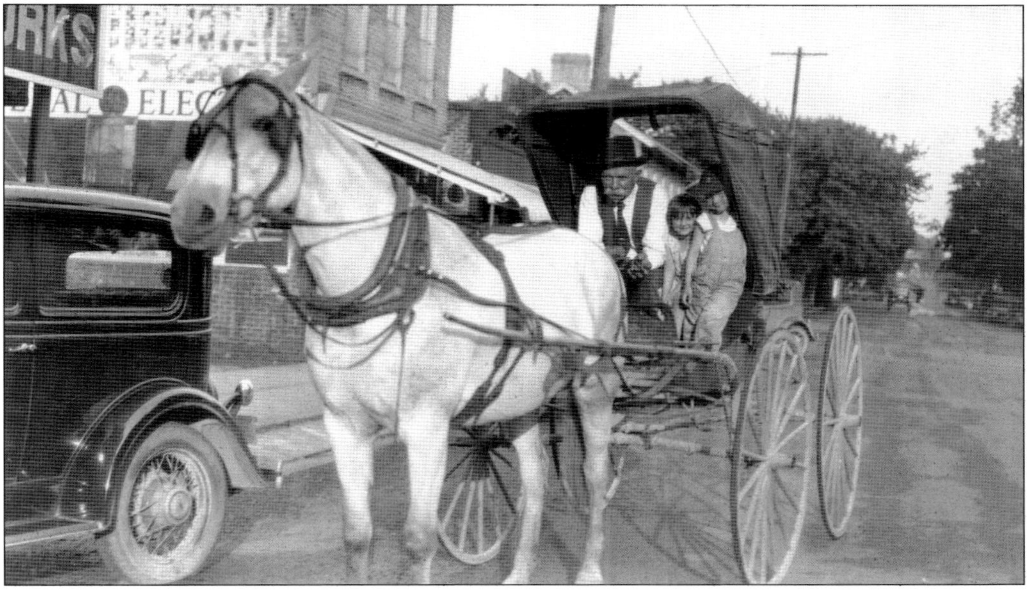

Williamsburg resident Kirby Knight takes young family members for a ride down Main Street in his wagon. (Photograph courtesy of Tim and Windy Ferree.)

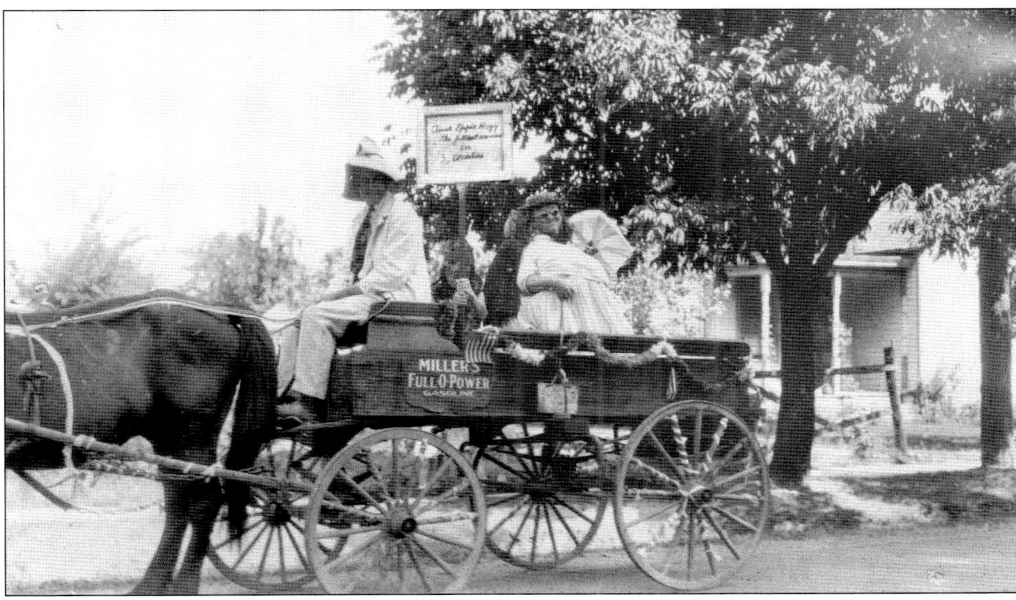

Williamsburg residents Harry Stamm, Violet Ellis, and women identified on the back of this photograph as Mrs. Berry and Mrs. Jones ride in a wagon advertising "Miller's Full-O-Power Gasoline." (Photograph courtesy of Jeanne Hancock.)

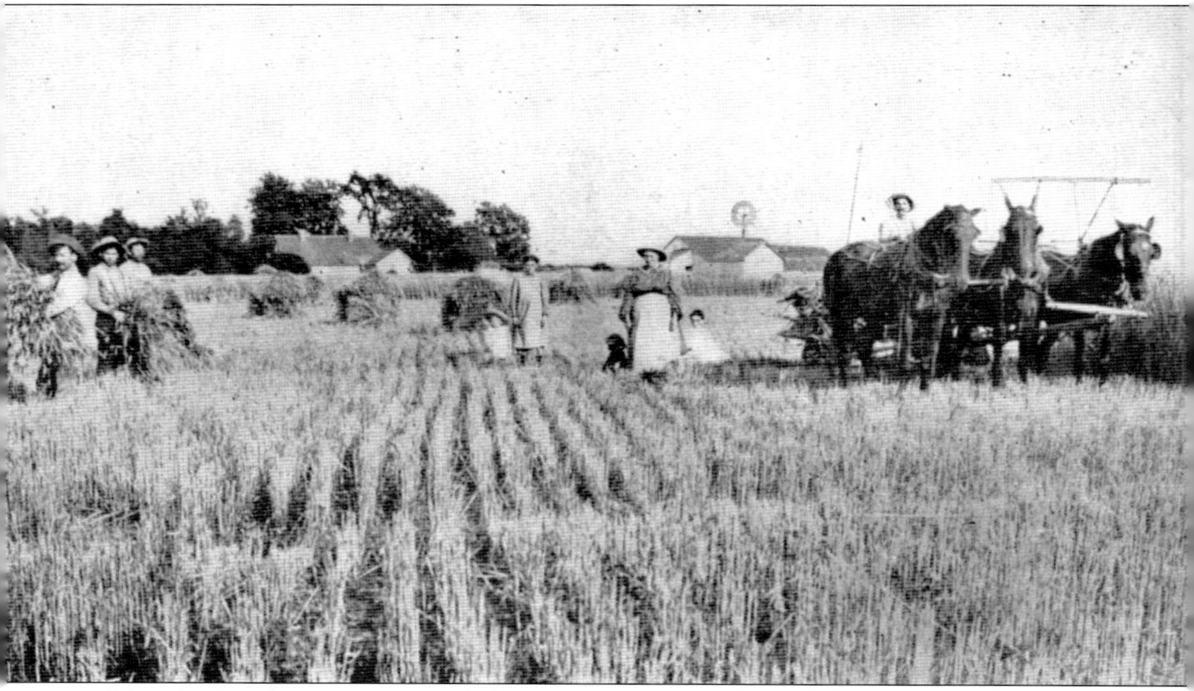

After the Revolutionary War ended in 1783, the state of Virginia ceded all its claims to land north of the Ohio River to the federal government but kept the area between the Little Miami and Scioto Rivers to use as payment to its war veterans for their service. Land bounties ranging from 100 acres for privates to 15,000 acres granted to a major general were given to the veterans. Many sold their bounty land for economic reasons while others preferred to remain in already settled parts of the country. Some saw their bounty as a chance to begin a new life and moved to the wilderness where they established farms. This early postcard photograph shows a group of farmers harvesting their crops near Williamsburg. Fine farms growing corn and soybeans and raising livestock can still be found in the surrounding areas of Williamsburg and Batavia. (Photograph courtesy of Tim and Windy Ferree.)

Two

Early Business

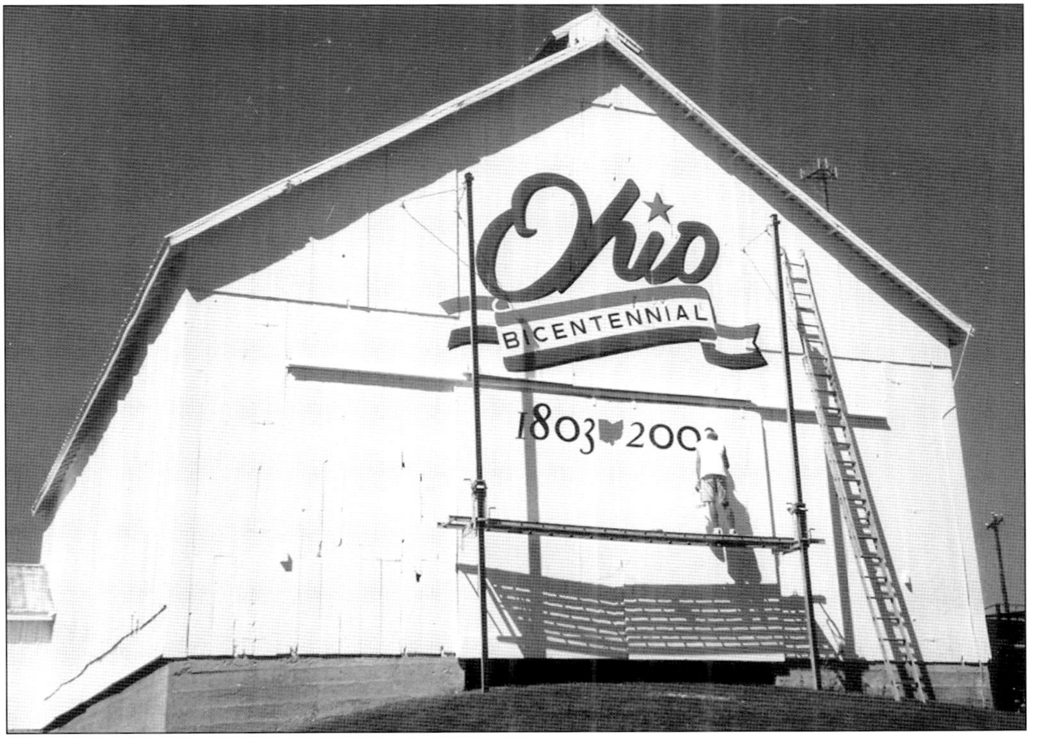

To celebrate its 200th anniversary in 2003, the Ohio Bicentennial Commission began a barn painting program as a unique way to get free, highly visible advertising. It grew into a cultural phenomenon with over 2,000 Ohio barn owners volunteering their barns for artist Scott Hagan to paint. This bicentennial barn is the only one in Clermont County and stands on McKeever Pike just outside Williamsburg. (Photograph courtesy of the Clermont County Historical Society.)

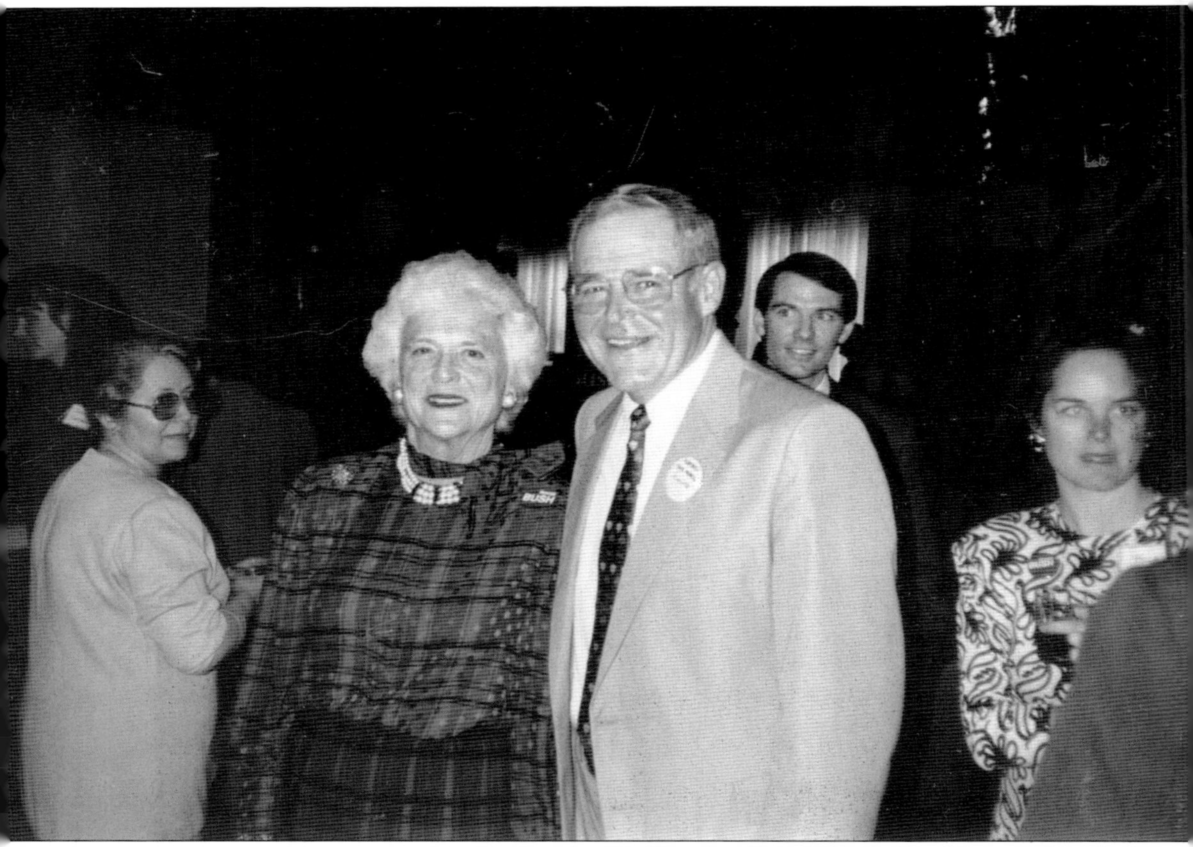

Lou Moore, pictured here with former first lady Barbara Bush (with Ohio's senator Rob Portman in the background), is the fifth generation to stand at the helm of his family's business, Moore Funeral Homes of Batavia. Established in 1820 as a carriage and casket maker, Moore Funeral Homes is believed to be the oldest continuously run family funeral business in the United States. (Photograph courtesy of Lou Moore.)

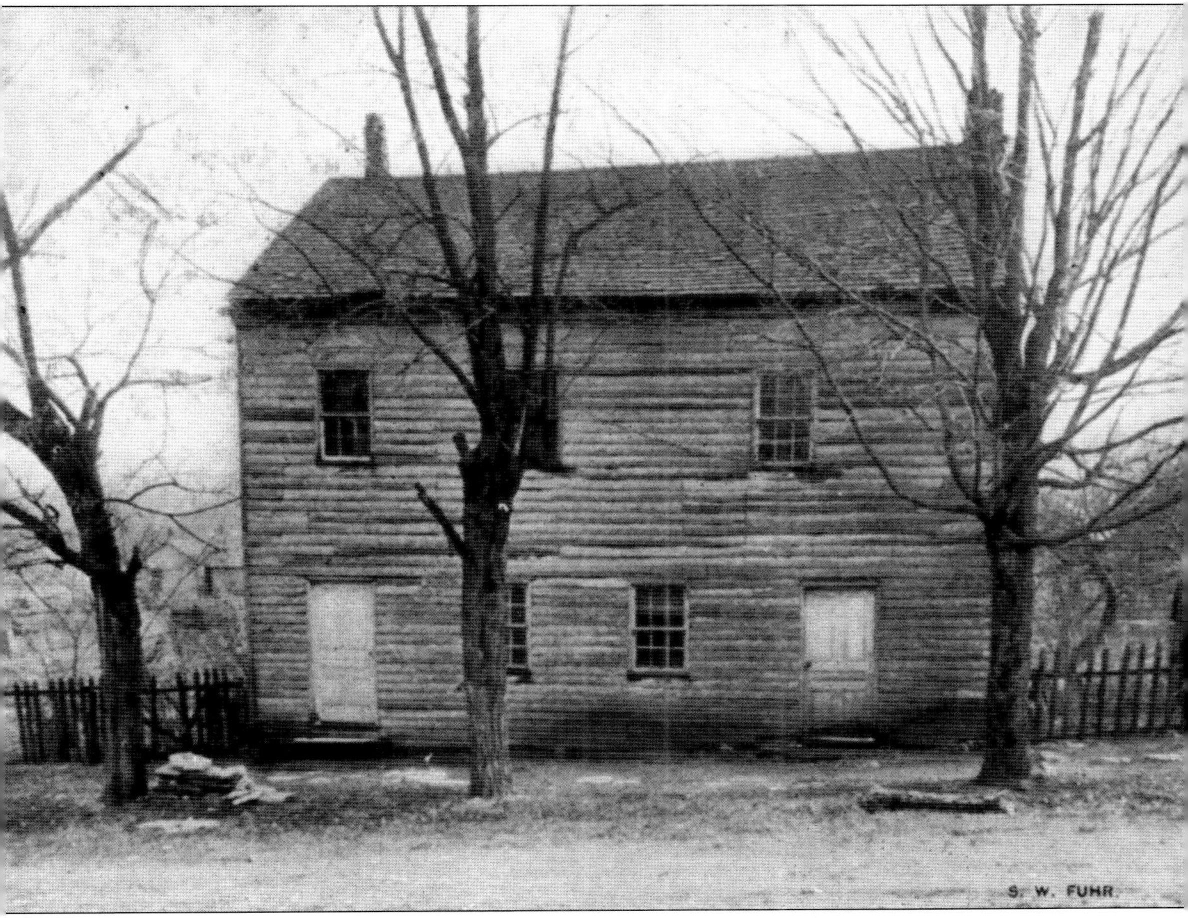

In 1802, Thomas Morris built this two-story frame tavern in Williamsburg to handle the town's increasing business. Early records state that the first court was held at the Morris Tavern and the jail was located in the lower story of Morris's log cabin. The town's first whipping post stood nearby, designed so the offender could stand or hang by the wrists while as many as "fifty save one" lashes were carried out. Described as a tall, fine-looking man with a noble mind, Thomas Morris became a state senator and was then elected to the US Senate in 1833, where he served until 1839. A firm abolitionist, Morris made an unsuccessful bid for the vice presidency on the Liberty Party ticket in 1844. (Postcard courtesy of Hazel Arnold.)

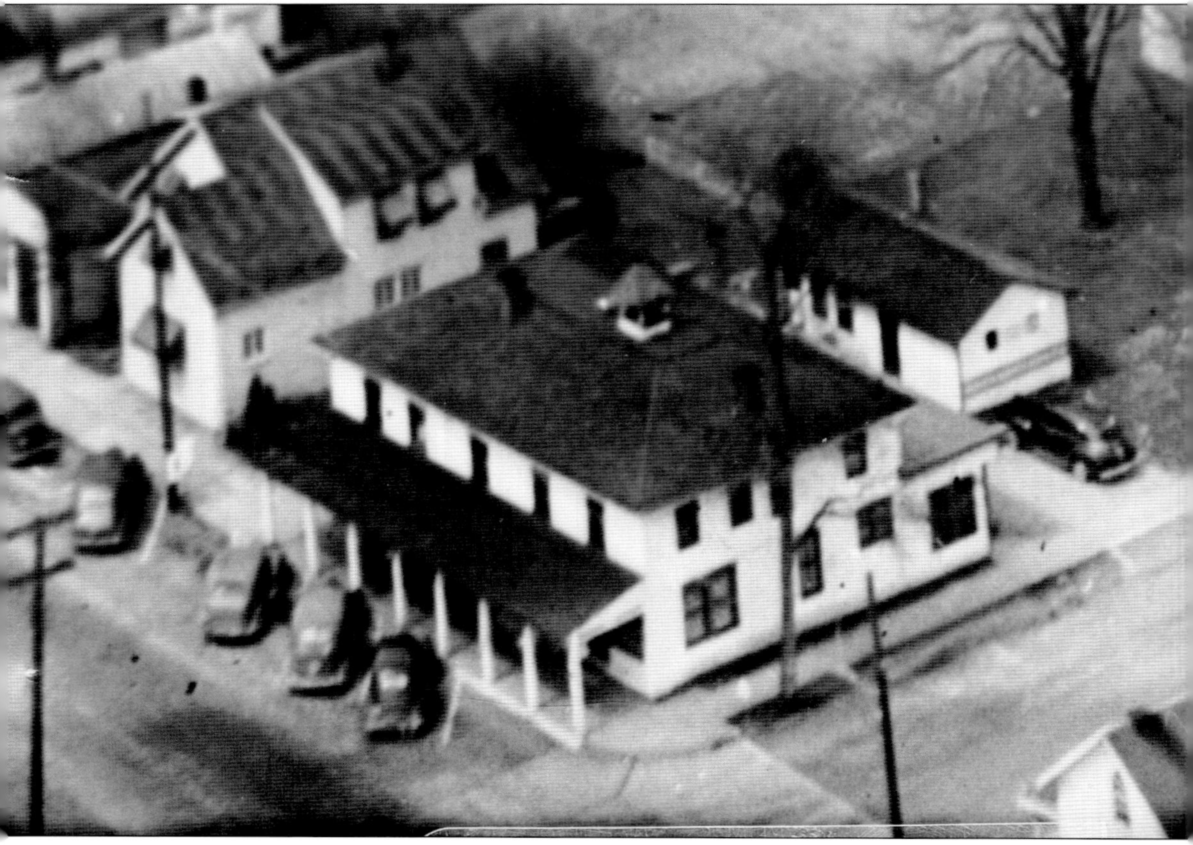

Taverns were an important part of early Williamsburg life. The Atchley House was built in 1835 by Daniel and George Everhart and sold around 1854 to John Atchley. It is part of the present Valley View Inn (pictured) standing at Front and Main Streets. Another early tavern was kept by James Kain in his cabin on Front Street. Legend says that in 1806, Aaron Burr rented a room there. Local Revolutionary War veterans, taking offense to Burr's presence, staged a protest outside the tavern, marching up and down the street playing the "Rogues' March." In 1816, Kain opened another tavern at the corner of Third and Main Streets. It is no longer standing. (Photograph courtesy of Hazel Arnold.)

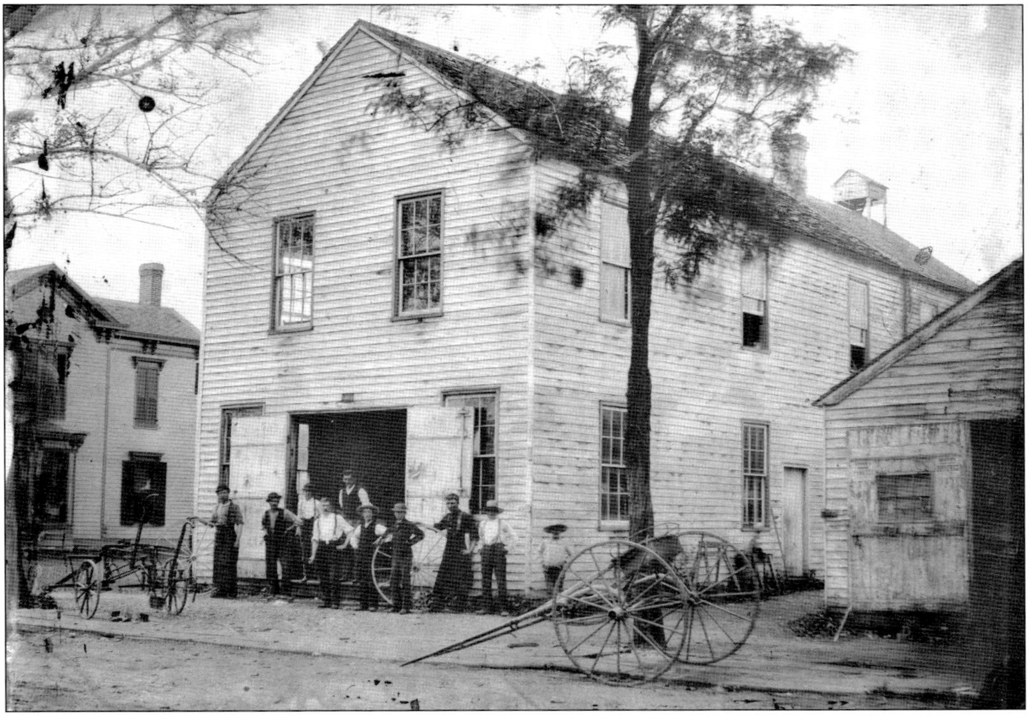

Moore Funeral Homes in Batavia is reported to be the oldest family run funeral home business in the country. The company began as a carriage factory on the site of the present Wh. Stirling Moore Funeral Home on Spring Street in Batavia. Around 1860, Hiram U. Moore became one of the first funeral directors in the country. In this 1861 photograph, from left to right, are James McTomany, John Zuermuhley, George Zuermuhley, John Griffith, Rem Lane, Chris Halbisch, and Ralph McKay. (Photograph courtesy of Lou Moore.)

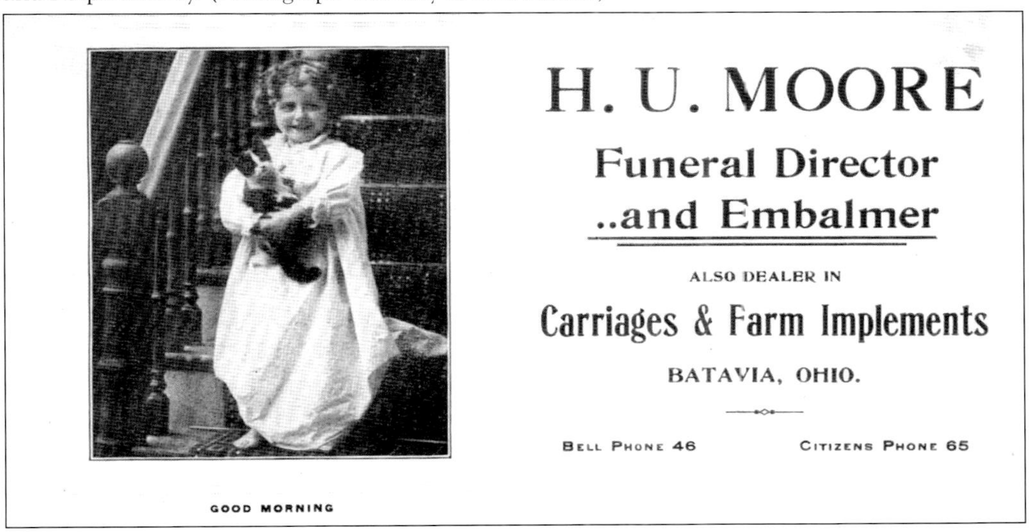

This photograph shows Hiram Ulysses Moore's business card. Note that the two-digit contact information consisted of two lines: the Bell line for general business, and the Citizen's line for personal calls. (Photograph courtesy of Steve Shinkle.)

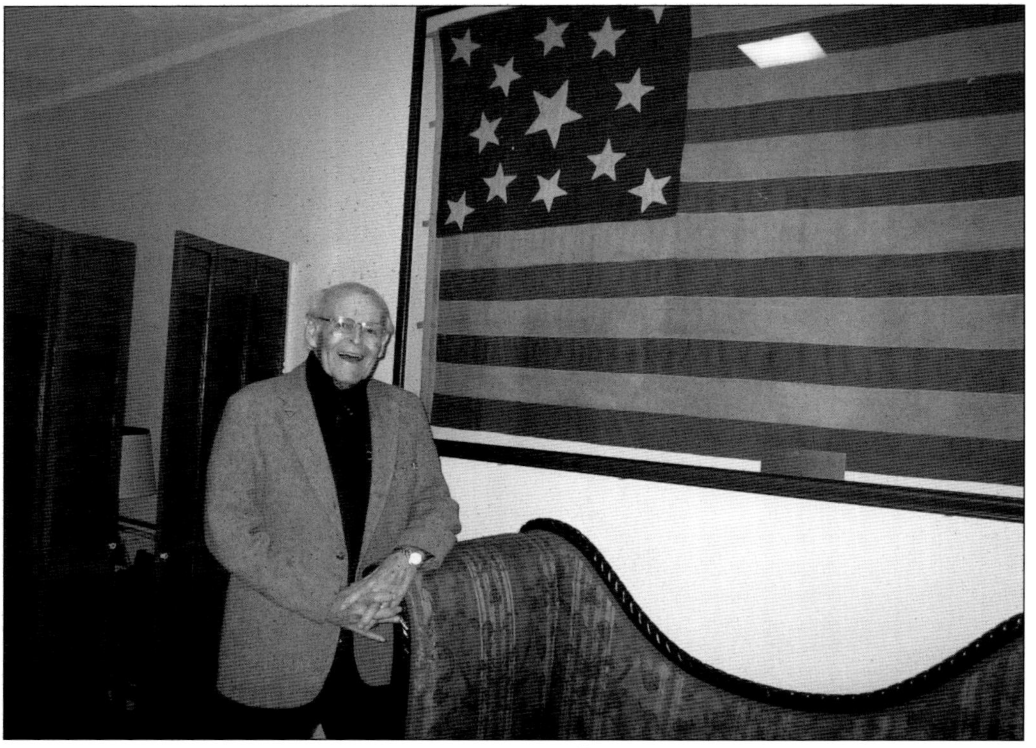

Batavia Funeral director Lou Moore stands in front of the 15-star US flag, which was used from 1795 to 1818 and sewn by his great-great-great grandmother Emma Marty during her overseas journey by schooner to the United States. Emma's husband required her to accomplish two things before her marriage: learn to speak English and sew a US flag. (Author photograph.)

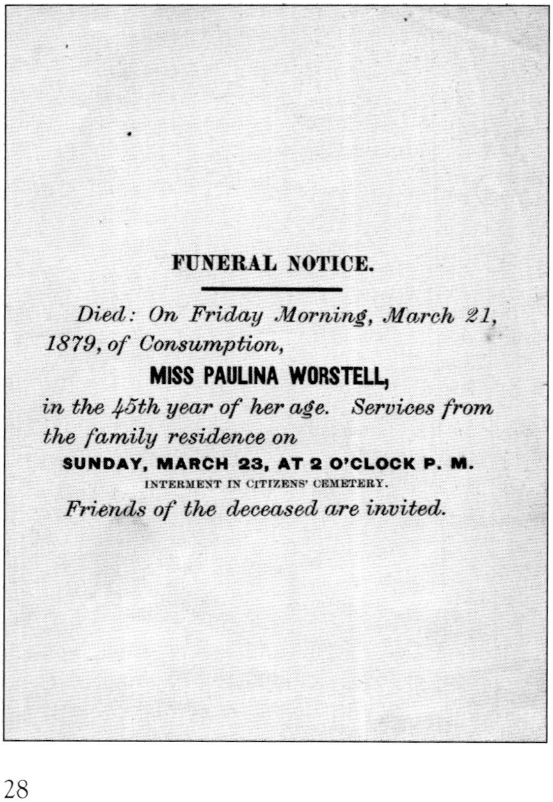

FUNERAL NOTICE.

Died: On Friday Morning, March 21, 1879, of Consumption,

MISS PAULINA WORSTELL,

in the 45th year of her age. Services from the family residence on

SUNDAY, MARCH 23, AT 2 O'CLOCK P. M.

INTERMENT IN CITIZENS' CEMETERY.

Friends of the deceased are invited.

Funeral notice cards in the mid- to late 1800s gave varying amounts of information and could be plain or fancy in design. After a death, the announcement card was displayed around town so friends could pay respects to the family. Paulina Worstell's announcement (left) indicates she died of consumption on Friday morning, March 21, 1879, at the age of 45. Her visitation and burial were two days later. (Photograph courtesy of Lou Moore.)

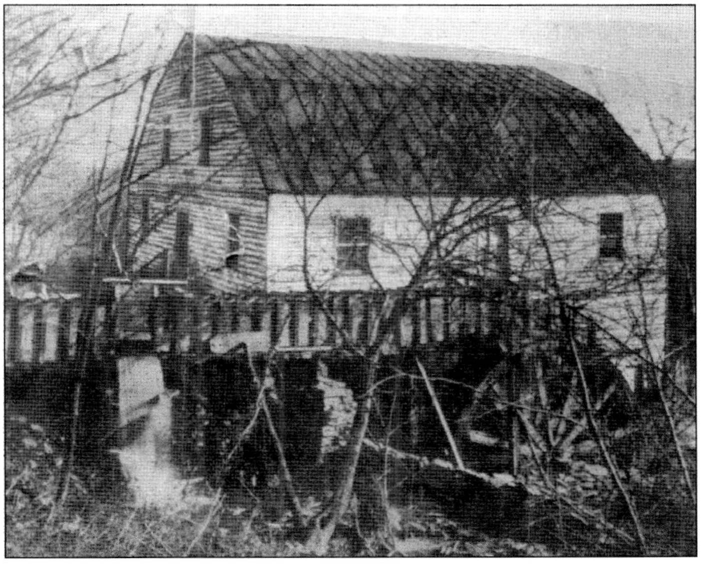

Gen. William Lytle and his partner, Gen. James Taylor, built this gristmill in Williamsburg. According to Lytle's papers, the work began in March 1797 by Robert Winslow, John Campbell, James Sterling, and Henry Dunham. Peter Wilson was chosen as the millwright because he had much experience in Kentucky. On February 9, 1799, a Mr. Beatie wrote, "the saw mill is generally going; the grist mill is in tolerable order." (Photograph courtesy of the Clermont County Historical Society.)

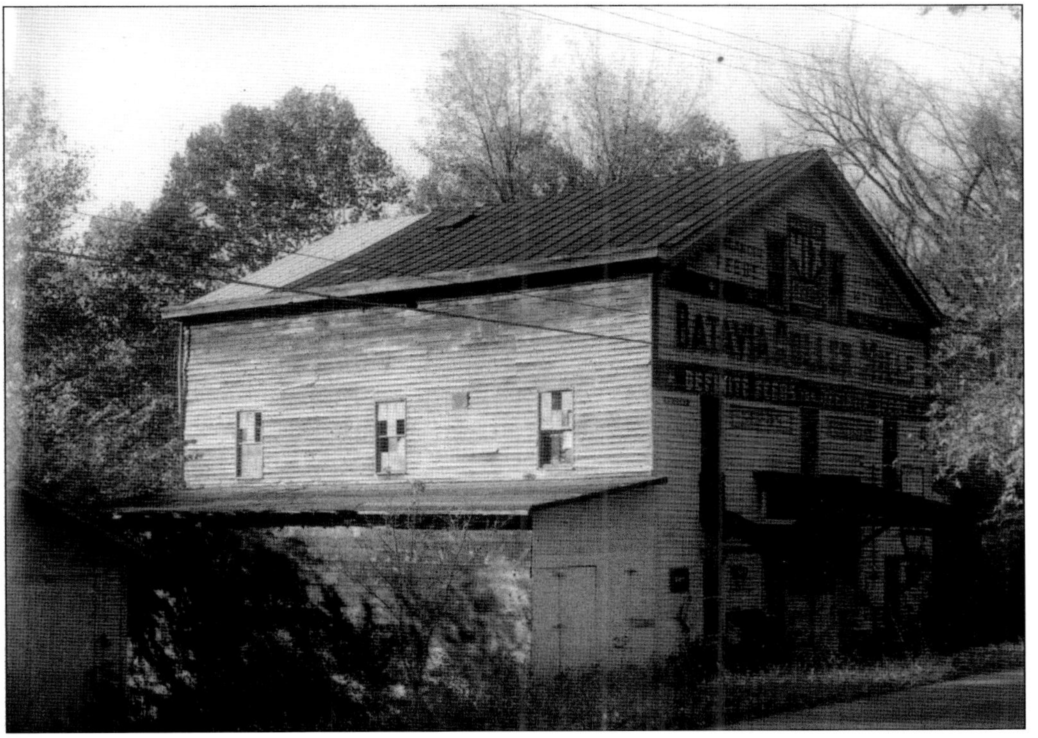

Located on Old South Riverside Drive in Batavia, this may be the oldest mill site in Clermont County, since millwright Peter Wilson selected it in 1795. George Ely was the first to operate a saw mill there. In 1816, Capt. Charles Moore purchased the property, and in 1840, he and his sons built a water-powered gristmill to grind wheat and corn. The mill was eventually steam powered and then gas driven and operated until 1961 under the name Batavia Roller Mills. The building collapsed with age and was demolished in 1990; however, the stone foundation remains. (Photograph from the Sharp Collection, courtesy of the Clermont County Library.)

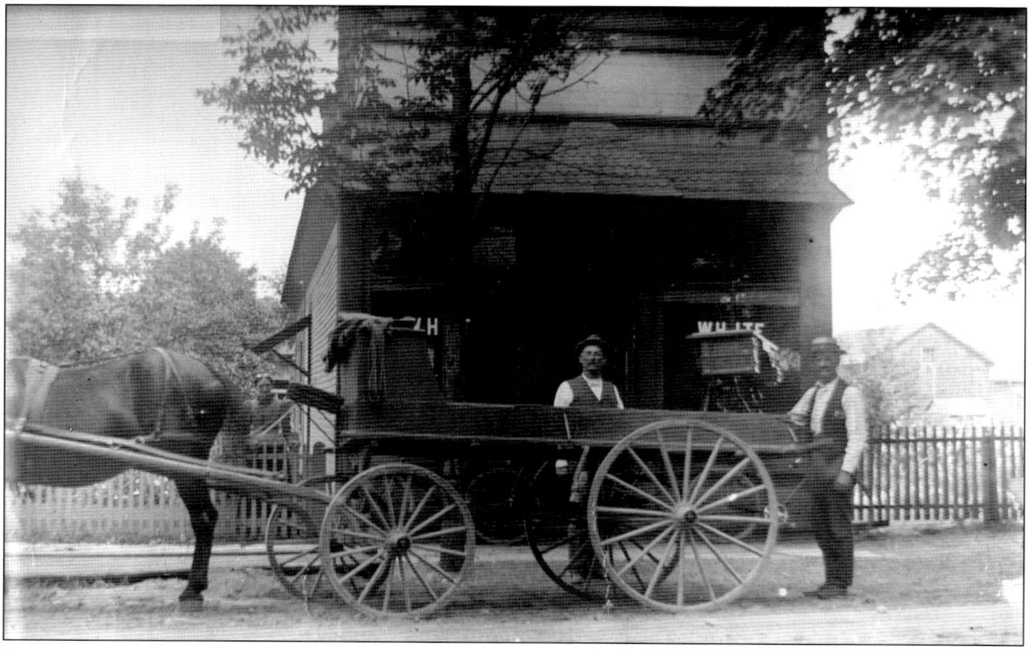

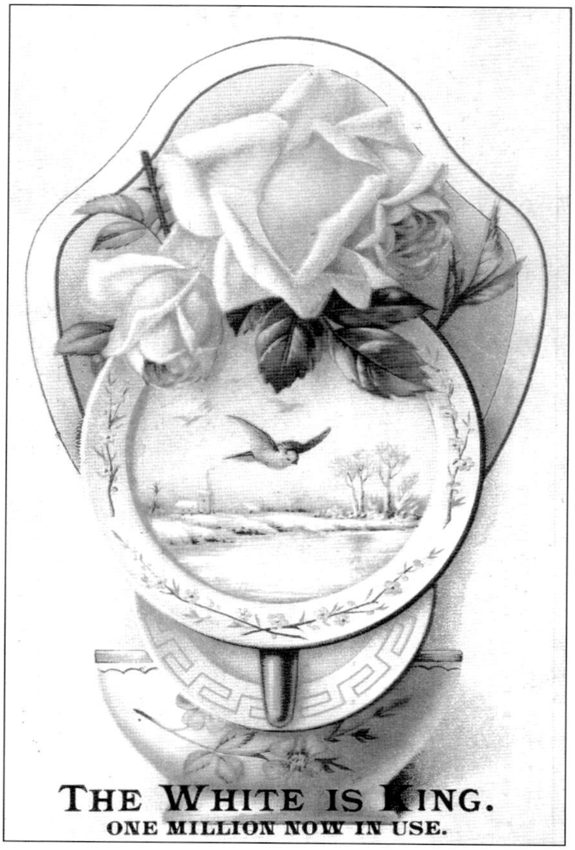

W.H. Baum was a dealer in White sewing machines in Batavia. In a public advertisement he wrote, "Having removed my business to my new building sitting on Second Street between Main and Spring Streets, I want you to know where I am at and what I am here for. I am here to supply your wants and if you want a new sewing machine for family use or manufacturing purposes, I want a chance with the other fellows to sell you the best so drop me a postal and find out my new methods for selling sewing machines."

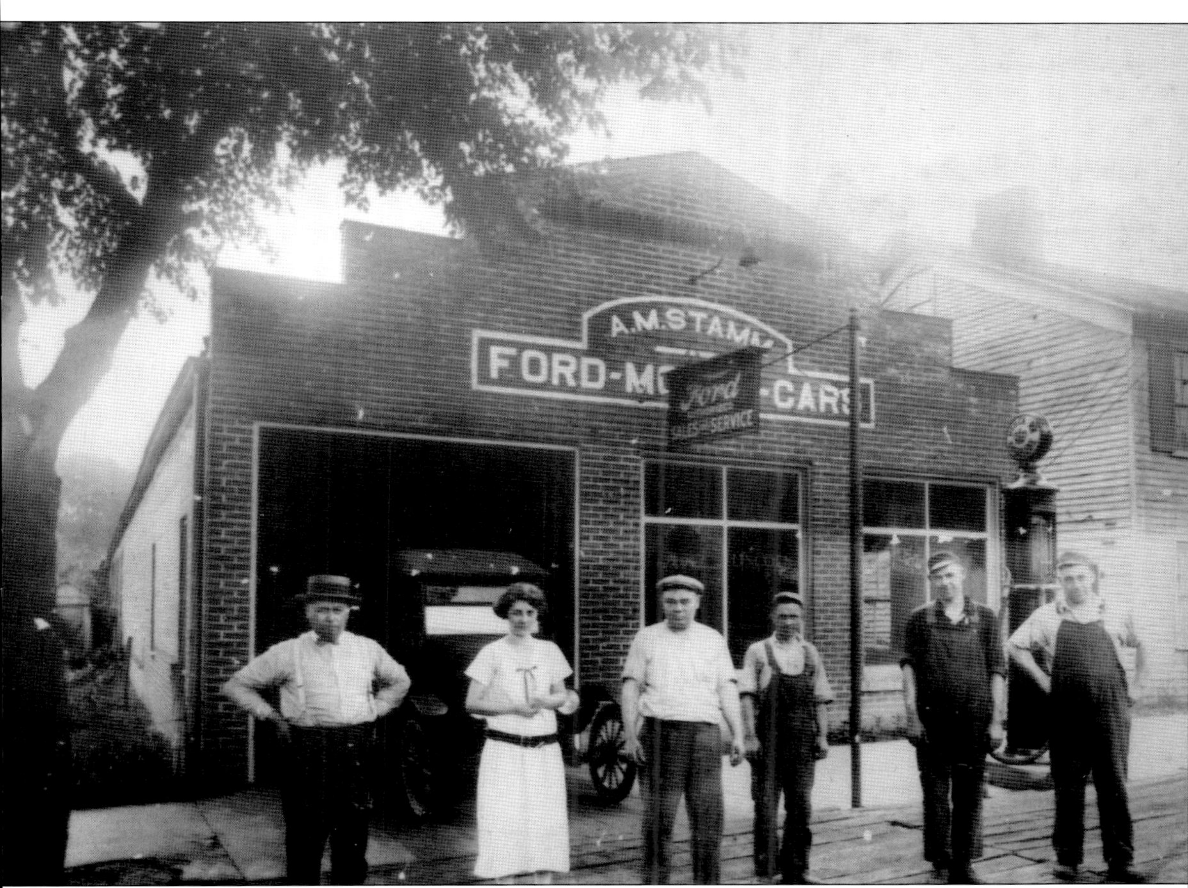

This 1928 photograph shows Stamm's Garage, which was located on Williamsburg's Main Street. Pictured from left to right are Albert Stamm, Bernice Beech, Harry Stamm, Lewis Duckwall, Mr. Clark, and Ernest Weeks. The Stamm family operated a Ford dealership at the garage during the 1920s and 1930s. The automobiles required assembly and sold for around $500. The first meeting of the Williamsburg Fire Department was held at Stamm's on June 10, 1935, and Harry Stamm was appointed the first fire chief. (Photograph courtesy of Jean Hancock.)

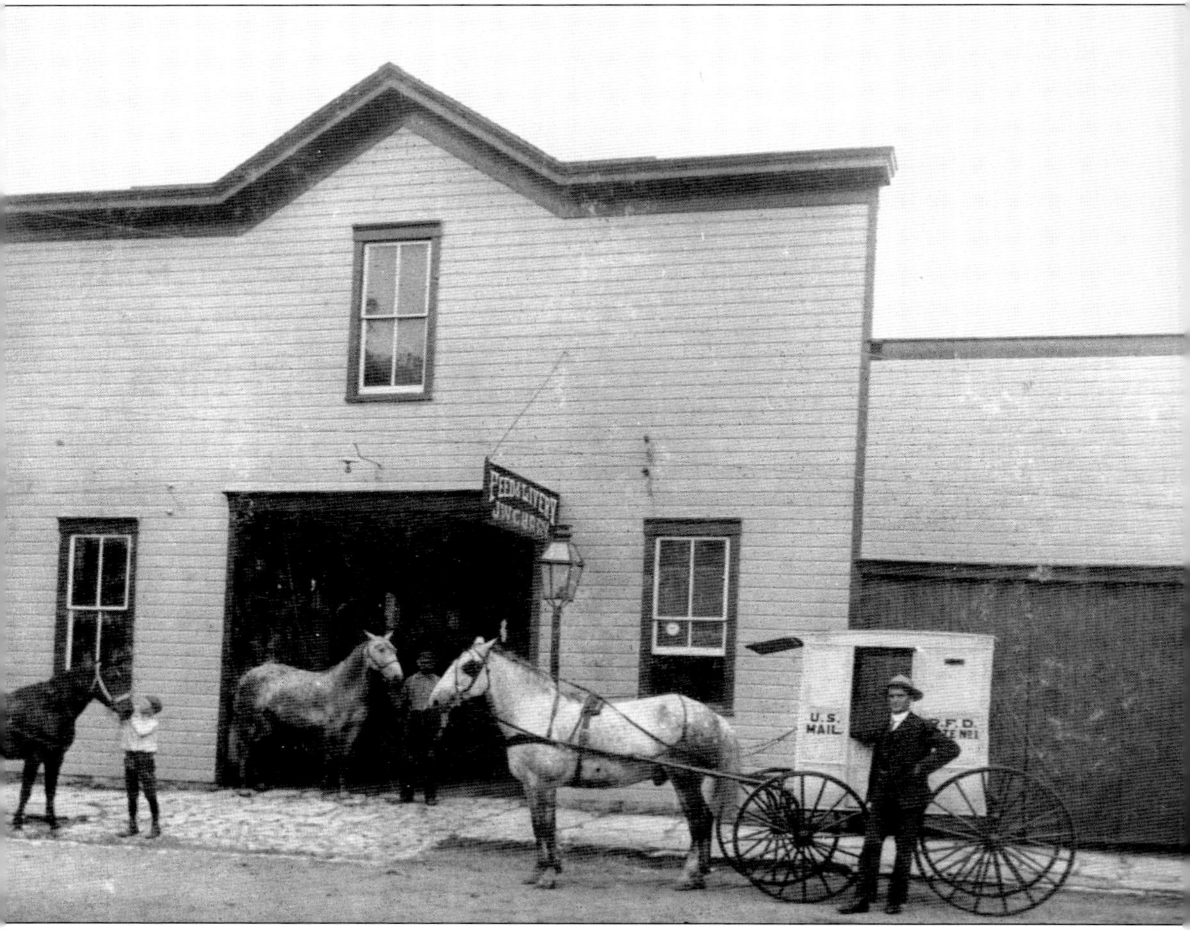

J.W. Curry offered feed and livery services from his business on Front and Walnut Streets in Williamsburg. At right is US mail carrier Will Ireton with his No. 1 RFD delivery wagon. (Photograph from the Sharp Collection, courtesy of the Clermont County Library.)

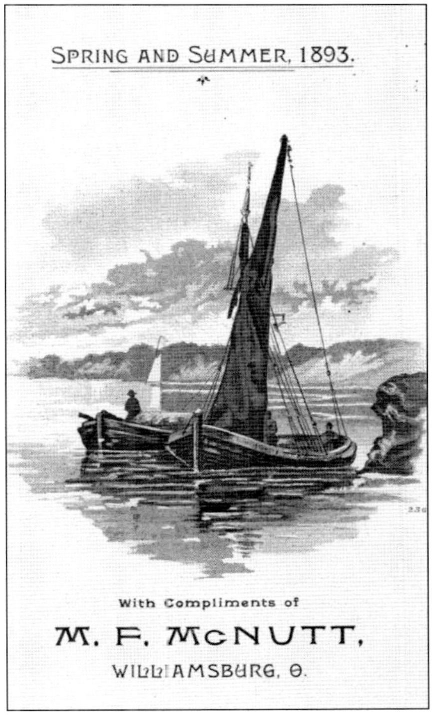

In the book *Clermont and Clermonters*, the Williamsburg dry goods stores of John Foster and C.H. McNutt are described as "being known throughout the area for their wide and excellent stock of merchandise." In 1893, McNutt announced his establishment would be known as the One Price Cash Store. New merchandise included spring cutaway suits for $8, while plow shoes were a bargain at 89¢. (Photographs courtesy of Tim and Windy Ferree.)

To my Friends, Patrons and the Public,

GREETING:

I wish to announce to you an important and radical change in my business, viz: I have adopted the system of ONE PRICE FOR CASH, and my store will be known as THE ONE PRICE CASH STORE. This will be painted in plain letters over the door, so you may not mistake the place. We have just received a very large stock of goods, bought with care and for *cash*, and we can promise you *latest styles, good quality and low prices*. Our stock consists of Dry Goods, Notions, Boots and Shoes, Clothing, Hats and Caps, Carpets and Oil Cloths, Wall Paper, Trunks, Valises, Ladies' and Gents' Furnishing Goods, etc. Will call your attention briefly to some of our attractions in the several departments.

SPECIAL.

Access to latest Metropolitan Fashions on our counters, free.

Men's Fine Wool Spring Cutaway Suits, $8.00, worth $12.00.

Men's Whole Stock Plow Shoes, 89 cents, worth $1.25

1st.—Dry Goods.—In domestics will be found an elegant assortment. Prints, Muslins, Ginghams, etc., at lowest prices. A special feature of this department will be Dress Goods, in the latest styles and colorings. Henriettas, Whip Cords, Stefano Velours, Jacquard Novelties, Surahs, Bengalenes, Tailor Serges, Fancy and Staple Blacks, etc. Also, a large line of Changeable and Surah Silks, in all the popular shades. Also, a large line of cheap and fine quality linings, as well as a large line of low-priced dress fabrics. Don't fail to give us a call.

2nd.—Shoes—Here we lead again. We carry the Douglas line for men and boys, the Drew-Selby line for ladies, misses and children, all warranted, and other makes. We can do you good. Come and see us. Buttons put on shoes we sell, with wire fastenings, without charge.

3rd.—Clothing.—Let the men and boys come too; they'll find our styles and prices right, and plenty of goods to select from.

4th.—Hats and Caps.—New and stylish, in wool, fur and straw, for men and boys.

5th.—Notions.—Almost anything you want, in unusual large variety. You should see our Embroideries, Laces, Hosiery, Gloves, Corsets, Buttons, Underwear, etc., etc.

6th.—Carpets and Oil Cloths.—A new, clean, desirable stock, at correct prices.

7th.—Wall Paper.—A large stock, very pretty and cheap this year; in fact, our prices will surprise you for cheapness, especially borders. We trim wall paper free that we sell.

8th.—Trunks and Valises, at right prices. In Window Curtains and Curtain Poles, we carry a large line. Our stock will surely interest you. We think we can interest you and save you money by buying for cash from us.

I have engaged the services of Mr. George Wageman, who has been selling goods in Cincinnati for some time past, and we cordially invite you to come in and look at what we have, and we promise you kind and polite attention, and we feel canfident you will like our new method of doing business. Remember, we have one price to all, and that the LOWEST. Our stock must be seen to be appreciated.

Hoping to see you soon, I am, respectfully,

M. F. McNUTT, Williamsburg, Ohio.

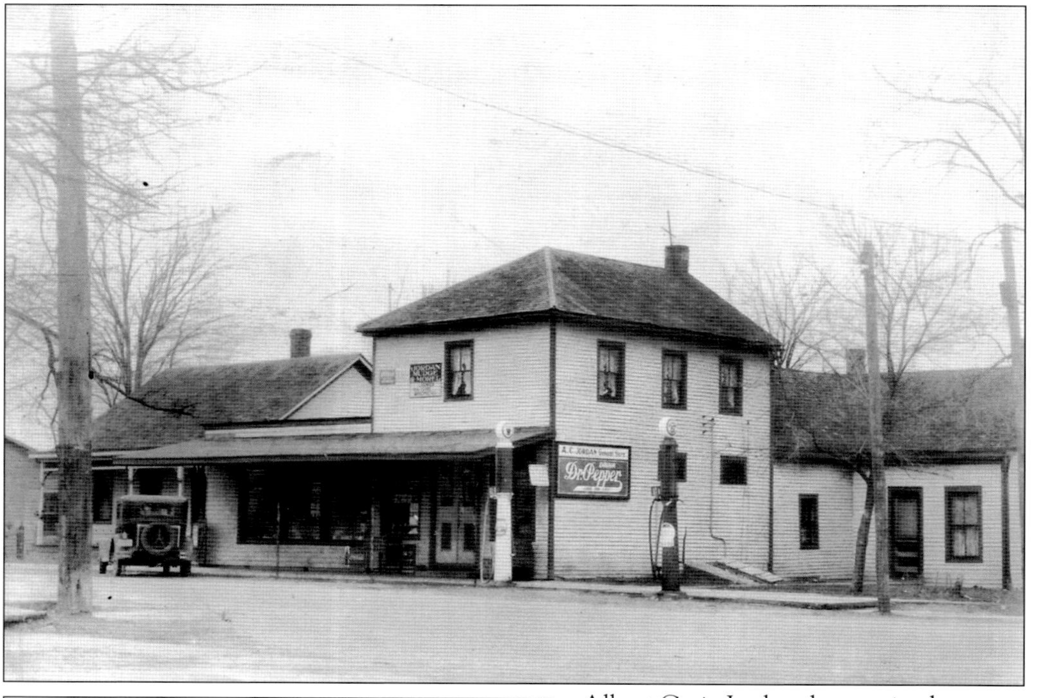

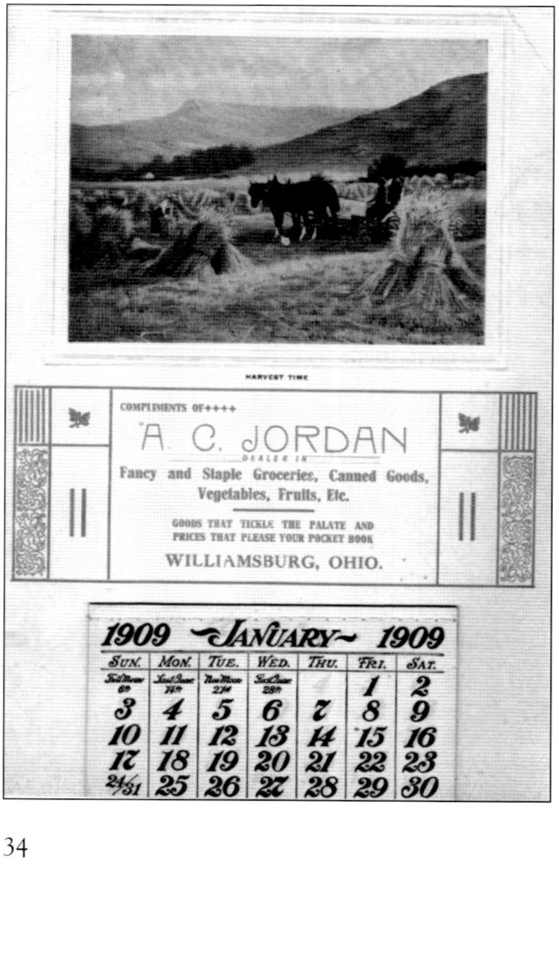

Albert Craig Jordan, known in the Williamsburg community as "A.C.," started the family business from his wagon taking it door-to-door selling Sayman Salve, a cure-all ointment. As the product list got larger and business grew, he built the A.C Jordan General Store (above) on Main Street in Williamsburg. The store's 1909 promotional calendar at left stated that they "sold goods that tickle the palate" and had "prices that please your pocket book." (Both photographs courtesy of Mark Jordan.)

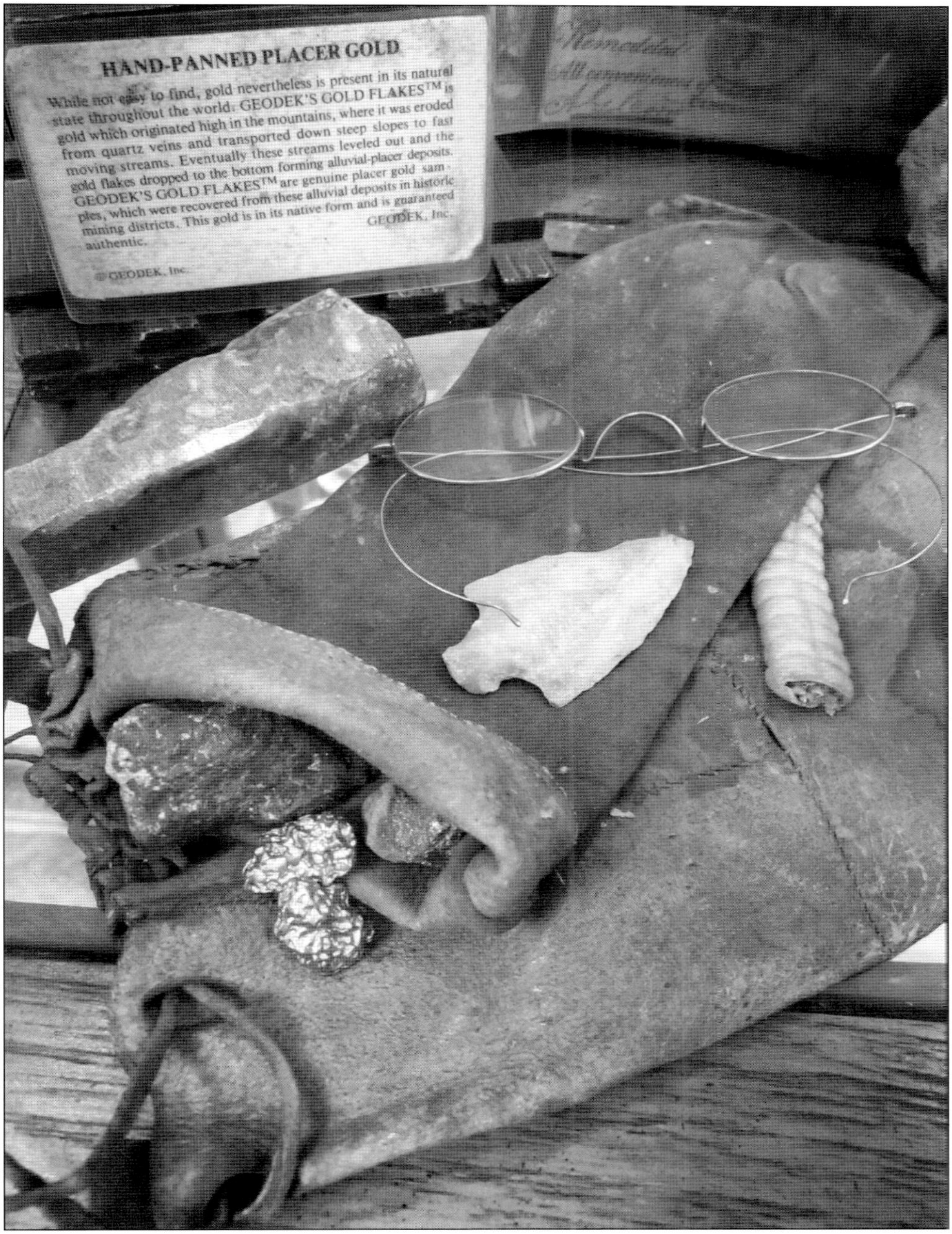

In 1868, hopeful prospectors returning from California descended upon Richland County in northeast Ohio and in the Batavia area near Elk Lick where it was rumored gold had been found. Soon after small traces of gold were discovered near Elk Lick, the Batavia Gold Mining Company was formed and flumes and buildings were constructed. Though small amounts of "placer" or "secondary" gold were found near Batavia and in Richland County, neither location produced enough to cover operating costs, and the mining companies closed after only a few months of operation. This photograph shows the bag in which Lou Moore's great grandfather kept gold that he found on his trek to California in 1849. (Author photograph.)

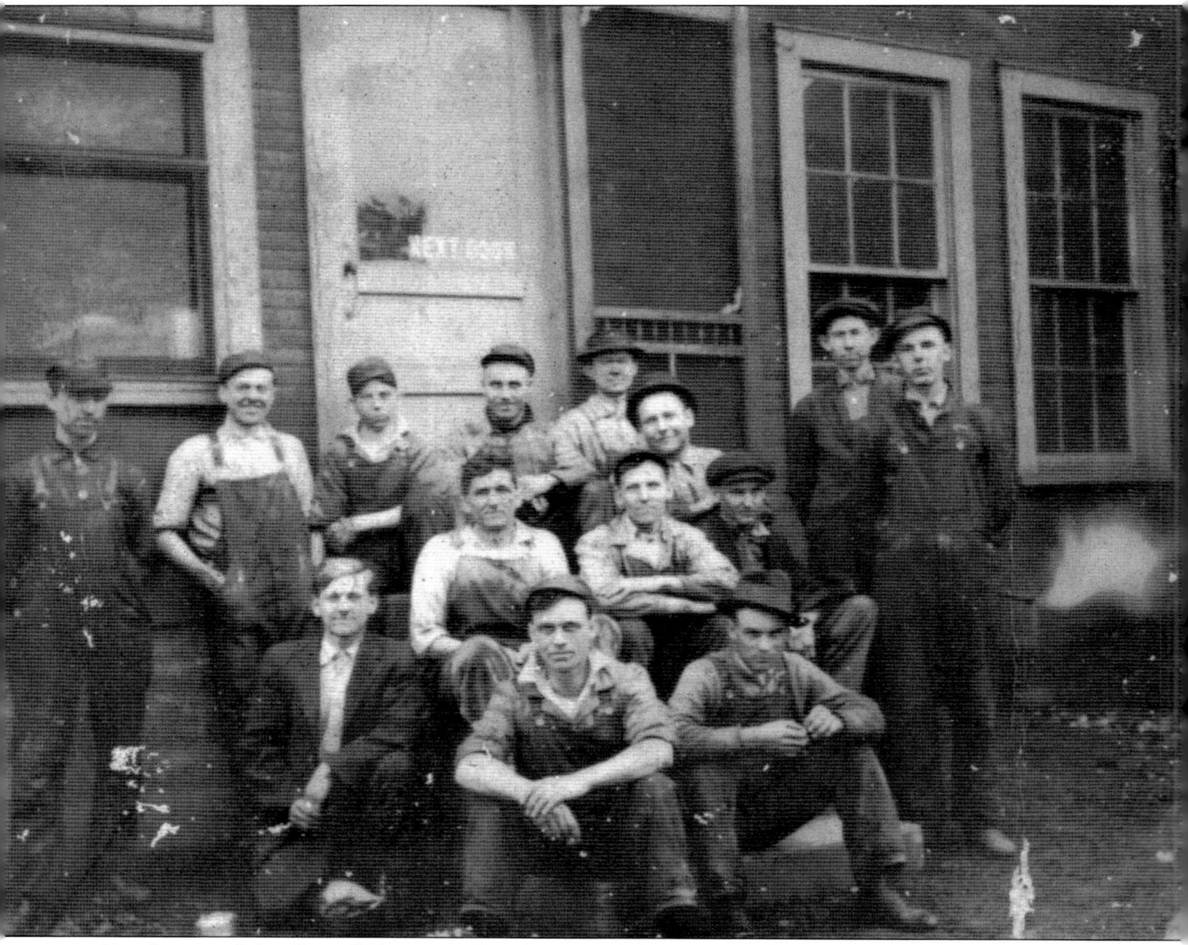

Employees of the Carroll-Jamieson Machine Tool Company take a break from work in this early photograph. The company was established by Percy French Jamieson in 1903 in Batavia. In 1933, Jamieson partnered with A.V. Carroll of Williamsburg to make lathes that are now popular with collectors of vintage machinery. (Photograph courtesy of Steve Shinkle.)

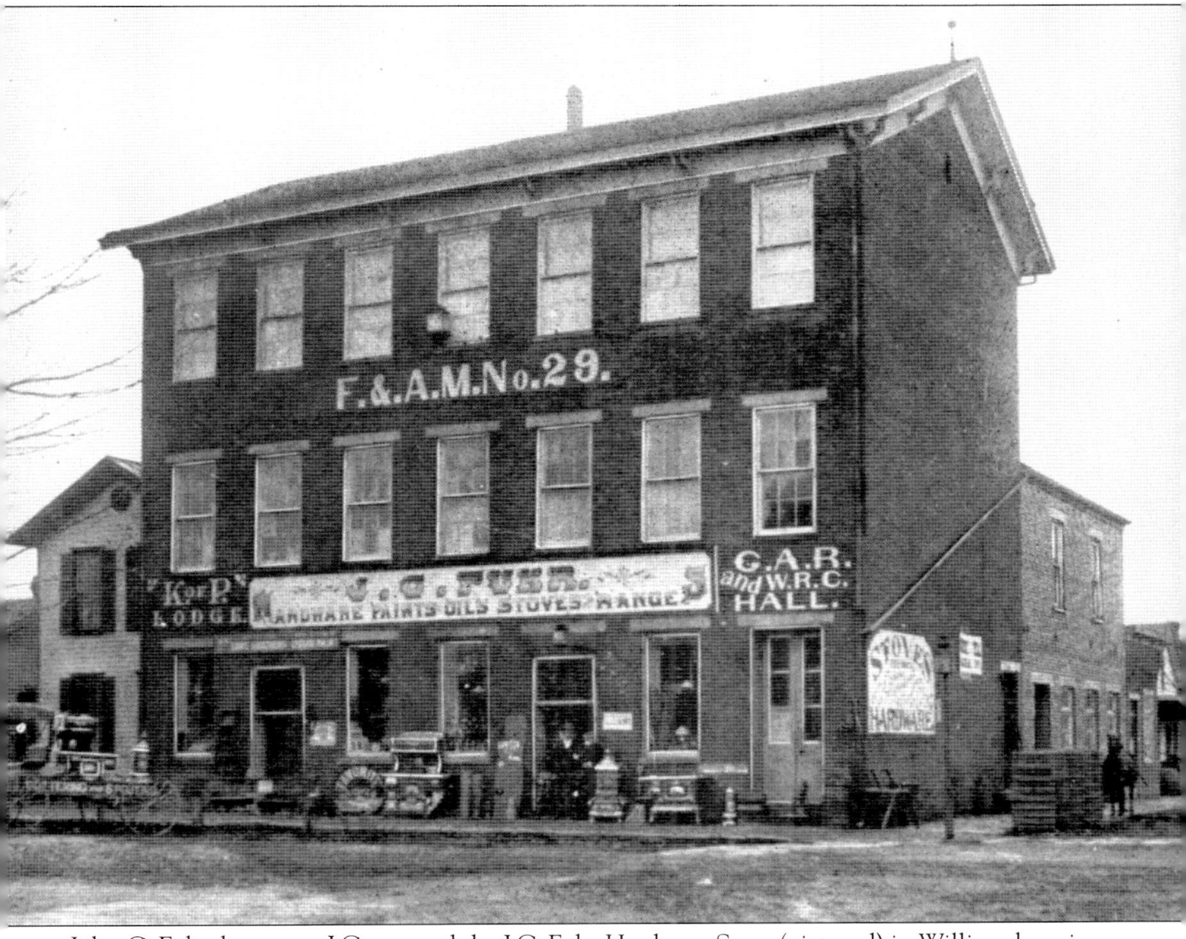

John C. Fuhr, known as J.C., opened the J.C. Fuhr Hardware Store (pictured) in Williamsburg in 1886. He also helped found the Farmers and Merchants Bank, the Williamsburg Furniture Company, and the Williamsburg Brick Company. (Photograph courtesy of Tim and Windy Ferree.)

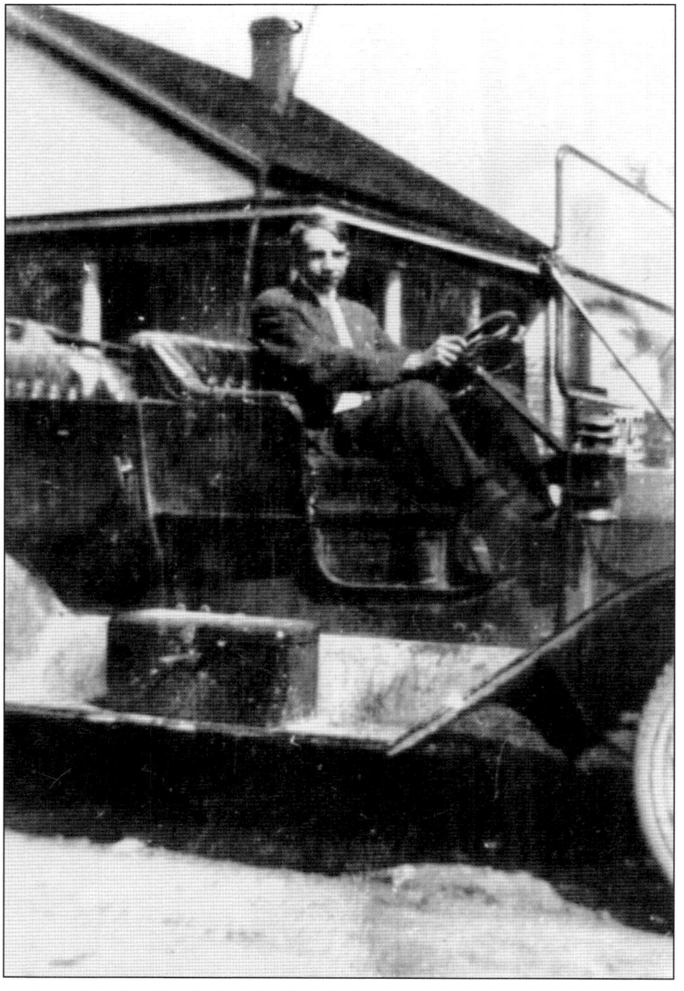

Ralph Fuhr shows off his new car in this photograph. Ralph was the son of John C. Fuhr, a well-trained sheet metal worker, who worked in several cities before moving to Williamsburg from Cincinnati in 1885. John C. Fuhr married Cora Walker, the only daughter of Ludlow Walker and Nancy J. Smith. (Photograph courtesy of Tim and Windy Ferree.)

The Fuhr family had large gatherings at its reunions, such as the one pictured here. John C. Fuhr was born in 1863 to John and Katharina Deuter Fuhr in Hessen, Germany. He was the first of three brothers to immigrate to America, arriving in New York in the midst of President Garfield's assassination on July 3, 1881. J.C., as he was known, and his wife, Cora, were the parents of John Roy, Stanley Walker, Ralph Deuter Fuhr, Lida Fuhr Smith, and Mary Katharina Fuhr. (Photograph courtesy of Tim and Windy Ferree.)

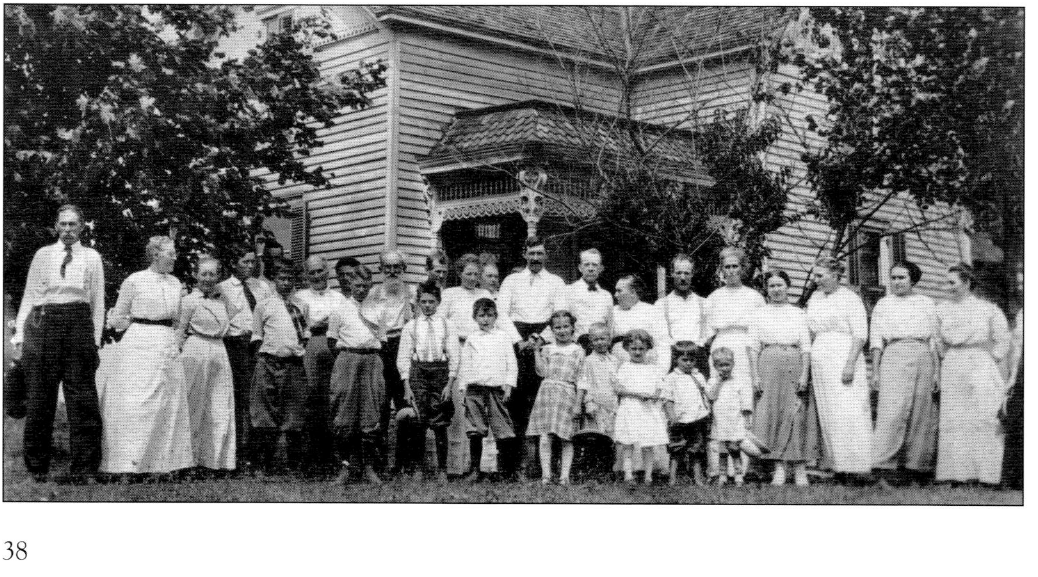

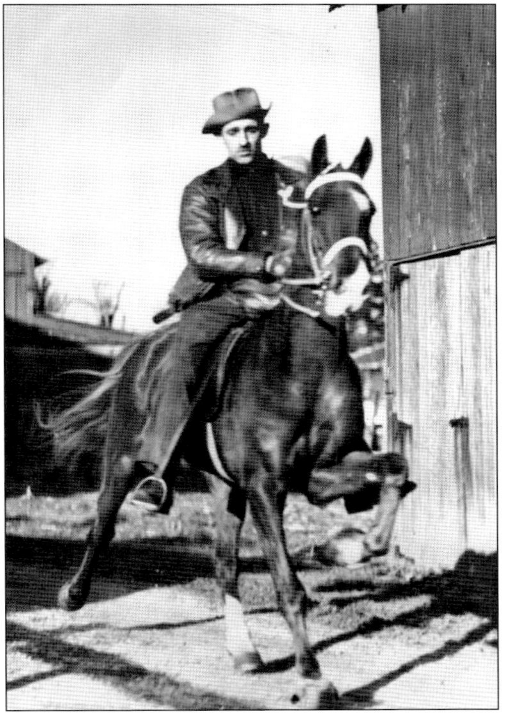

Williamsburg resident Arthur Peed is pictured showing off his horsemanship skills. Peed, whose nickname was "Poke," was the brother-in-law of Roy and Ralph Fuhr. He and Roy managed the Fuhr Hardware Store for several years. (Photographs courtesy of Tim and Windy Ferree.)

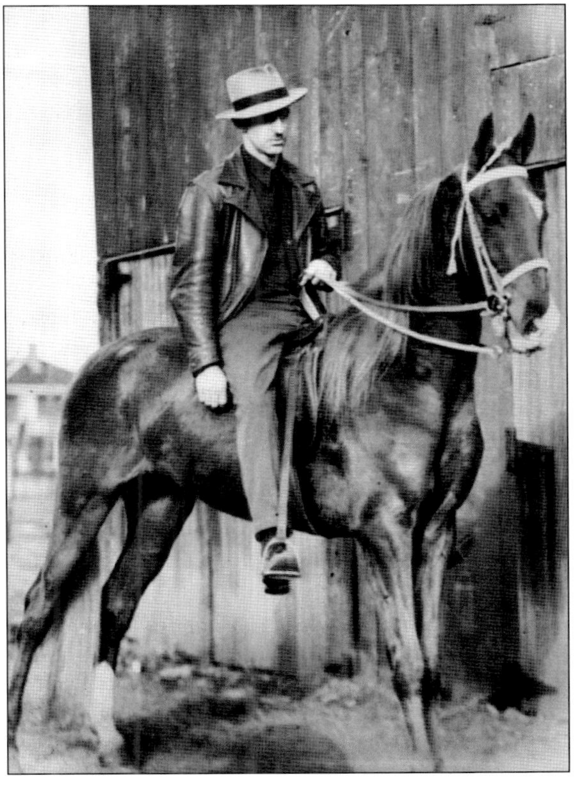

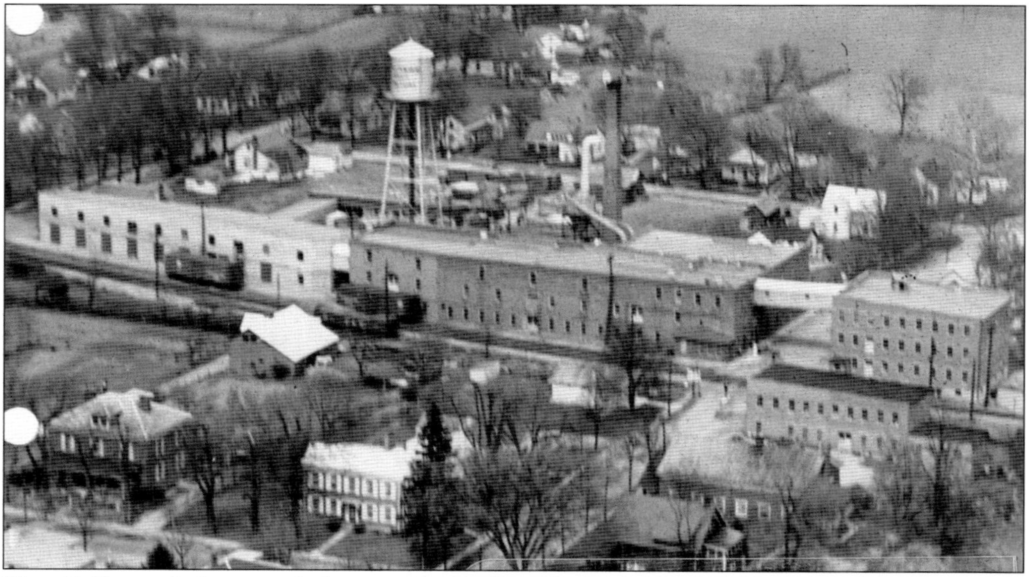

This 1945 aerial photograph features the Williamsburg Chair Factory. As early as 1820, splint seated chairs were made by hand and manufactured in Williamsburg. In 1848, Volney Stockton began making chairs by machine, and as many as 10 to 12 dozen chairs were made weekly by the four or five men who worked in the factory. (Photograph courtesy of Tim and Windy Ferree.)

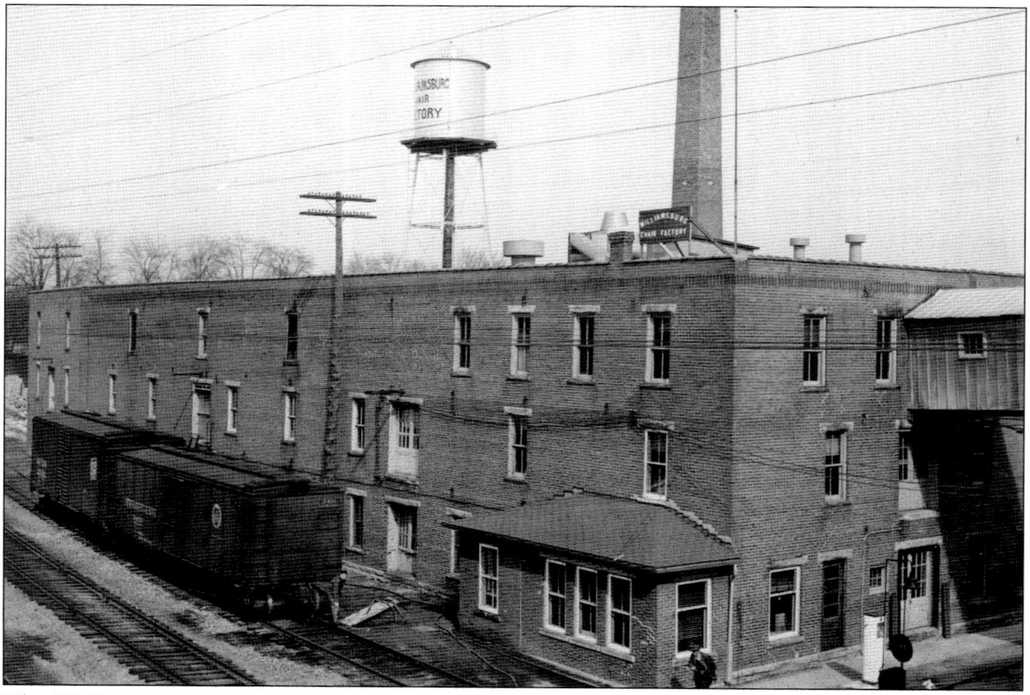

The Williamsburg Chair Factory, established in 1896, was owned and operated by J.H. White and George Dillman. By 1903, when White bought out Dillman, the factory was considered the great industry of the town, employing as many as 30 men. (Photograph courtesy of Tim and Windy Ferree.)

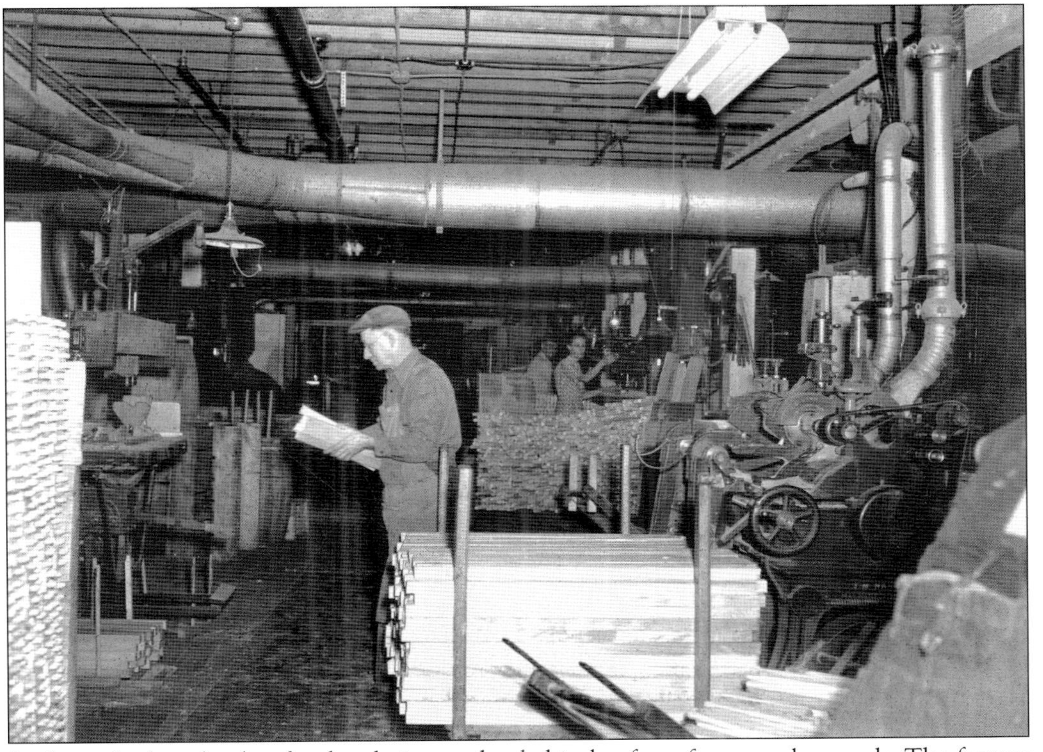

In the early days, lumber for the chairs was hauled in log form from nearby woods. The factory had 15 machines and most of the labor was done by hand. As many as 12 dozen chairs were made per day and then hauled from Williamsburg to the Ohio River, where they were put on riverboats. Others were sold directly from the factory. By 1936, the factory had increased to 73,000 square feet and employed 100 men, who turned out as many as 65 dozen chairs. An ad in the 1936 *Williamsburg Times* boasted that the factory used 650 tons of coal for heating and powering the plant, along with 35,000 gallons of paints, varnishes, and stains; 850,000 feet of lumber, and 100 tons of wrapping paper to prepare the furniture for shipping. (Photograph courtesy of Tim and Windy Ferree.)

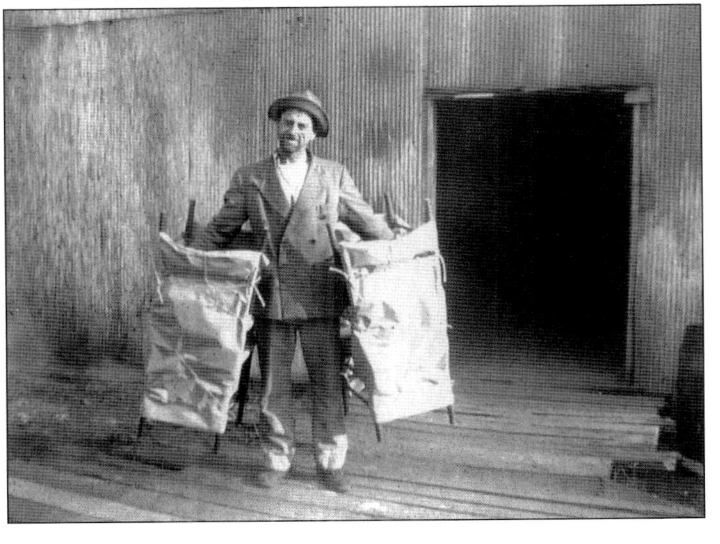

Wilbur Shoemake carries two finished chairs wrapped for shipping. The factory was conveniently located on Williamsburg's Walnut Street across the tracks from the train depot. (Photograph courtesy of Hazel Arnold.)

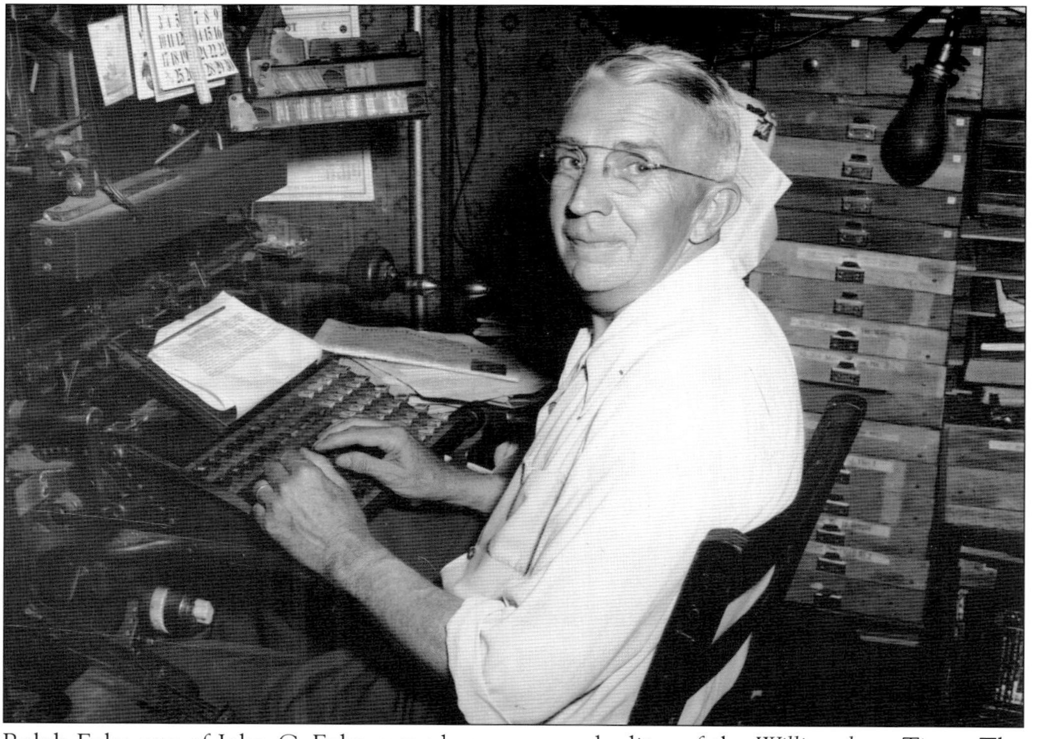

Ralph Fuhr, son of John C. Fuhr, served as owner and editor of the *Williamsburg Times*. The paper ran its first issue on December 15, 1920. In addition to his editorial duties, Fuhr was also known as "Radio Ralph" because of his interest in early radio. (Photograph courtesy of Tim and Windy Ferree.)

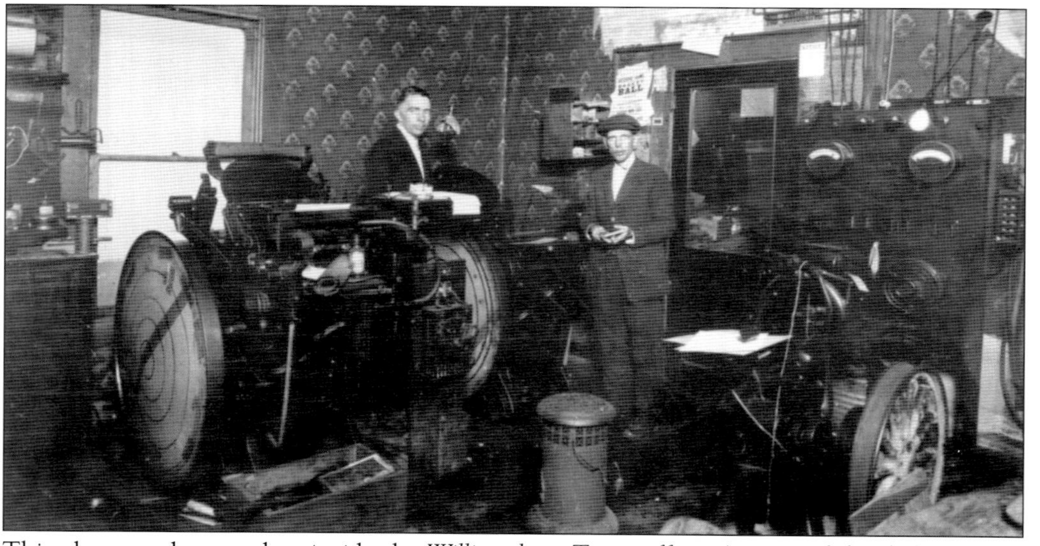

This photograph was taken inside the *Williamsburg Times* office. As part of the dedication of the new bridge in downtown Williamsburg, the newspaper offered a double deal for rural route subscribers only. Readers could get a year's subscription to the *Williamsburg Times* and the *Cincinnati Times Star* for only $4.25. (Photograph courtesy of Tim and Windy Ferree.)

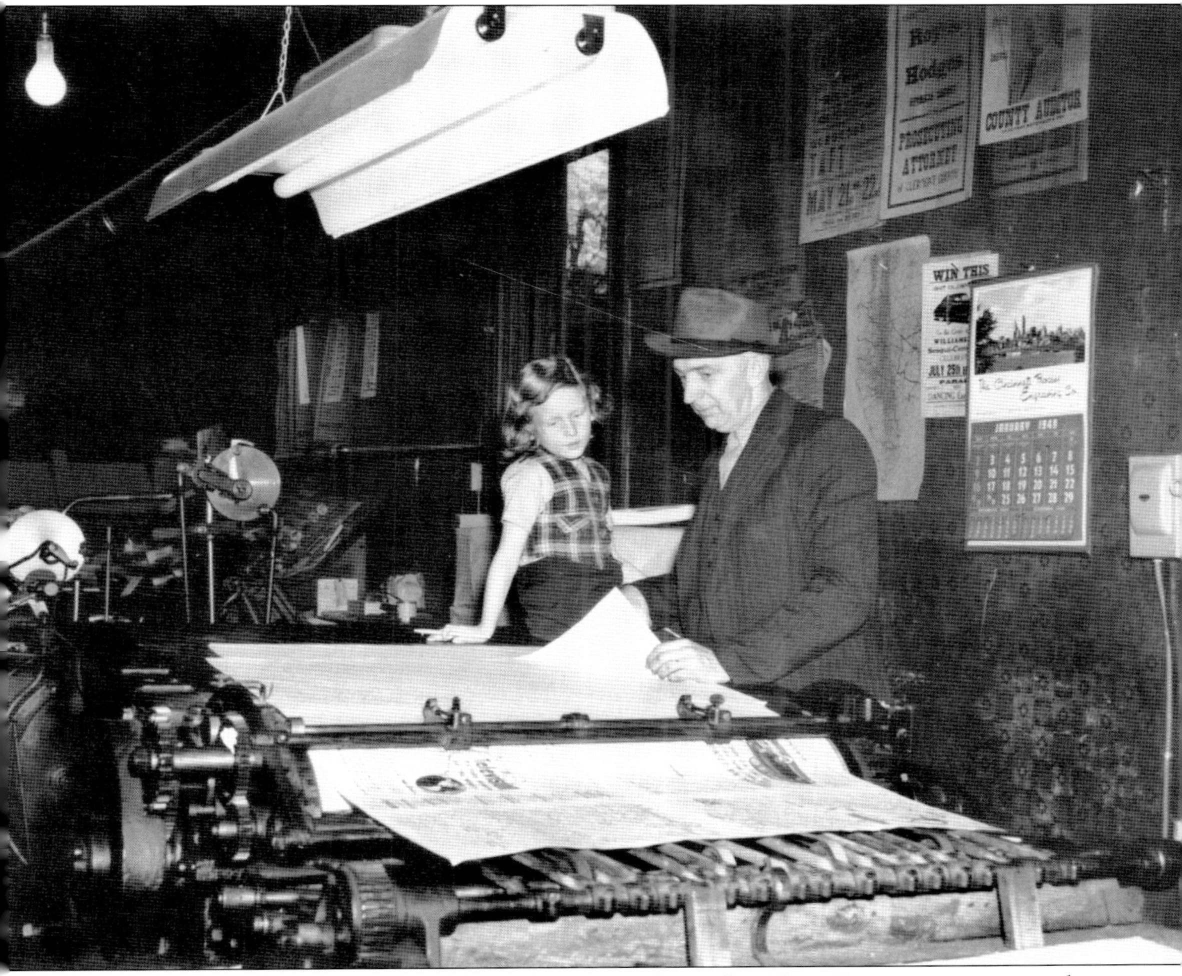

Ralph Fuhr shows his young granddaughter, Patricia, the *Williamsburg Times* newspaper on the presses in this 1949 photograph. Ralph served as the newspaper's owner and editor from 1920 until the 1960s, when Ralph's son D.J sold it to Charles Danbury and Kermit Smith. (Photograph courtesy of Hazel Arnold.)

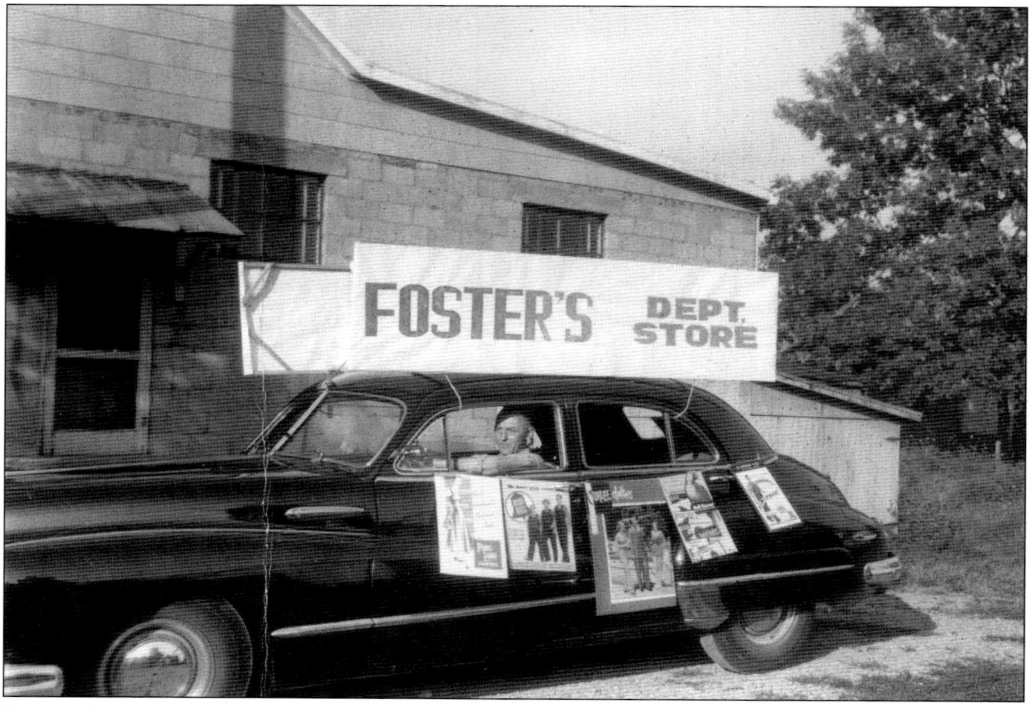

Foster's Department Store was known for selling home furnishings, men's and women's clothing, window treatments, wallpaper, and complete dry goods such as shoes, suits, and clothing. Foster's closed in the late 1970s. (Photograph courtesy of Tim and Windy Ferree.)

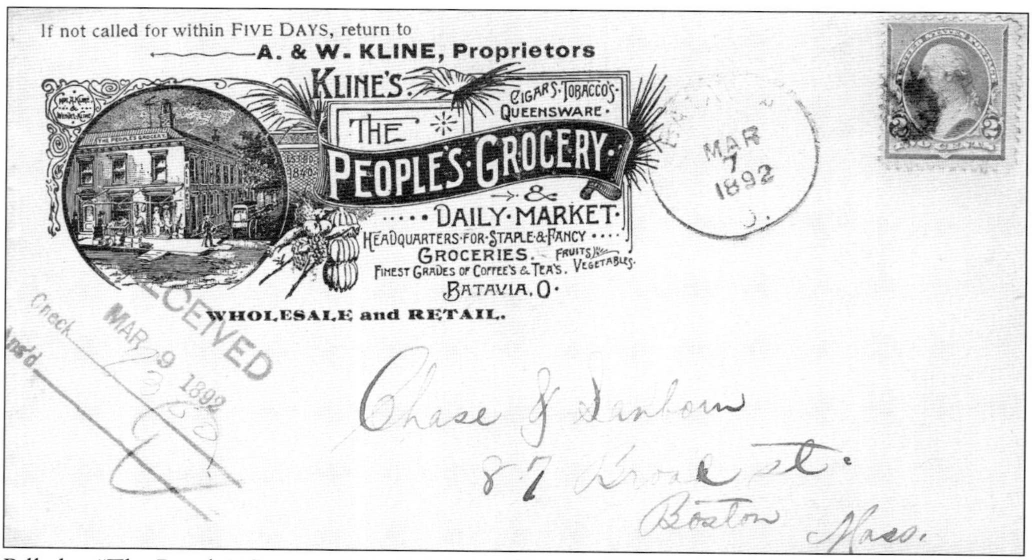

Billed as "The People's Grocery & Daily Market," Kline's Grocery Store of Batavia was established in 1892 by proprietors A. & W. Kline. They advertised themselves as the headquarters for staple and fancy groceries, finest grades of coffees and teas, and fruits and vegetables. (Photograph courtesy of Steve Shinkle.)

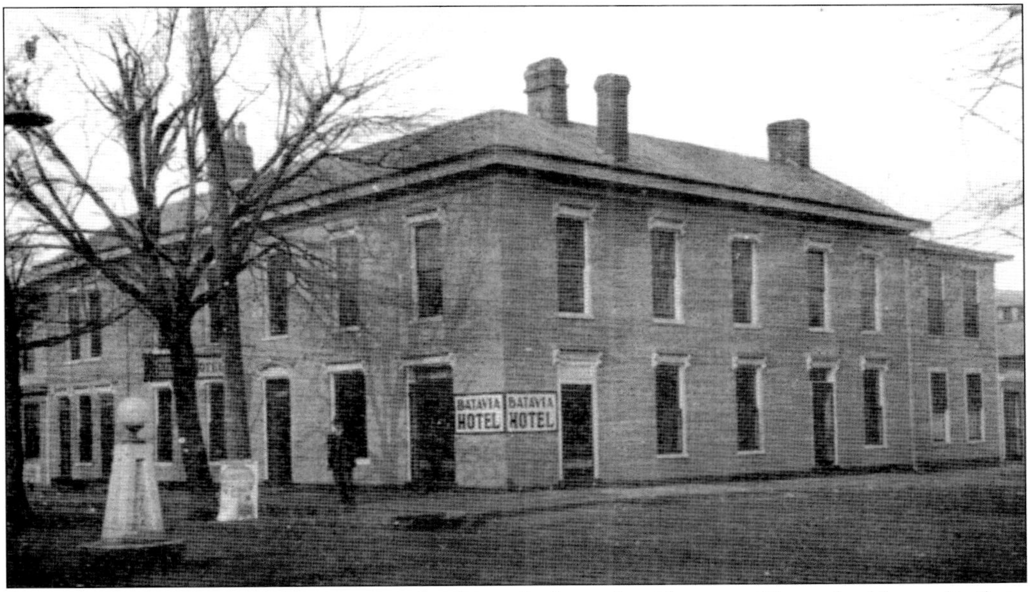

Located on Main Street, the Batavia Hotel stood where the Clermont House had been. Built in 1898 by the Maham family, it boasted of being "equipped with all modern conveniences of heat, electricity, telephones, and telegraphs with a free hack running to all passenger trains," according to a 1936 article in the *Williamsburg Times*. (Photograph courtesy of Steve Shinkle.)

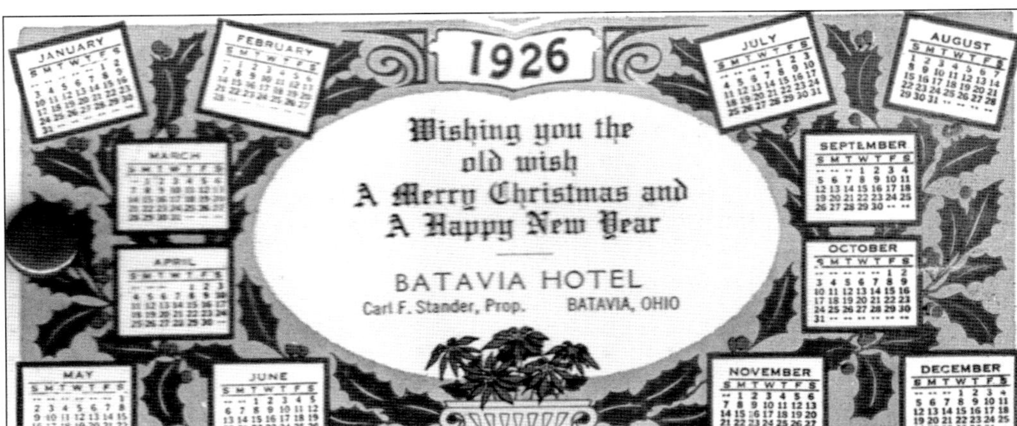

As the county seat, Batavia drew visitors from all parts of Ohio, Indiana, and Kentucky. Blotters like this one from the Batavia Hotel were effective tools in advertising. (Photograph courtesy of Steve Shinkle.)

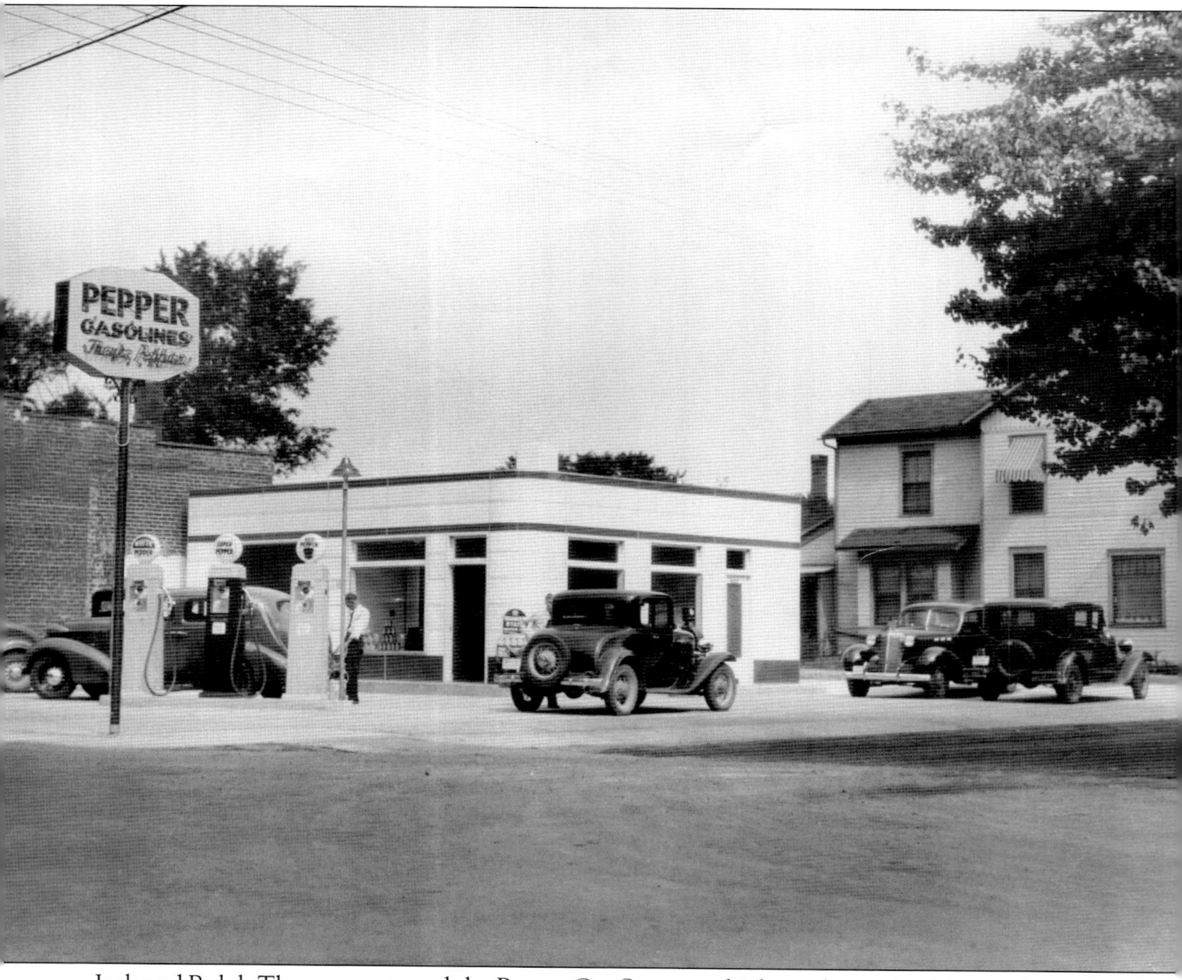

Jack and Ralph Thompson started the Pepper Gas Station, which was located at Main and Second Streets in Williamsburg. The Thompsons operated the station for a few years before selling it to Ernest Ruffner, who turned it into an Ashland Oil station in the 1940s. Pepper gasoline was advertised as "outstanding among the nation's finest motor fuels on mileage, power and pep." This c. 1930s photograph shows Main Street when it was still a sand and gravel road. (Photograph courtesy of Hazel Arnold.)

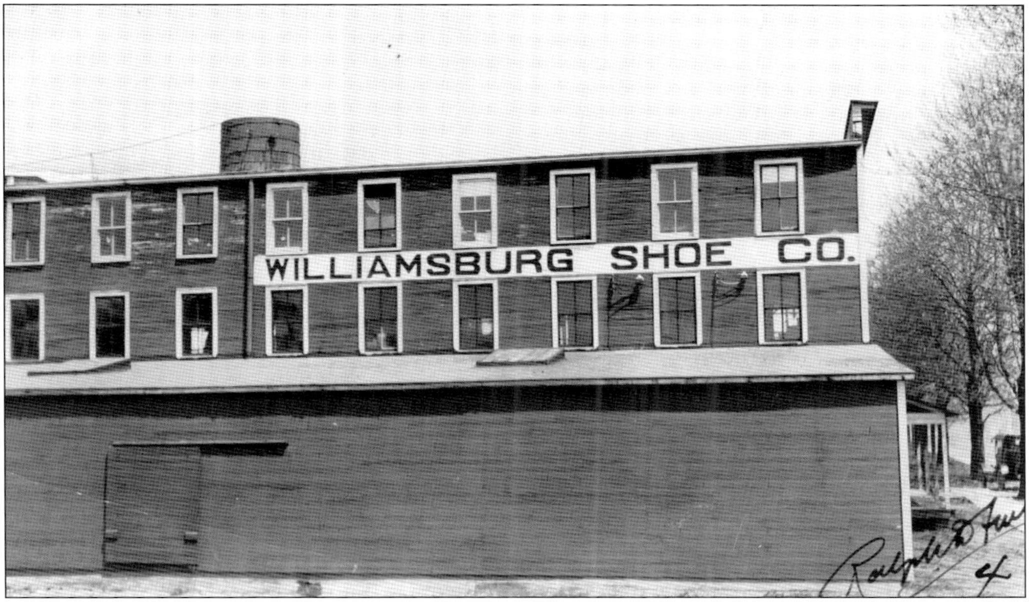

The Williamsburg Shoe Factory was a mainstay for town residents who found jobs there during the Great Depression. The company began as the Jones Heel Company in the mid- to late 1800s, became the Williamsburg Shoe Factory, and then was renamed the Sullivan Shoe Factory in the 1920s. (Photograph courtesy of Tim and Windy Ferree.)

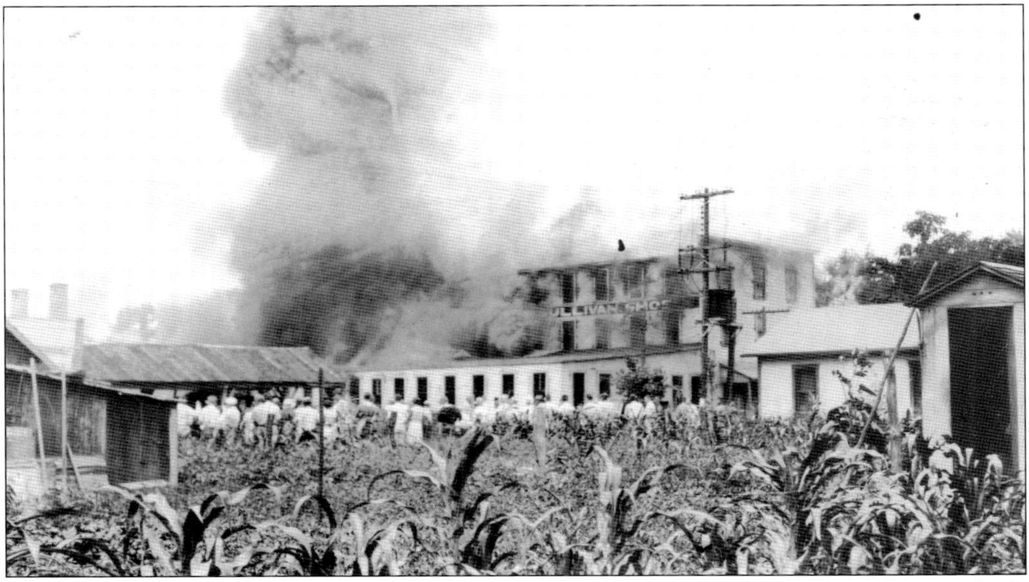

This photograph shows the smoldering remains of Williamsburg's Sullivan Shoe Factory, which burned in the 1930s. (Photograph courtesy of Tim and Windy Ferree.)

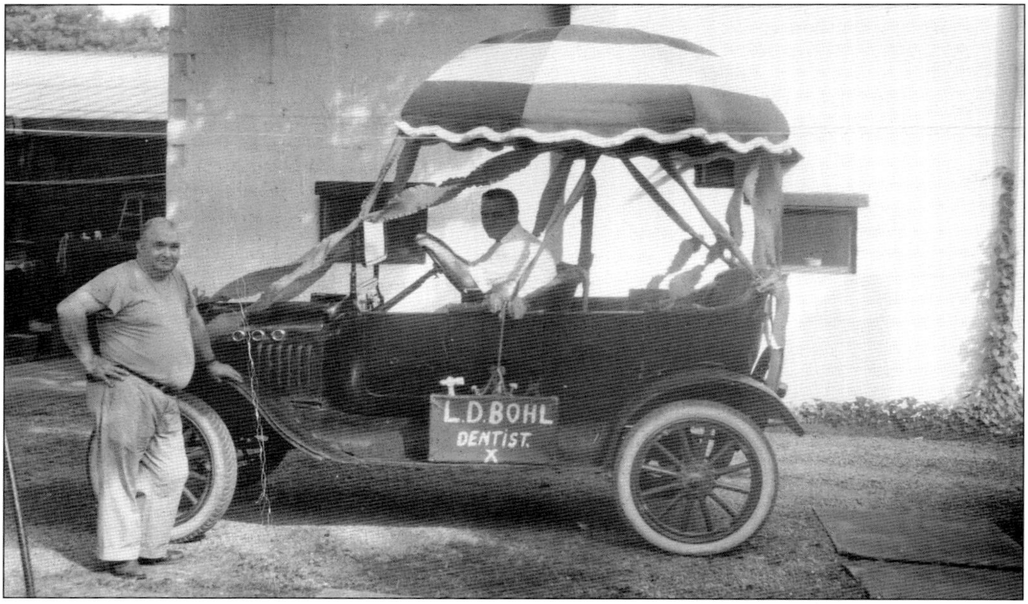

On July 5, 1927, Dr. Leslie Bohl established an office in his home at 122 W. Main Street in Williamsburg. In 1930, he moved his office to the second floor rooms of the Croswell Bus Line building. He continued his practice until 1944, when he moved his office to 284 W. Main. He and his son Dr. Roy Bohl provided over 50 years of quality dental service to hundreds of patients. (Photograph courtesy of Hazel Arnold.)

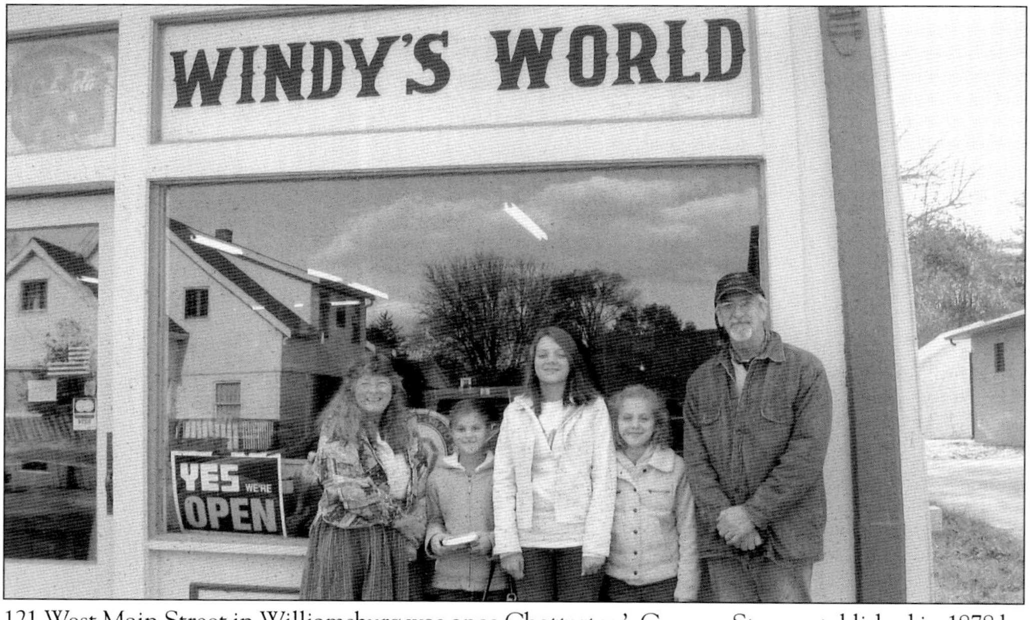

121 West Main Street in Williamsburg was once Chatterton's Grocery Store, established in 1878 by Charles Phillip Chatterton. The family-operated store was in business for nearly a century before closing its doors in 1973. In 1975, Windy Ferree (left) and her husband Tim (right) became the proprietors of Windy's World, an old-fashioned dry goods store that sells fabric, sewing and weaving supplies, and antiques and collectibles. (Photograph courtesy of Tim and Windy Ferree.)

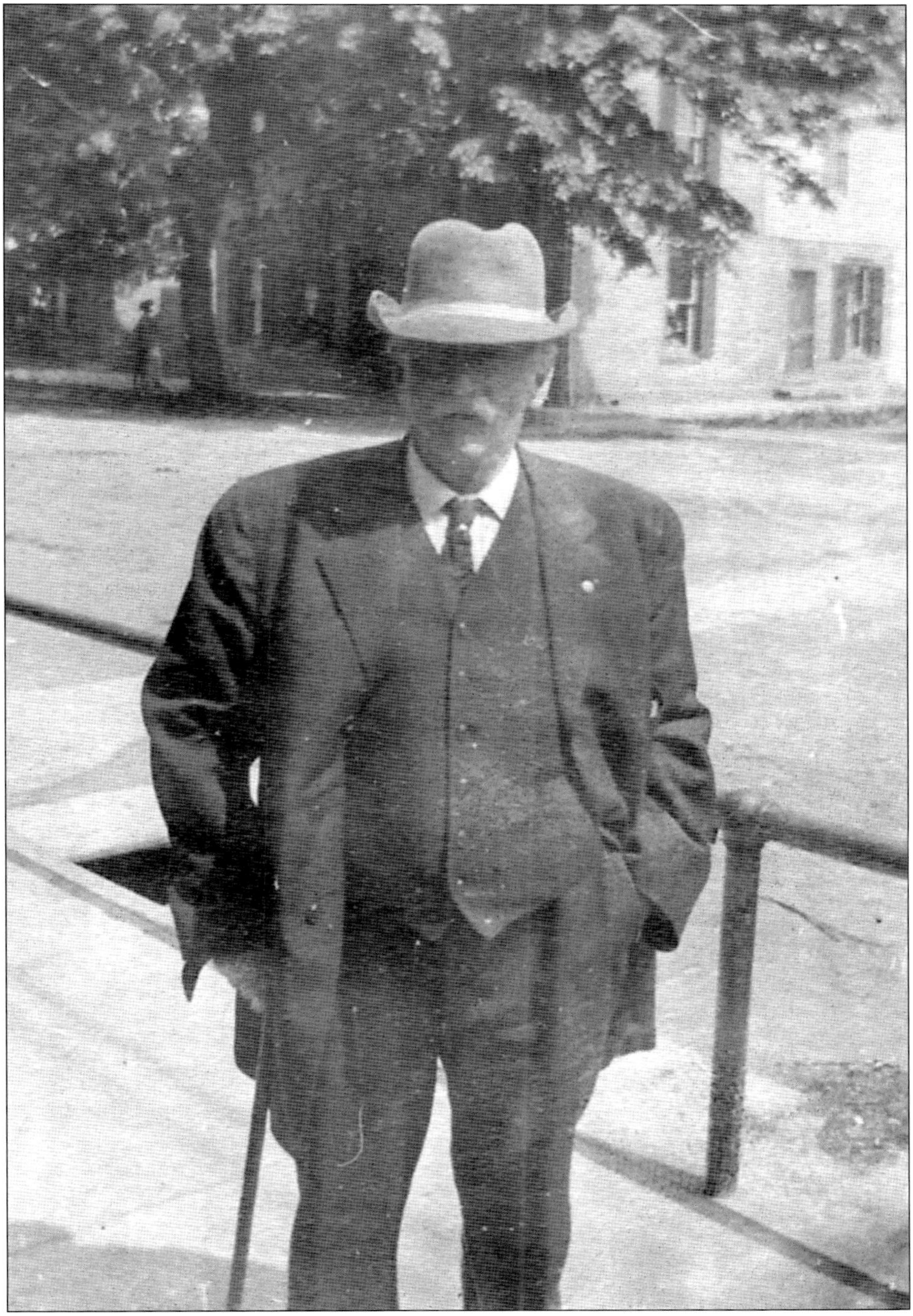

Dr. George Hines lived on Gay Street in the former home of Underground Railroad stationmaster Dr. Leavitt Thaxter Pease. Doctor Hines was a highly respected doctor who practiced from the late 1800s through the 1920s. His son Harry Hines owned the drugstore in Williamsburg, and went on to become the chief operating officer and cashier of the town's Building and Loan and then eventually became the town's postmaster. (Photograph courtesy of Tim and Windy Ferree.)

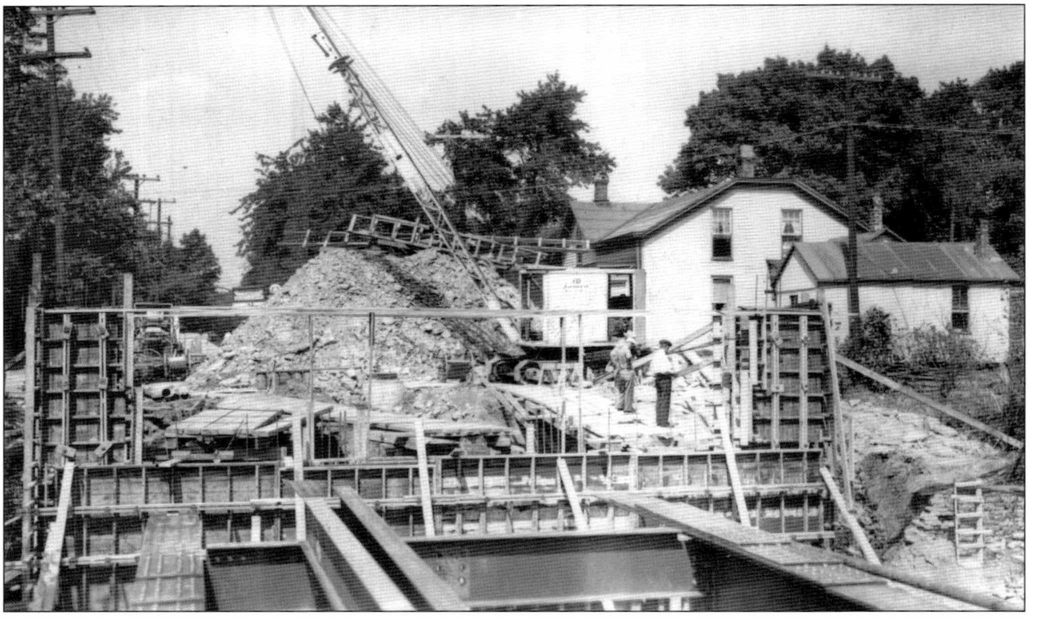

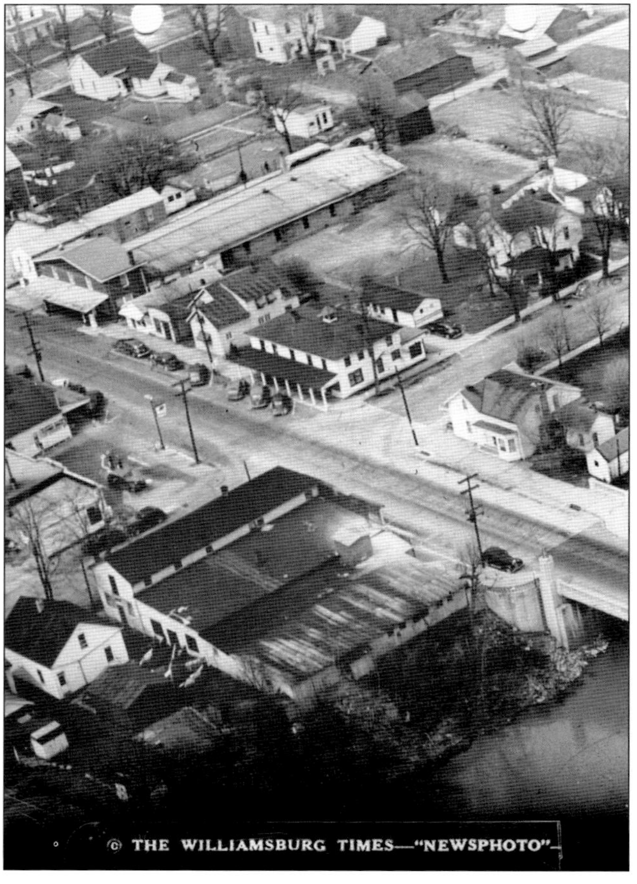

This c. 1930s photograph shows the temporary bridge built in Williamsburg over the East Fork of the Little Miami River, which was intended to handle traffic while the new concrete bridge was being constructed. (Photograph courtesy of Hazel Arnold.)

Taken in April 1947 for the *Williamsburg Times*, this aerial photograph is of the southeast section of Williamsburg. It shows the new concrete bridge over the East Fork of the Little Miami River, constructed from 1935 until 1936 to replace the town's beloved covered bridge. (Photograph courtesy of Hazel Arnold.)

Three

Serving the Country

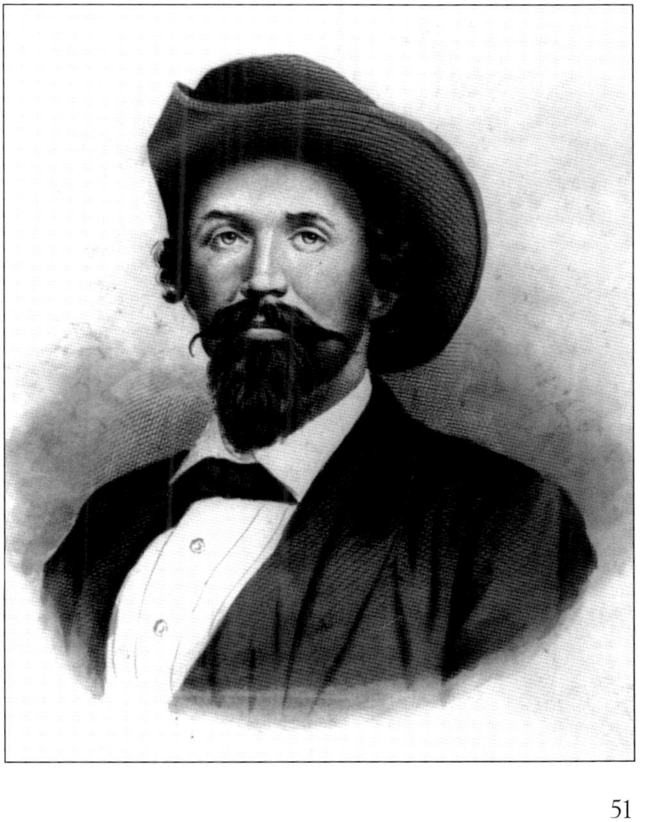

On July 19, 1863, Confederate general John Hunt Morgan and his tired entourage of 2,000 soldiers arrived in Williamsburg after riding 92 miles in 35 hours. Morgan and six of his officers stayed at the Kain Tavern and over 100 soldiers took supper there. Morgan, who reportedly stayed in Room 9, confiscated all the mail from the Williamsburg post office looking for military news and money. (Photograph courtesy of the US Library of Congress.)

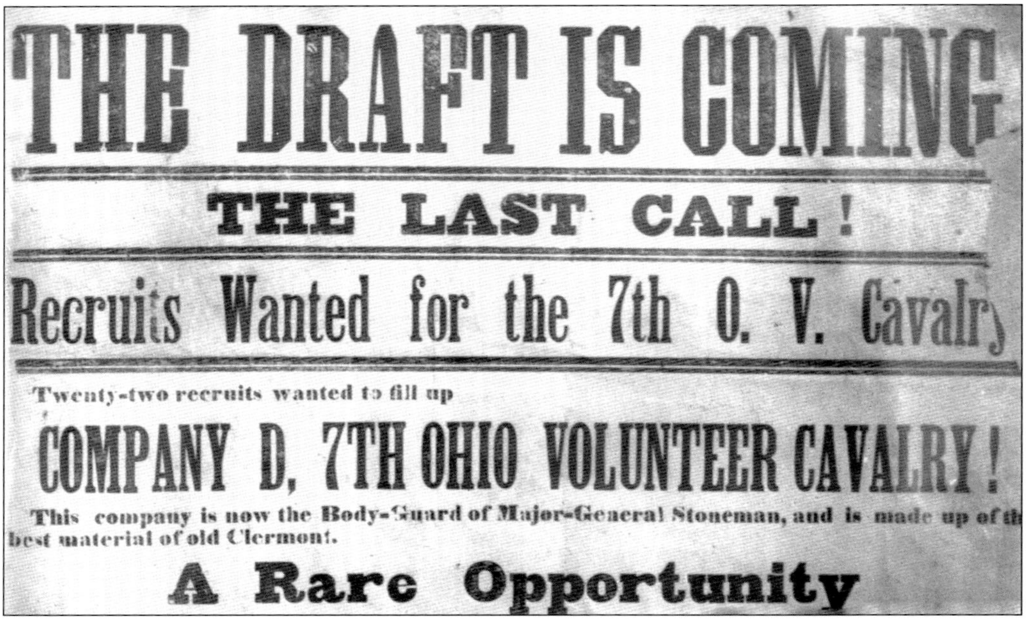

Nearly 5,000 Clermont County men enlisted during the course of the Civil War, placing the county in the top third in the state by percentage of eligible men who served. They served in every military branch, from the infantry and cavalry to artillery and Navy, and were represented at the battles of Bull Run, Gettysburg, Antietam, Shiloh, Vicksburg, and Chickamauga. (Photograph from the Sharp Collection, courtesy of the Clermont County Library.)

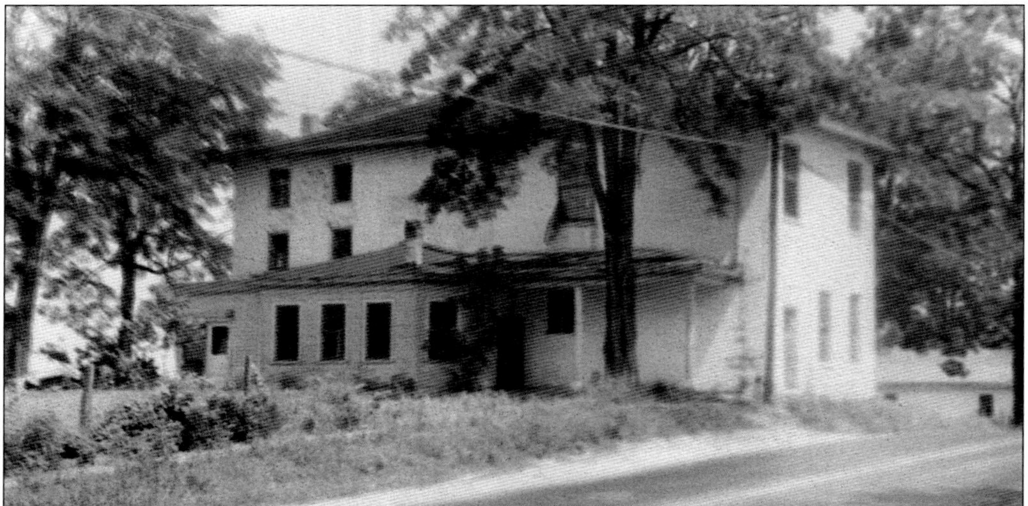

After building this c. 1815 home at Main and Broadway in Williamsburg, William Lytle transferred ownership to his brother John. Built of brick with stone trimming and always painted white, it held a commanding view of the town. It is believed that Gen. John Hunt Morgan and his officers made their headquarters there. Carved on its doorsill were the words, "John Morgan July 14, 1863, 30,000 men," most probably put there by one of Morgan's men. The home stayed in the Lytle family until 1889. Mrs. William Beckett was the last owner before it was torn down. (Photograph courtesy of Tim and Windy Ferree.)

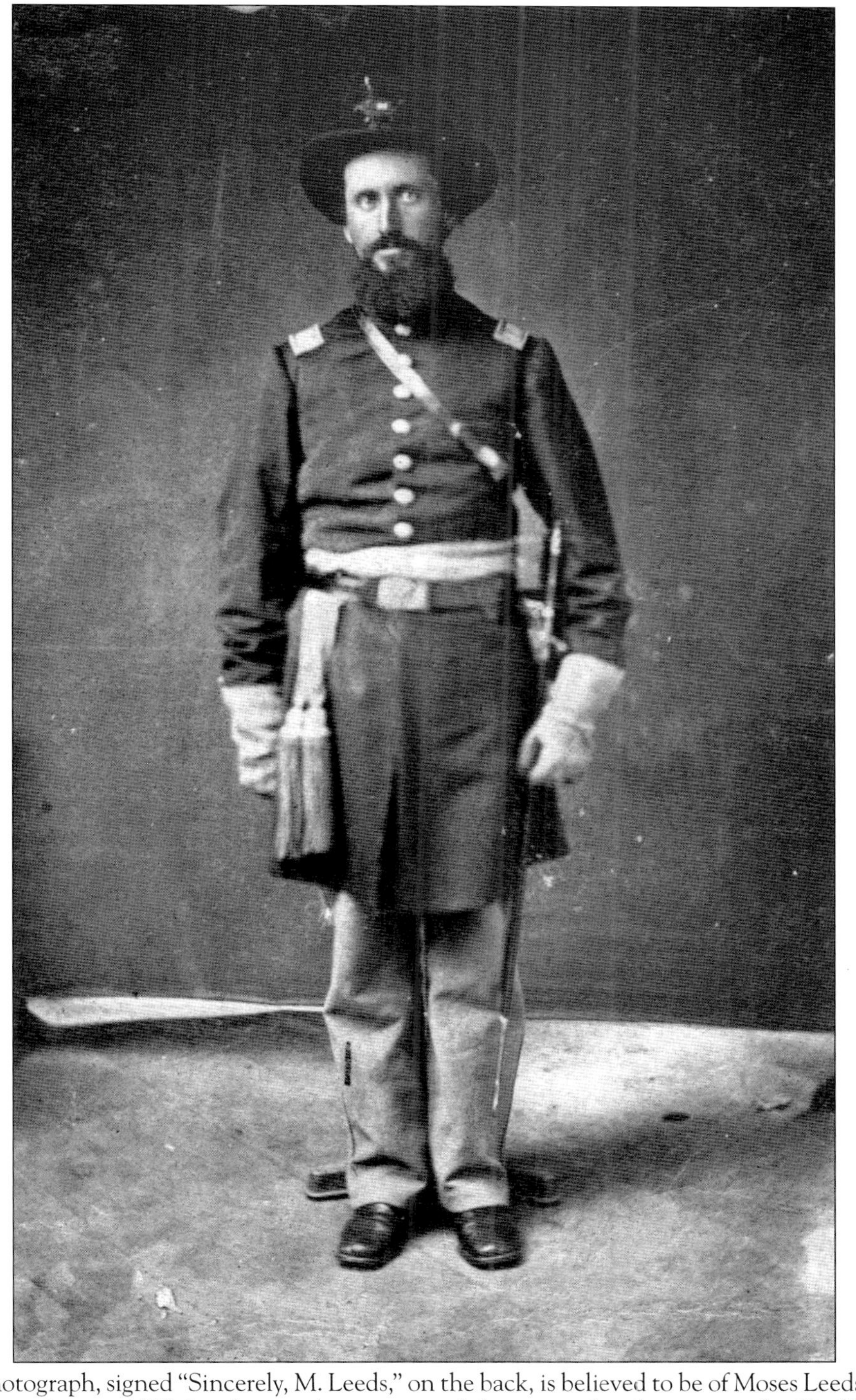

This photograph, signed "Sincerely, M. Leeds," on the back, is believed to be of Moses Leeds. Born in Williamsburg in 1838, Leeds gave three years and three months of service in the Civil War in Company B, 5th Ohio Cavalry, fighting at Pittsburg Landing, Bull Run, and others. (Photograph courtesy of Tim and Windy Ferree.)

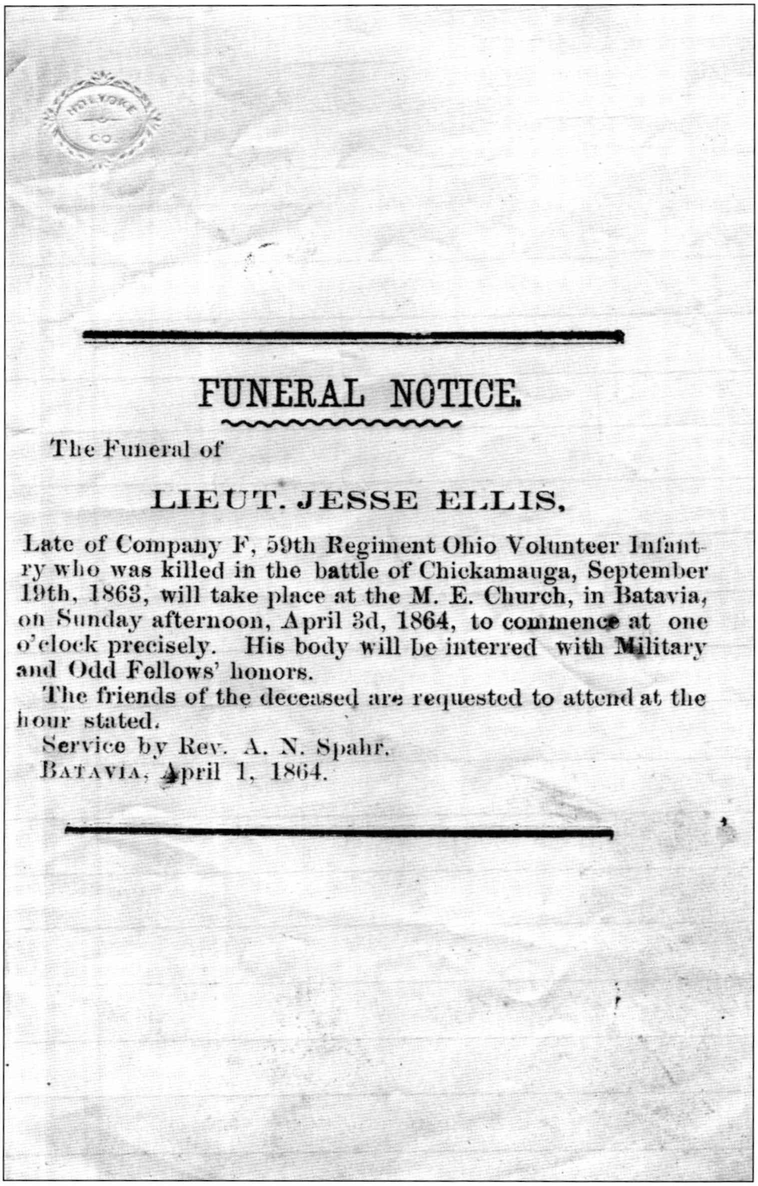

FUNERAL NOTICE.

The Funeral of

LIEUT. JESSE ELLIS,

Late of Company F, 59th Regiment Ohio Volunteer Infantry who was killed in the battle of Chickamauga, September 19th, 1863, will take place at the M. E. Church, in Batavia, on Sunday afternoon, April 3d, 1864, to commence at one o'clock precisely. His body will be interred with Military and Odd Fellows' honors.

The friends of the deceased are requested to attend at the hour stated.

Service by Rev. A. N. Spahr.

BATAVIA, April 1, 1864.

Batavia resident Jesse Ellis, 37 years old, was the town's first Civil War casualty. In *The History of Batavia, Ohio* by Rosanna Hoberg, an anonymous writer recalls Ellis's funeral, saying, "I remember the death of our Jesse Ellis, for whom the G.A.R Post at Batavia is named. He was in the 59th regiment, a lieutenant, and was killed at the Battle of Chickamauga. I remember when the news of his death reached Batavia, and how deeply it affected the people. His body was found on the battlefield and brought home for burial. I remember the funeral very distinctly . . . There were soldiers from Camp Dennison who marched in the funeral procession. It all seemed very imposing and solemn . . . There was a large flag over the coffin. The band played a funeral march with muffled drums. After the coffin was lowered into the grave, the soldiers, four of them, I think, possibly more, fired over his grave, an old military custom . . . There was a large gathering of people at the funeral and it is all clear in my memory." (Photograph courtesy of Lou Moore.)

This house, located at 180 Gay Street in Williamsburg, was the home of Underground Railroad stationmaster Dr. Leavitt Thaxter Pease and his wife, Nancy Ann Fee. Doctor Pease, an advocate of human freedom and civil rights, moved to Williamsburg in February 1835 and practiced medicine for over 40 years. (Author photograph.)

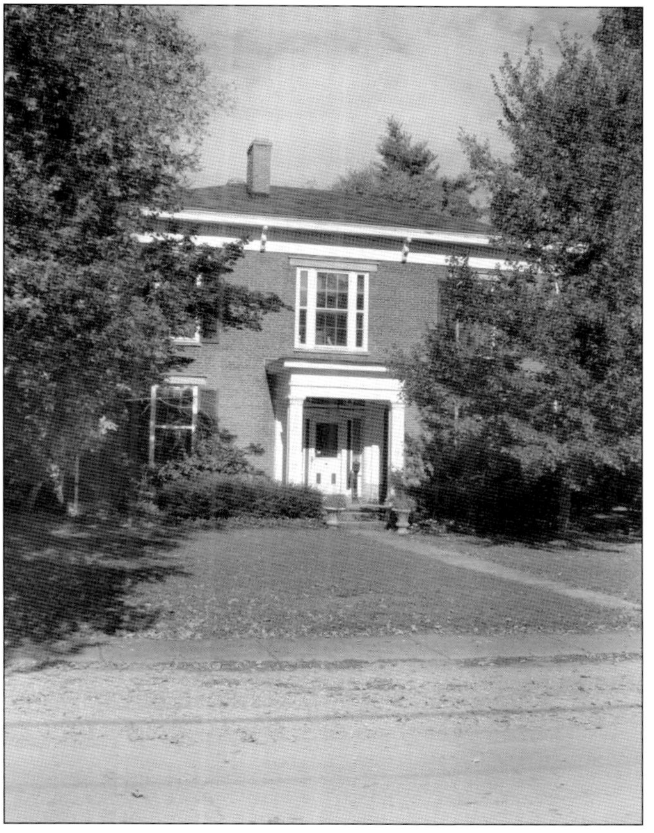

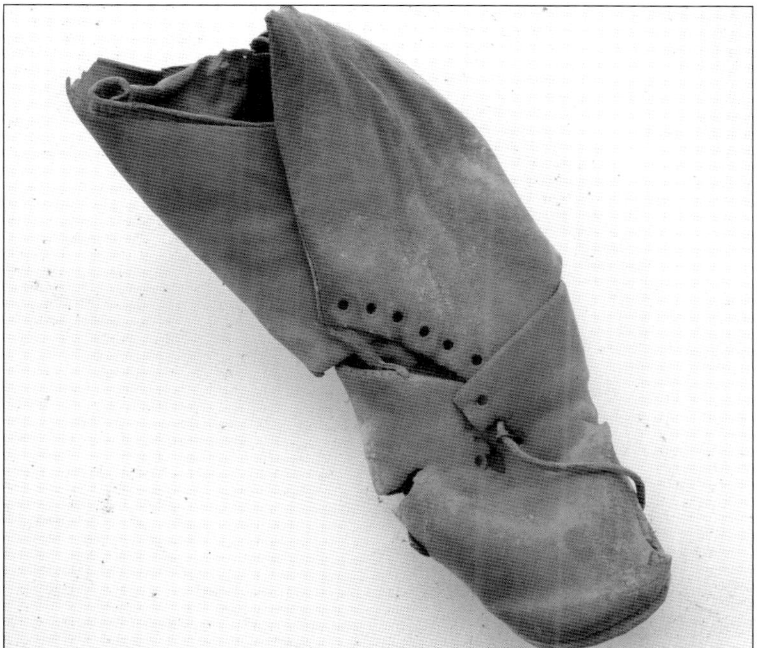

This old leather shoe was found in a hidden closet when the Pease house was in the process of renovation. It is believed to be part of the supplies kept for runaway slaves on their way to freedom in the North or Canada. (Author photograph.)

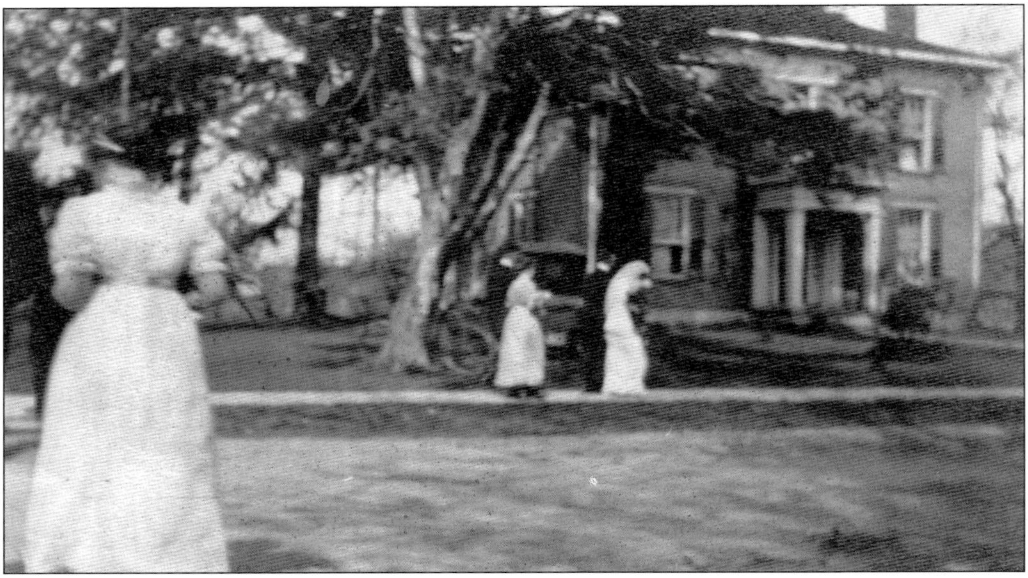

An antislavery Whig, Dr. Leavitt Pease served as an assistant Underground Railroad stationmaster to another Williamsburg resident, "Boss" Huber, who is credited with helping more than 300 men, women, and children escape slavery. Upon Huber's death, Pease became the stationmaster in Williamsburg. This 1913 photograph of the Pease home is of a wedding party who may have been married at the Williamsburg Presbyterian Church located just across the street. (Photograph courtesy of Tim and Windy Ferree.)

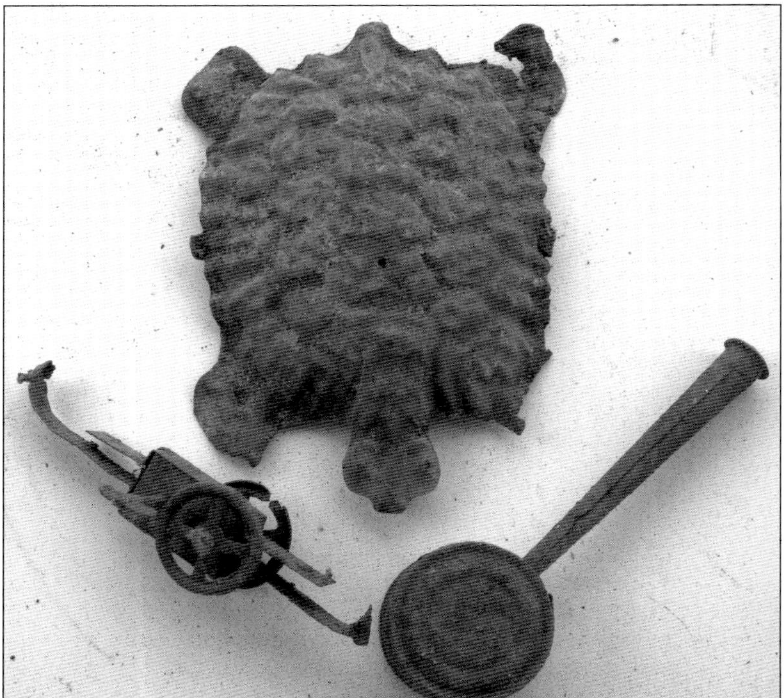

A child's rattle, turtle, and toy cannon from the Civil War era were found in a hidden closet when the Pease house was renovated. (Author photograph.)

Ludlow Walker, the father of Williamsburg resident Cora Walker Fuhr, served as a seaman aboard the Confederate gunboat Peaslee #36 of the Tennessee division of the Mississippi Squadron. (Photograph courtesy of Tim and Windy Ferree.)

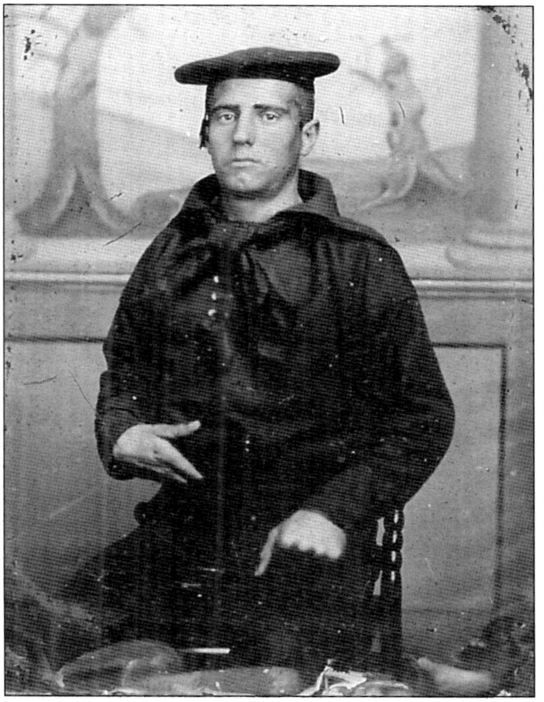

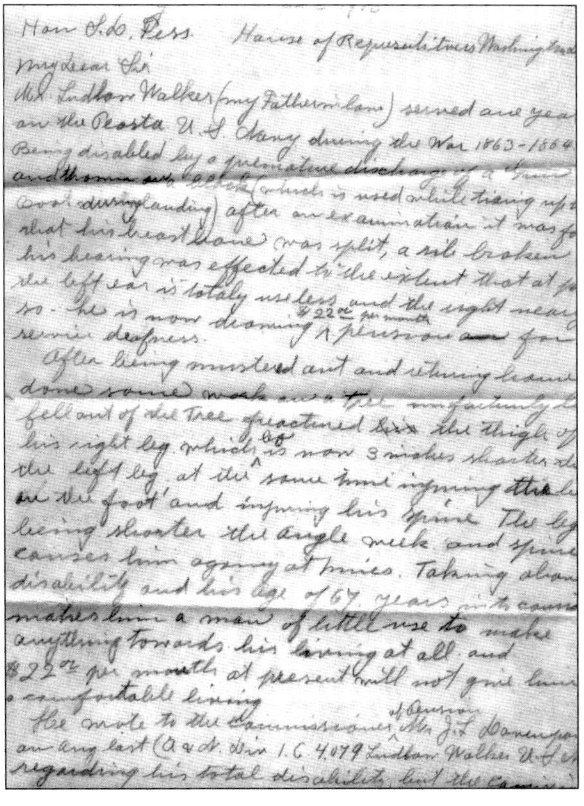

Hon S.D. Fess. House of Representatives Washington [illegible]
My Dear Sir
Mr Ludlow Walker (my Father in law) served one year
on the Peosta U.S. Navy during the War 1863-1864
Being disabled by a premature discharge of a [illegible]
and thrown [illegible] (which is used while tieing up
boat during landing) after an examination it was fo[illegible]
that his breast bone was split, a rib broken
his hearing was effected to the extent that at p[illegible]
the left ear is totaly useless and the right near
so - he is now drawing $22.00 per month pension for
service deafness.
After being mustered out and returning home
done some work on a [illegible] unfortunately [illegible]
fell out of the Tree fractured his the thigh of
his right leg which is now 3 inches shorter th[illegible]
the left leg at the same time injuring the [illegible]
in the foot and injuring his spine The leg
being shorter the angle week and spine
causes him agony at times. Taking above
disability and his age of 67 years [illegible]
makes him a man of little use to make
anything towards his living at all and
$22.00 per month at present will not give him
a comfortable living
He wrote to the Commissioner of Pension Mr J.L. Davenport
on Aug last (A & N. Div I.C. 4079 Ludlow Walker U.S. [illegible]
regarding his total disability but the Commi[illegible]

Ludlow Walker's papers state he was stationed at a gun when it discharged, blowing both Walker and another soldier, Lieutenant Vance, into the river. A witness testified, "Walker grabbed Vance by the stub of his right arm and with others helped him back aboard the boat." Walker, who lost his hearing in the accident, was receiving the handsome sum of $72 in disability by 1920. (Photograph courtesy of Tim and Windy Ferree.)

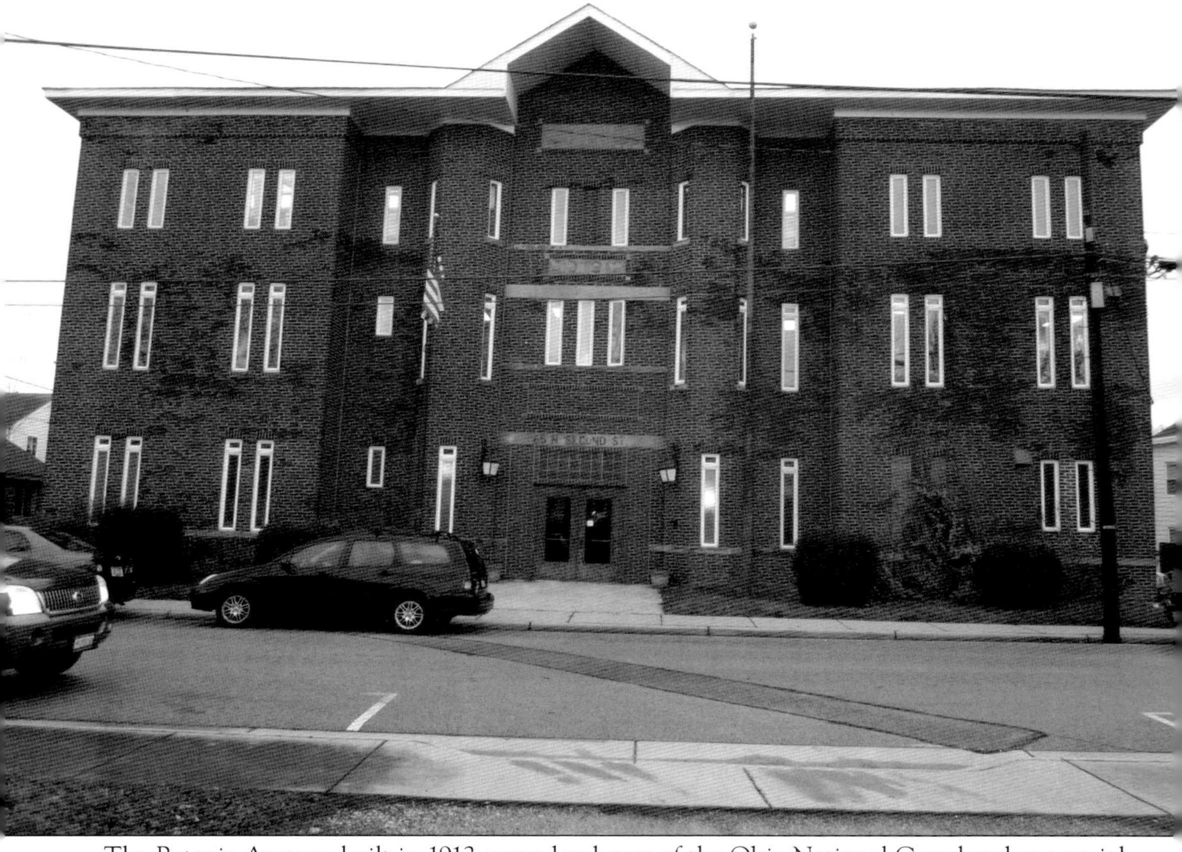

The Batavia Armory, built in 1912, served as home of the Ohio National Guard and as a social center for the town's citizens. Before schools had gymnasiums, basketball games were held at the Armory. It was busiest during the World War II years, when two county draft boards were established there. In 1994, voters rejected a bond issue to renovate the structure. It was auctioned off in 1998. (Photograph courtesy of the Clermont County Historical Society.)

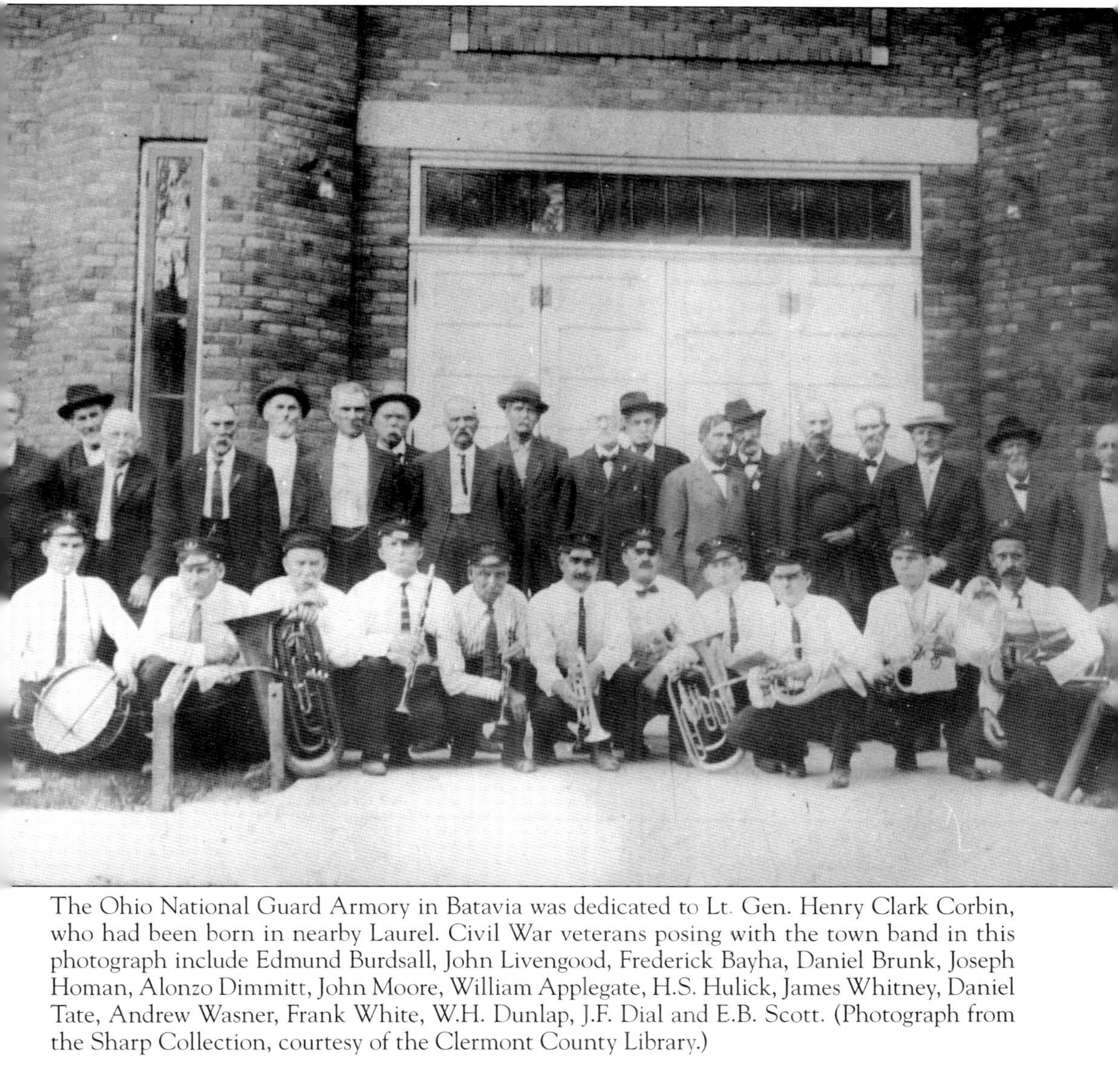

The Ohio National Guard Armory in Batavia was dedicated to Lt. Gen. Henry Clark Corbin, who had been born in nearby Laurel. Civil War veterans posing with the town band in this photograph include Edmund Burdsall, John Livengood, Frederick Bayha, Daniel Brunk, Joseph Homan, Alonzo Dimmitt, John Moore, William Applegate, H.S. Hulick, James Whitney, Daniel Tate, Andrew Wasner, Frank White, W.H. Dunlap, J.F. Dial and E.B. Scott. (Photograph from the Sharp Collection, courtesy of the Clermont County Library.)

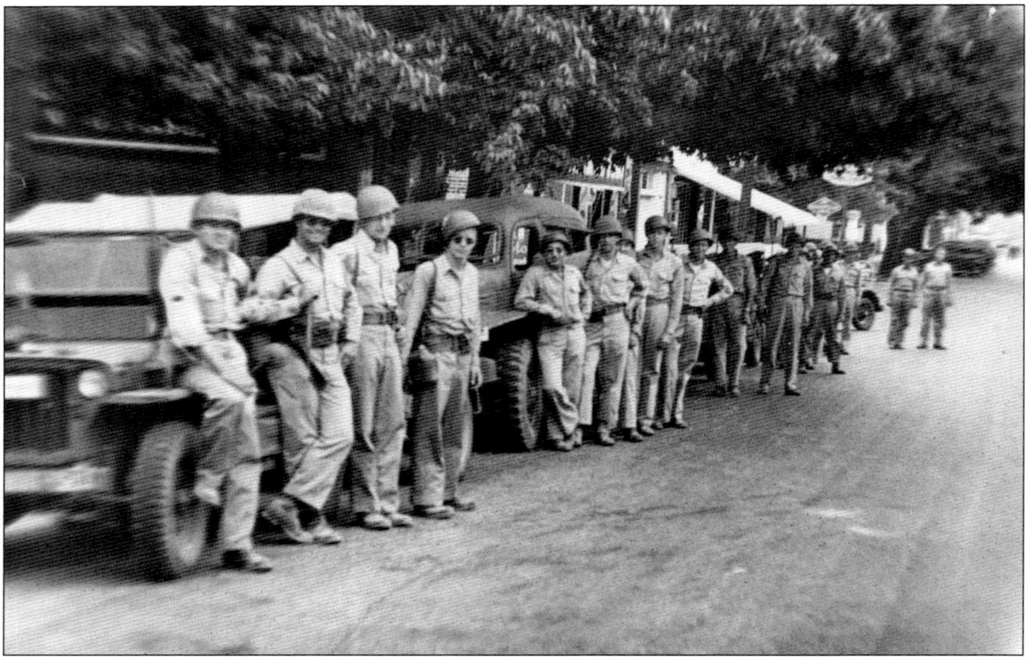

Whenever duty called, the men of Batavia and Williamsburg answered. This photograph shows World War II soldiers on Williamsburg's Main Street. (Photograph courtesy of Tim and Windy Ferree.)

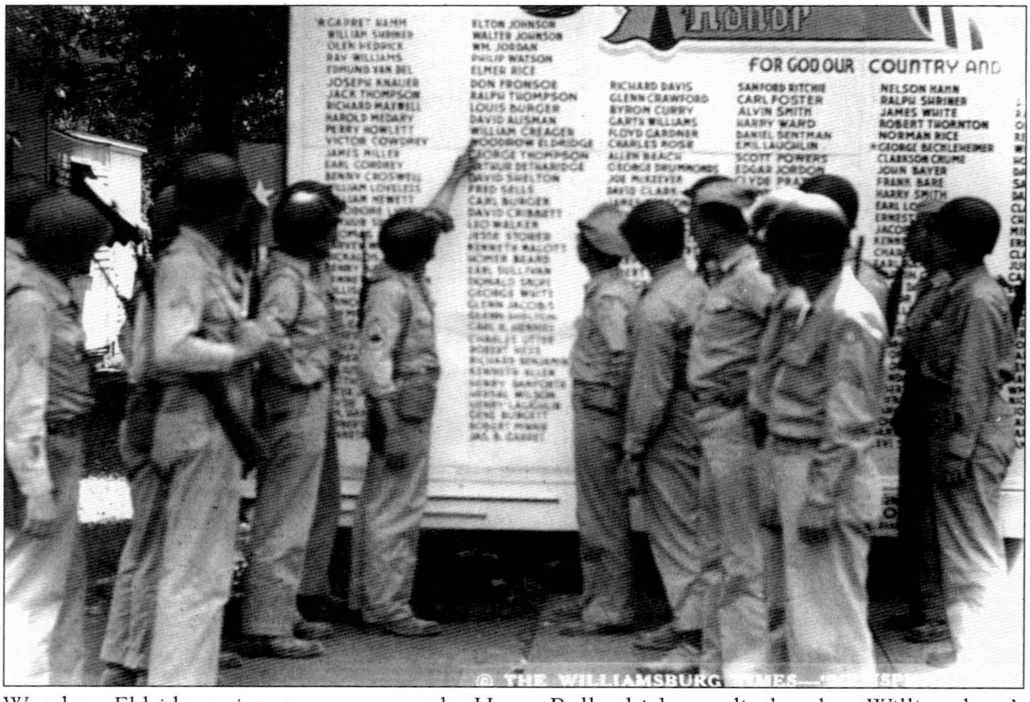

Woodrow Eldridge points to a name on the Honor Roll, which was displayed on Williamsburg's Main Street. (Photograph courtesy of Tim and Windy Ferree.)

Four

Ceremonies and Celebrations

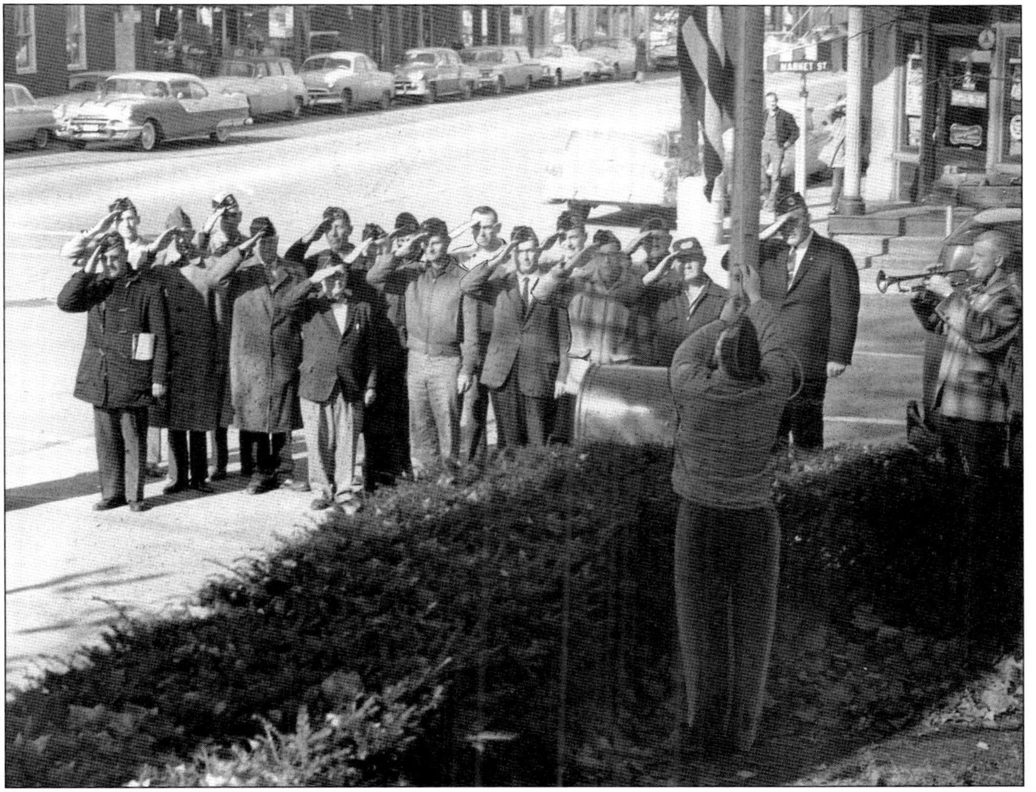

This c. 1950s photograph shows members of Batavia's American Legion, Frank W. Weaver Post, gathering for an Armistice and Veterans Day ceremony. Veterans of World War I, World War II, and the Korean conflict are shown offering a salute as Richard Brown sounds taps and post commander Lonnie Garner raises the Clermont County courthouse flag. (Photograph courtesy of the Clermont County Historical Society.)

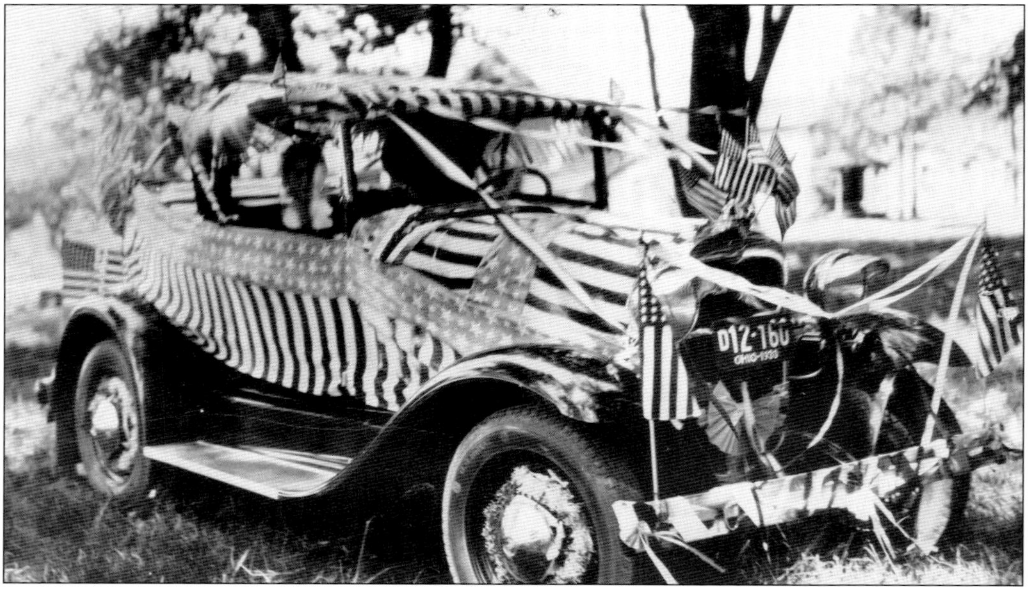

Businesses and residents of Williamsburg always looked forward to holiday celebrations. This photograph shows a hand-decorated car wrapped in the stars and stripes that participated in the 1930 Fourth of July parade. (Photograph courtesy of Tim and Windy Ferree.)

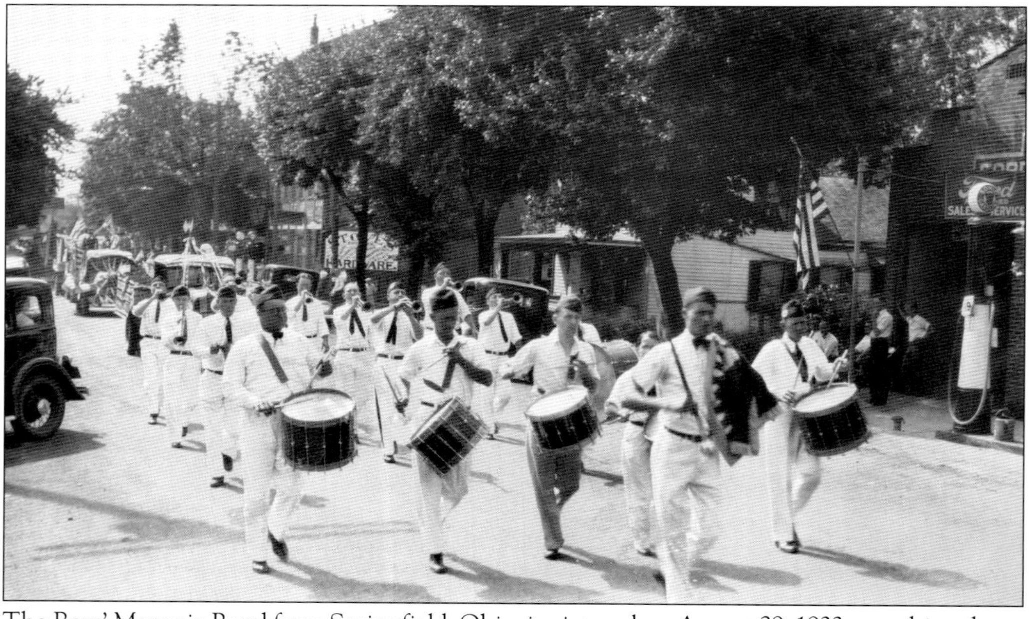

The Boys' Masonic Band from Springfield, Ohio, is pictured on August 29, 1933, marching down Williamsburg's Main Street between Second and Third Streets. Williamsburg has one of the oldest Masonic lodges in the Midwest. (Photograph courtesy of Tim and Windy Ferree.)

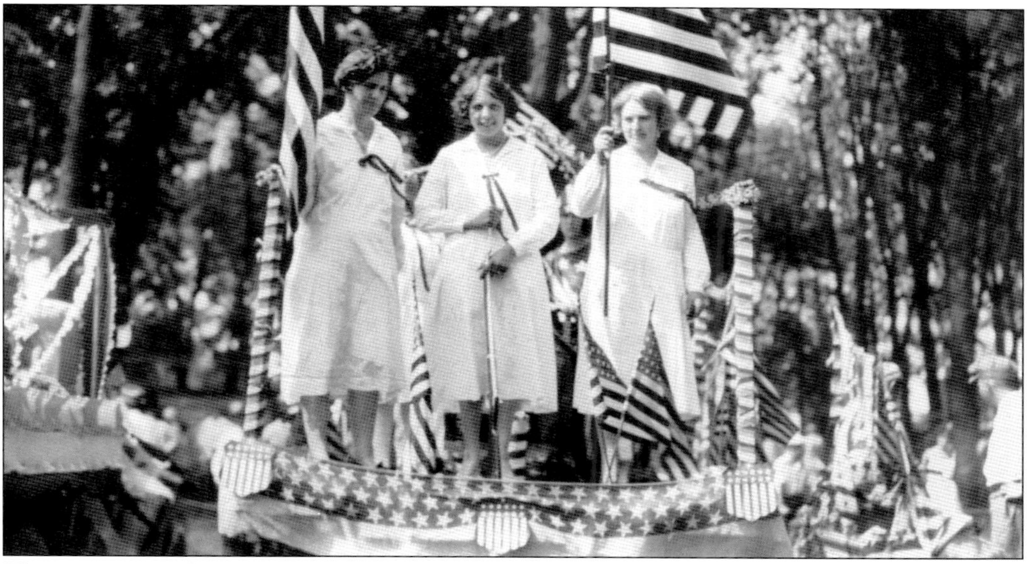

These women in the 1930 Williamsburg Memorial Day parade had great reason to celebrate, having attained the right to vote just 10 years before in 1920. Ohio's women began organizing conferences across the state as early as 1850 when they petitioned the Ohio Constitutional Convention for the right to vote. They were denied but did not give up. By 1861, married women in Ohio who were no longer living with their husbands were granted the right to own their property and to make contracts. Prior to this law, all property owned by a husband and wife became exclusive property of the husband if they separated or divorced. (Photograph courtesy of Tim and Windy Ferree.)

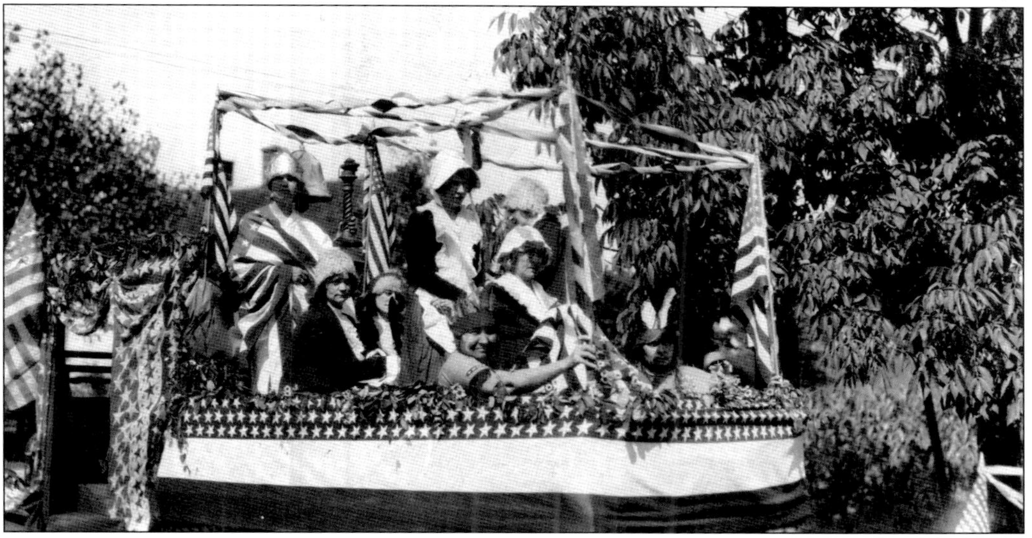

Williamsburg residents are dressed as pioneers and Indians in honor of the area's early history in this photograph from the 1930 Fourth of July parade. On April 10, 1792, in what has come to be known as the Battle of Grassy Run, frontiersmen Simon Kenton and Cornelius Washburn led a group of men against an encampment of Shawnee led by Tecumseh near Williamsburg. The Indians had stolen horses from the settlement in Limestone (Maysville), Kentucky, and crossed into Clermont County with the white men in pursuit. Shawnee women and children fled while the Indians drove off the Kenton party. (Photograph courtesy of Tim and Windy Ferree.)

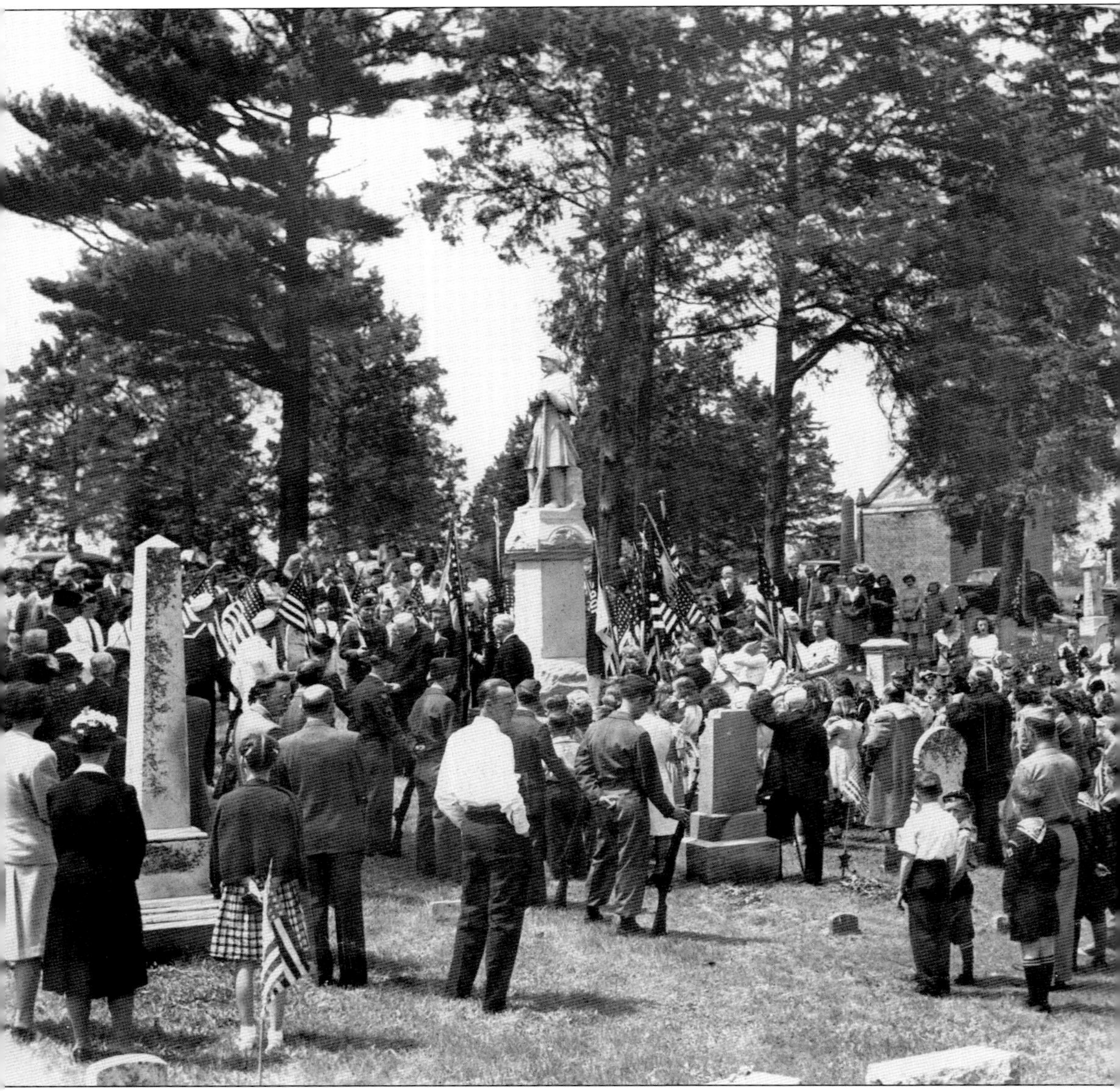

The statue of the Unknown Soldier dressed in Civil War uniform shown in this 1950s photograph still stands in the Williamsburg Township Cemetery as a memorial to fallen heroes who gave their lives in service to their country. Memorial Day ceremonies are still held at the cemetery at the Viet Nam memorial. (Photographs courtesy of Tim and Windy Ferree.)

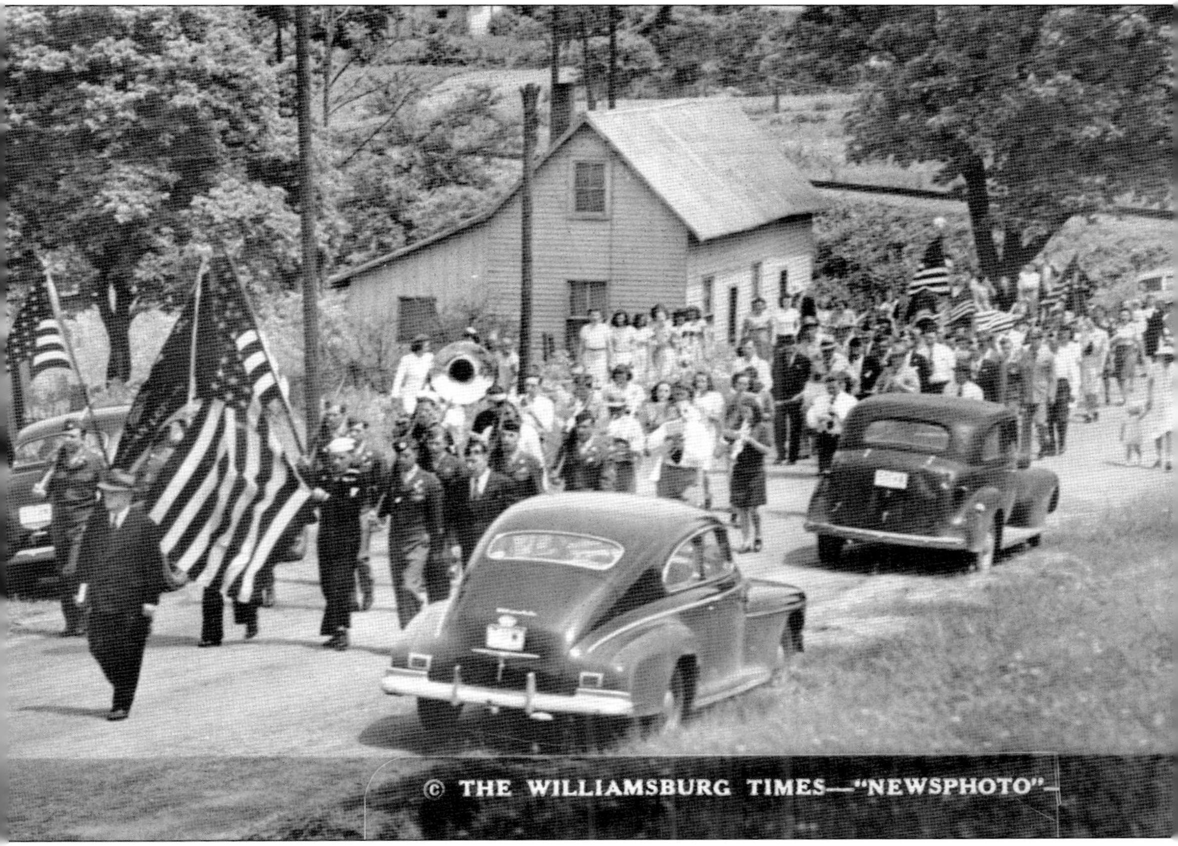

Memorial Day parades ended with a service at the Williamsburg Cemetery to honor those who died in war. Many of the town's pioneers are buried in the cemetery, including Underground Railroad activists Boss Huber and Dr. Leavitt Pease. (Photographs courtesy of Tim and Windy Ferree.)

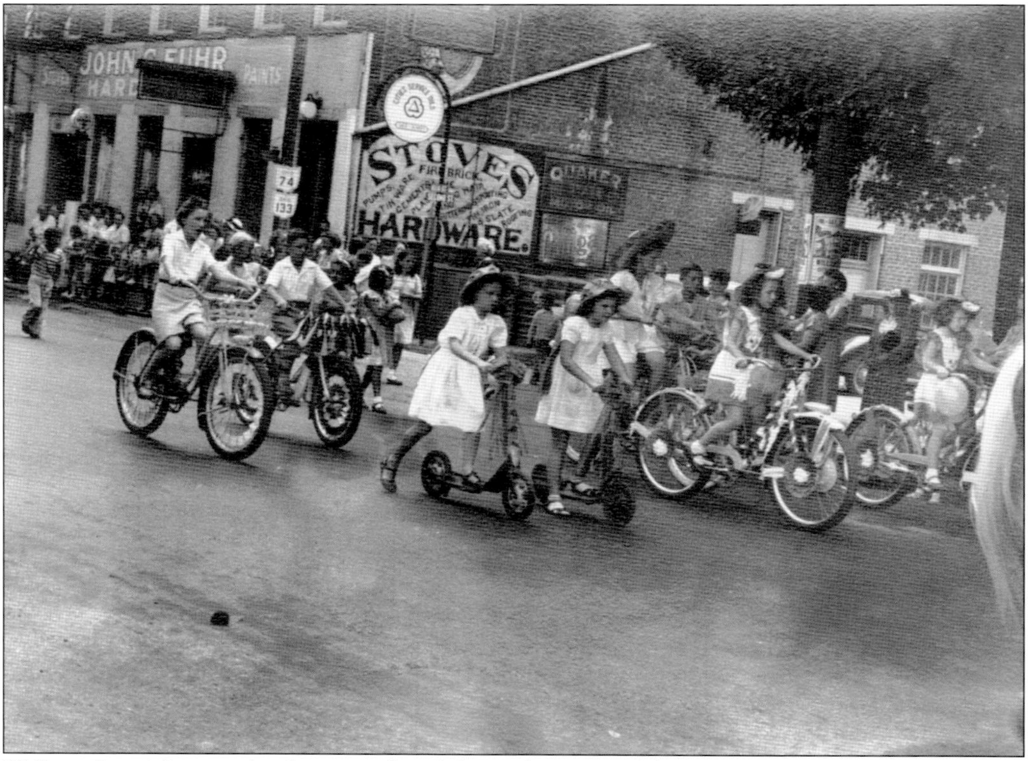

Williamsburg's boys and girls got on their bikes to be a part of the parade welcoming soldiers home from their service in World War II. (Photograph courtesy of Tim and Windy Ferree.)

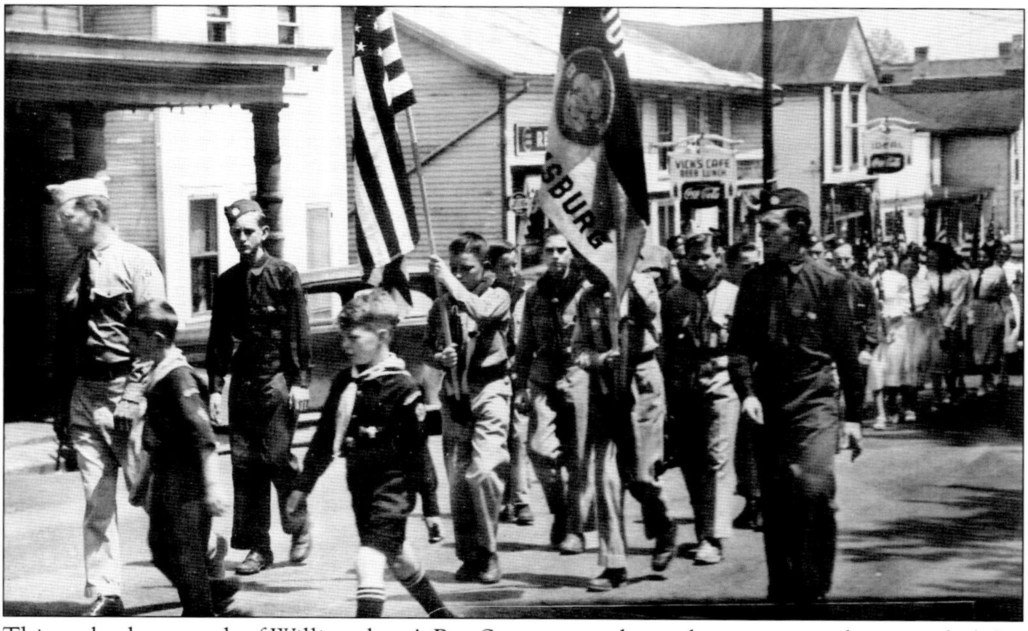

This early photograph of Williamsburg's Boy Scout troop shows the scouts marching in a holiday parade. (Photograph courtesy of Tim and Windy Ferree.)

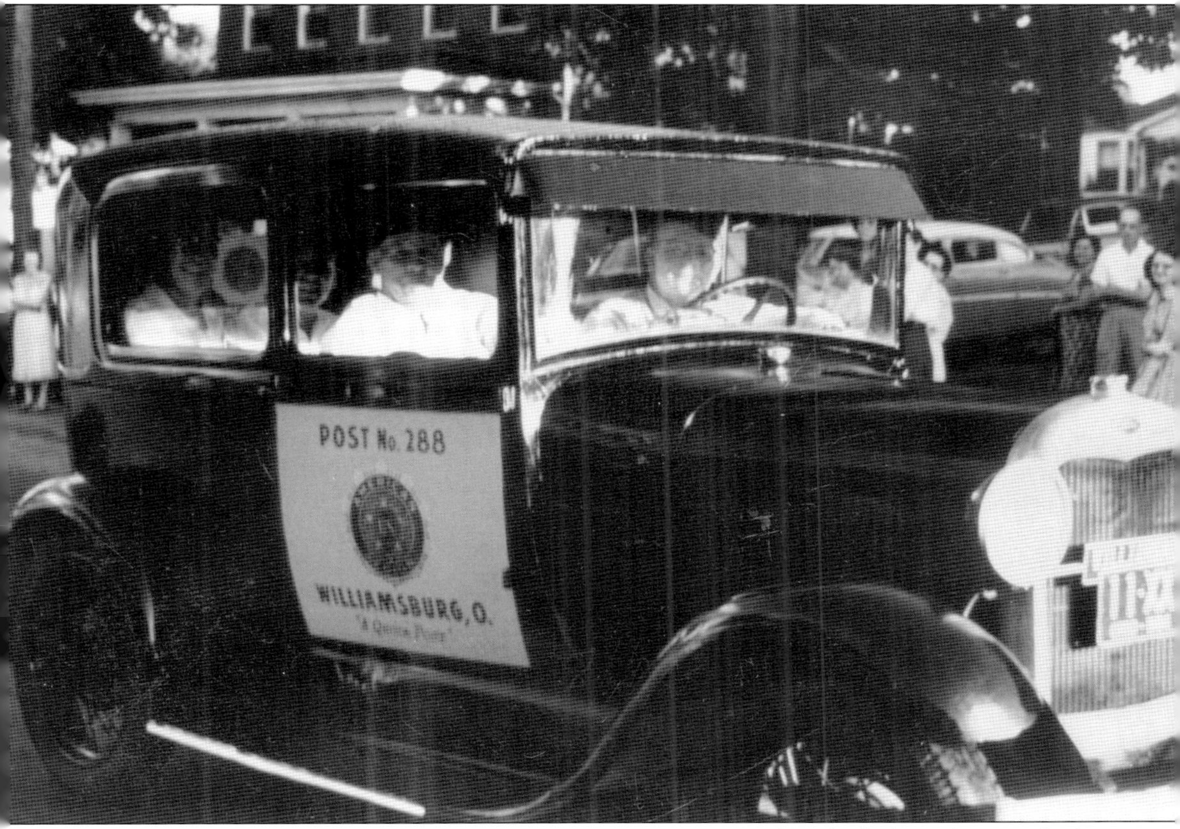

The American Legion Post in Williamsburg was established in 1920 and has had a long, distinguished history of helping fellow veterans. In this 1954 photograph, they have decorated a car for a holiday parade. (Photograph courtesy of Tim and Windy Ferree.)

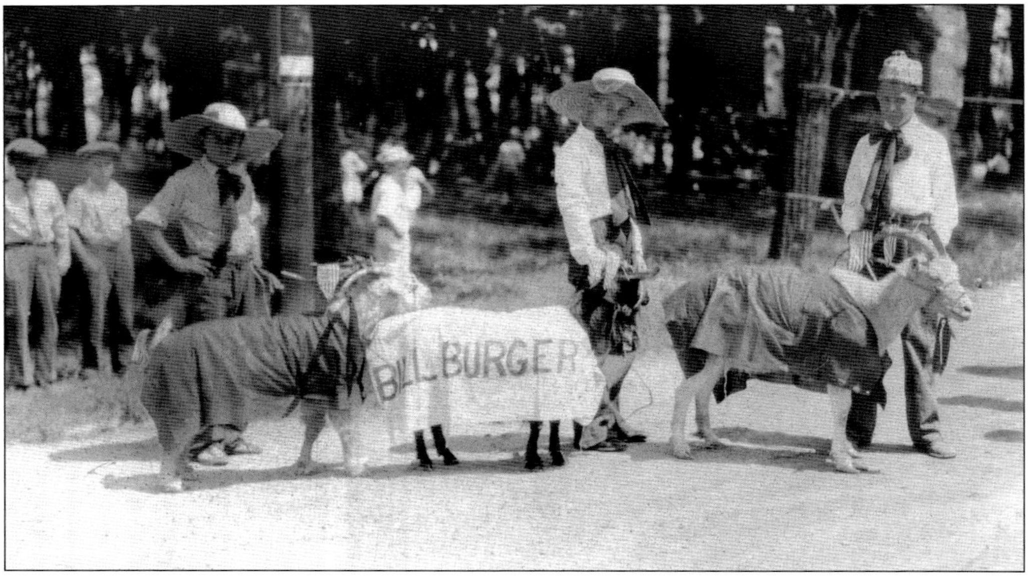

Even farm animals got involved in the fun of Williamsburg's parades. Burger's Meat Market on Main Street sponsored these goats and their young masters. (Photograph courtesy of Tim and Windy Ferree.)

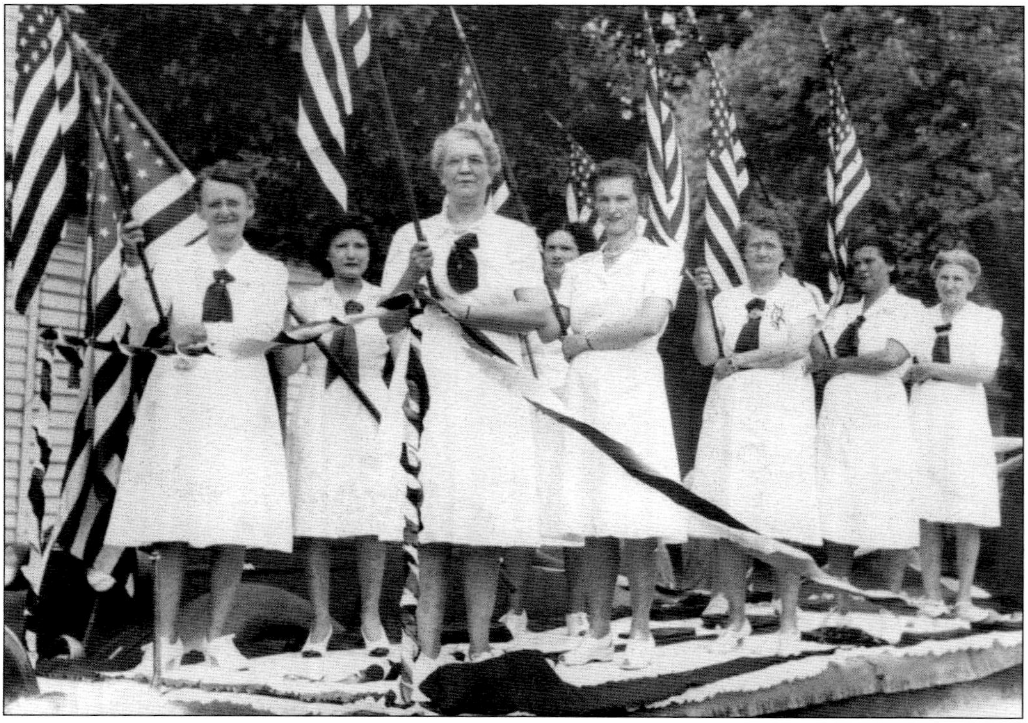

Pictured from left to right are Williamsburg ladies Mrs. Garman, Hazel Harry, Mildred Hornbach, Anna May Duchemin, unidentified, Lillian Watson, Mrs. Jordan, and unidentified showing off their patriotic spirit in the 1947 Fourth of July parade. (Photograph courtesy of Tim and Windy Ferree.)

Five

Politics and Civic Pride

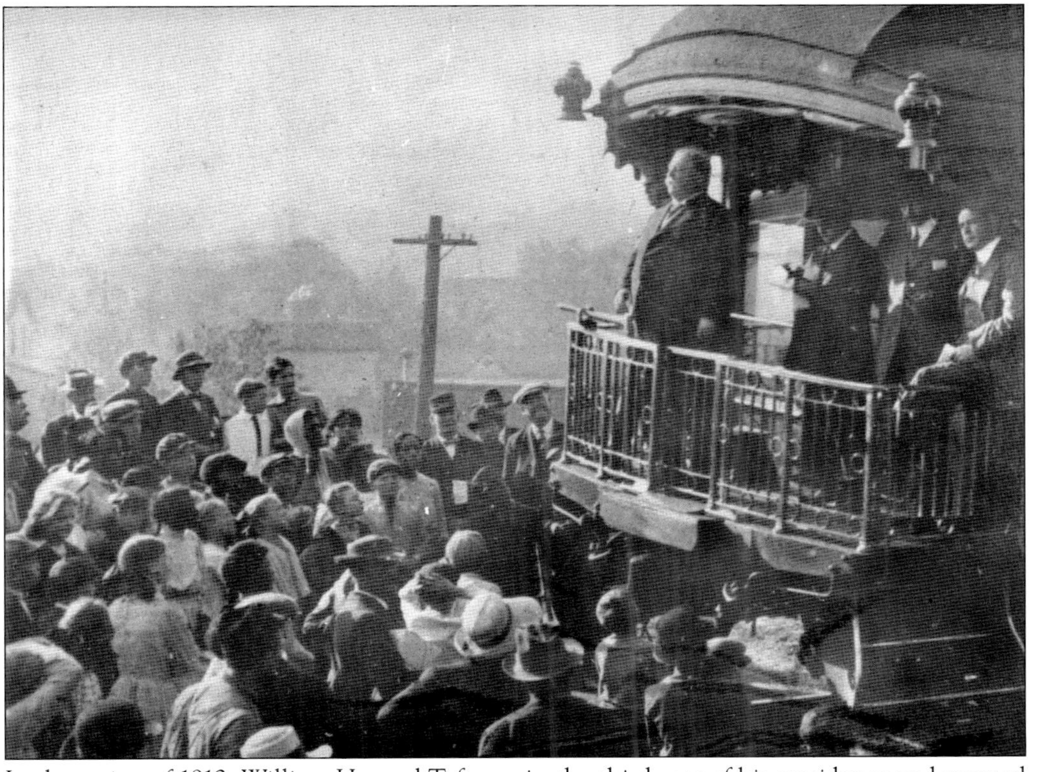

In the spring of 1912, William Howard Taft was in the third year of his presidency and stopped at the Batavia train station to make a speech from a railway car. Prior to this visit, the most distinguished guest to come to Batavia was Pres. Ulysses Grant when he and his family visited the Simpson-Griffith family, who were relatives. The village was packed with people waiting for the Grants to arrive from Georgetown. Their waiting proved fruitless, as the president had taken his carriage by way of Williamsburg. Said a cousin, "The president was doing his own driving. He was wearing just a soft hat and a dark business suit." (Photograph from the Sharp Collection, courtesy of the Clermont County Library.)

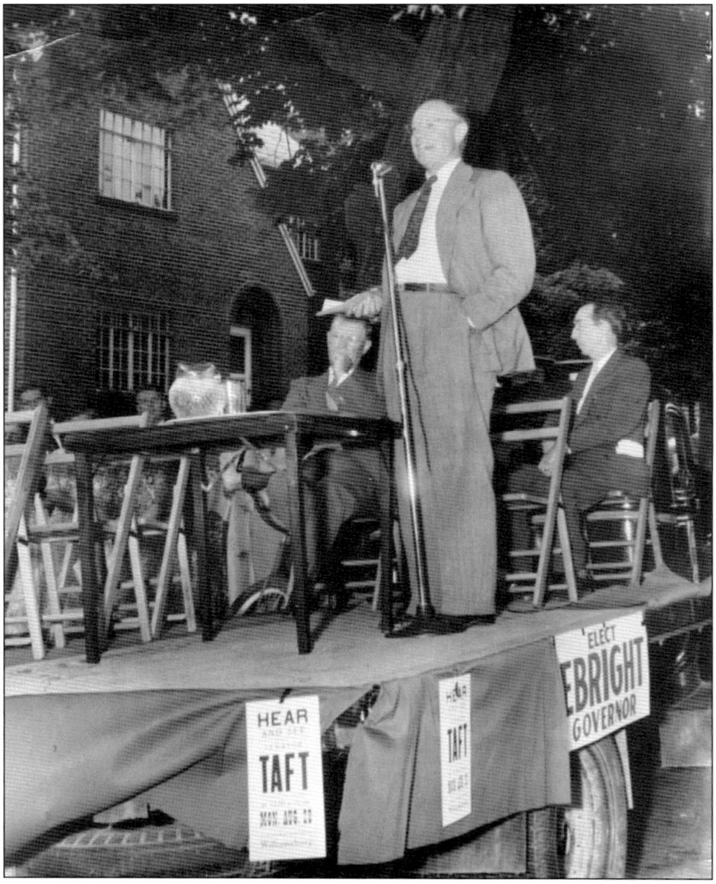

An Ohio senator from 1939 until 1953, Robert Taft Sr. is pictured campaigning on Williamsburg's Main Street. Taft was the son of former president William Howard Taft. (Photograph courtesy of Hazel Arnold.)

In this photograph, a large group of Williamsburg residents attend a political rally held on the grounds of the town square. This plot of land was specifically donated by the Lytle family for the sole purpose of providing a place for public gatherings. To this day, it must still be used for this purpose or the land must return to the Lytle family.

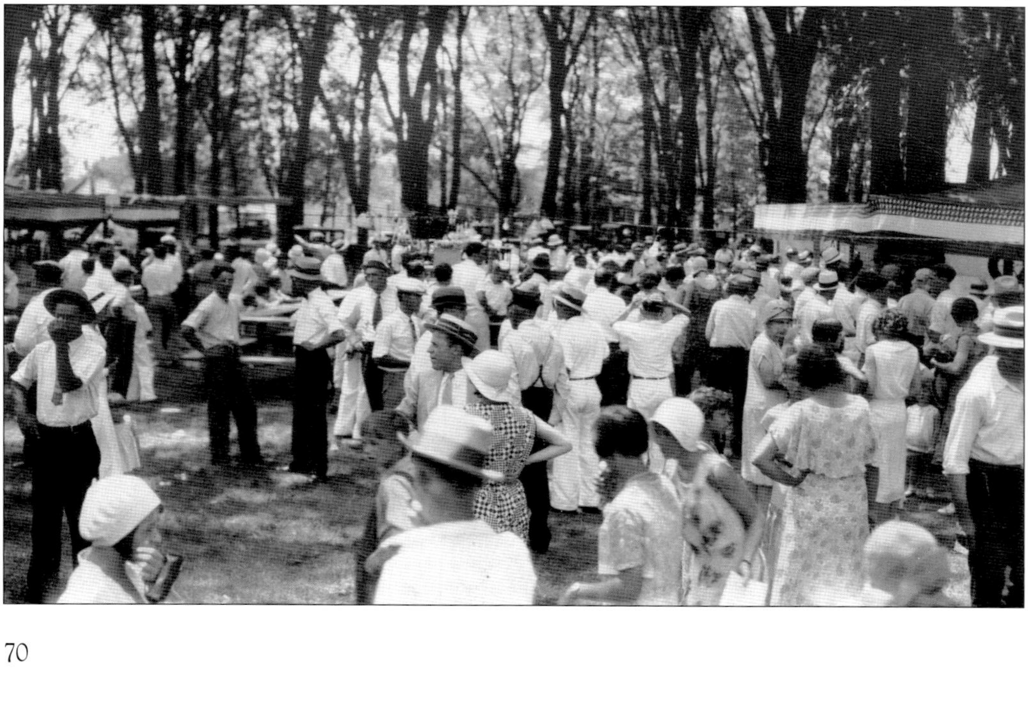

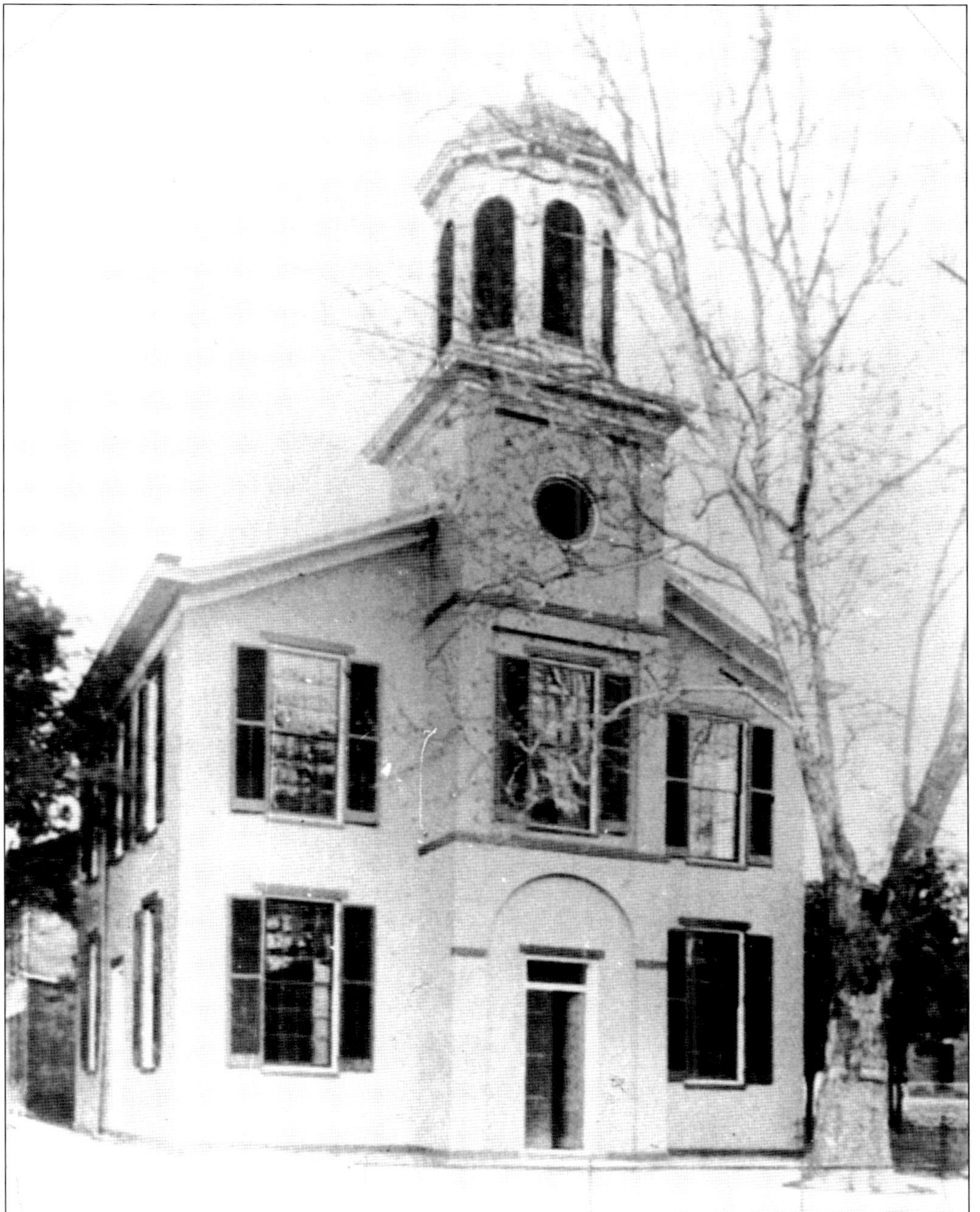

According to the 1883 *Clermont Gazetteer and Directory*, in 1817, Brown County was formed from Clermont, taking with it four townships and leaving Williamsburg only a short distance from the boundary line. This led to proposals to change the county seat to New Richmond, on the Ohio River, or to Batavia, further west. After much debate and heated quarrels, the county seat was permanently moved to Batavia in 1824. All courts were held at the M.E. Church until 1829, when the courthouse (above) was completed. It was torn down to make way for a new building in 1935. (Photograph courtesy of Molly Cribbet.)

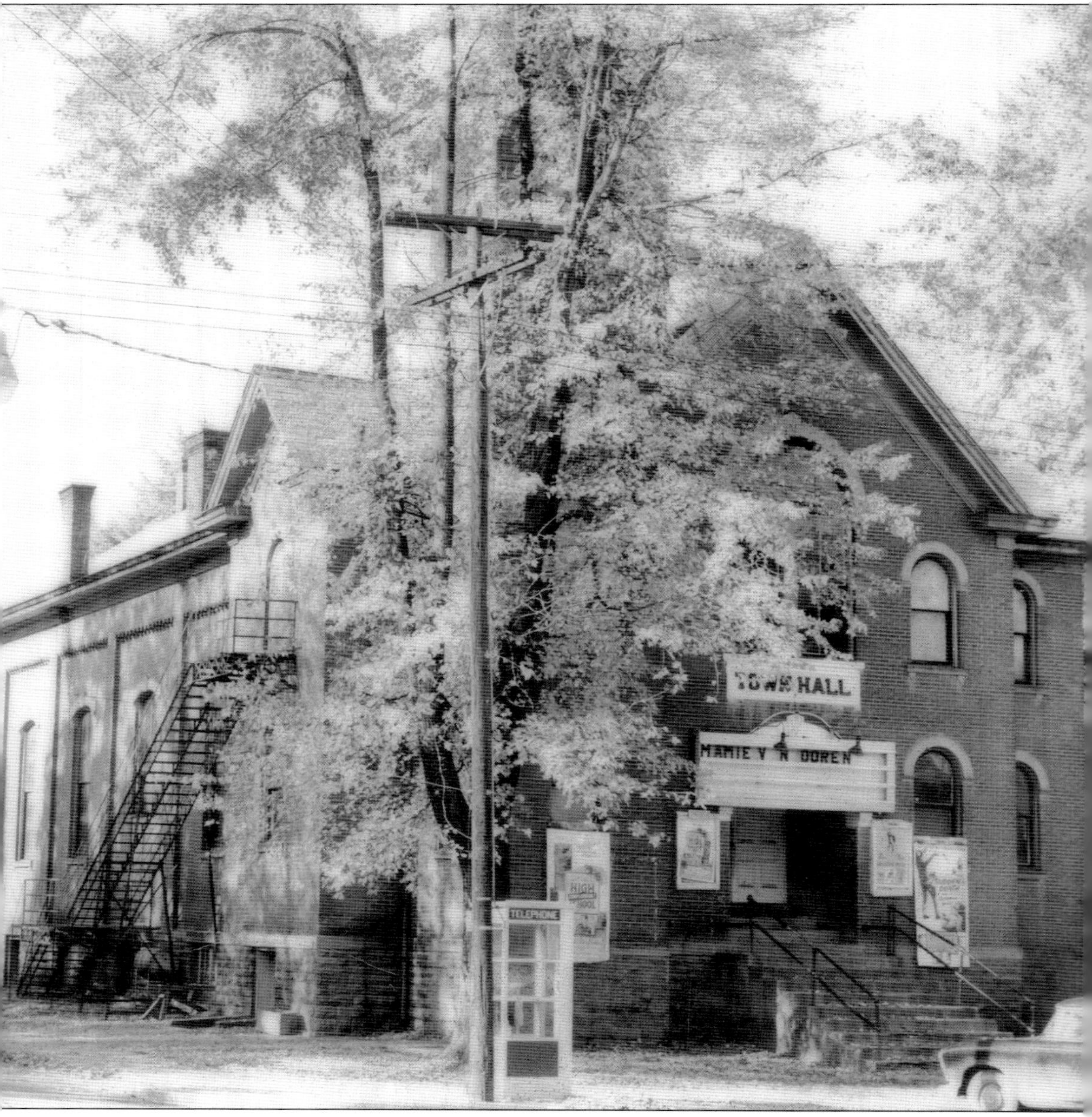

In 1880, officials complained that the old jail, built in 1842, was insecure, with inmates having easy access to communicating with people on the street. This jail and sheriff's residence, which was built in the 1890s, was torn down around 1936, the same time the new Clermont County Courthouse was built on Main Street. (Photograph courtesy of the Clermont County Historical Society.)

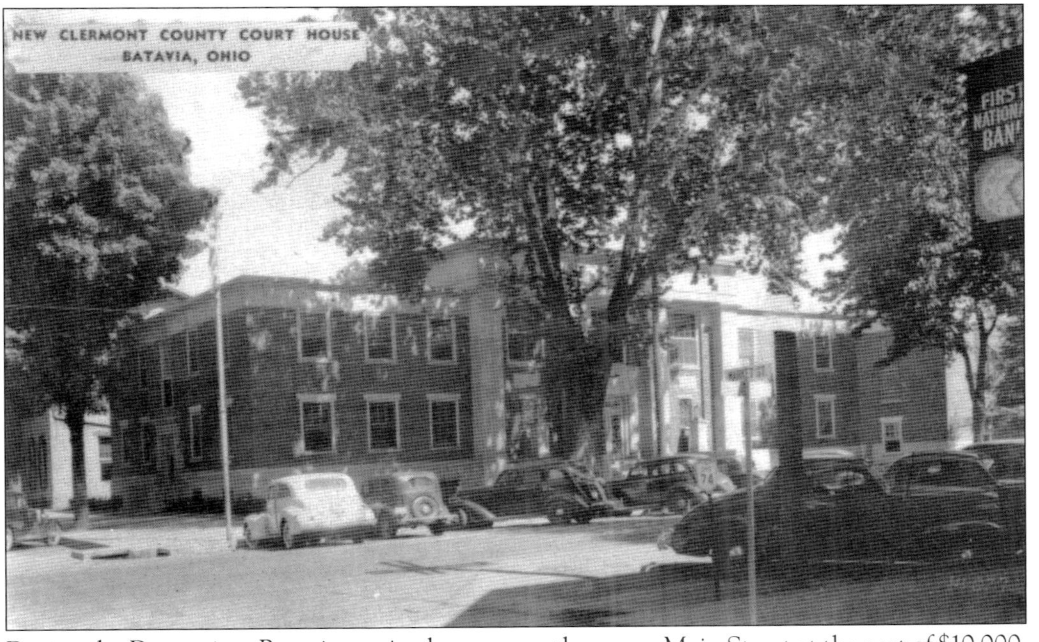

During the Depression, Batavia received a new courthouse on Main Street at the cost of $10,000. It was built in a Greek-inspired utilitarian style and is two stories tall on top of a partially exposed basement. The building was doubled in size in 1998, when the new portion was built adjoining the original structure where the previous jail had stood. (Photograph from the Sharp Collection, courtesy of the Clermont County Library.)

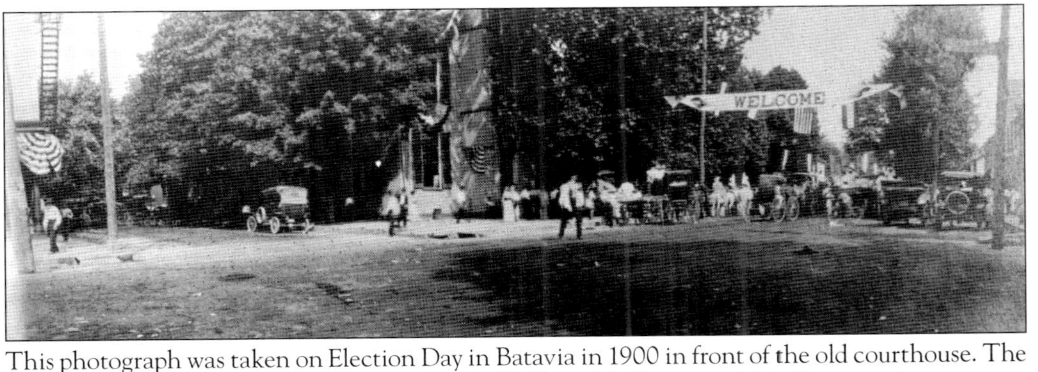

This photograph was taken on Election Day in Batavia in 1900 in front of the old courthouse. The presidential candidates, Republican president William McKinley and his Democratic opponent William Jennings Bryan, were a rematch of the 1896 election. McKinley won 292 electoral votes and chose New York governor Theodore Roosevelt as his vice president.

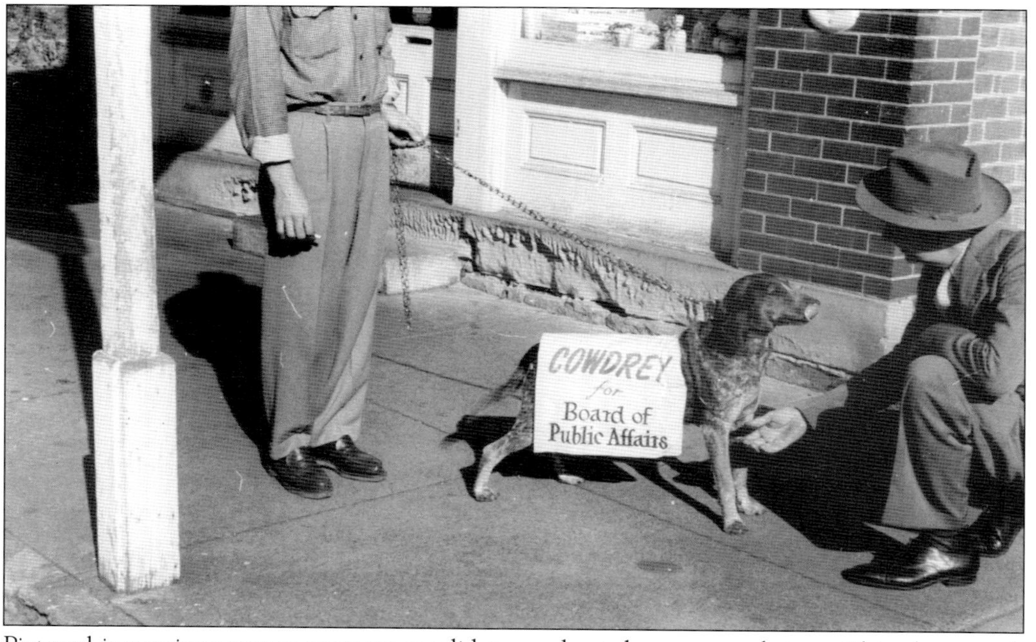

Pictured is a unique way to promote candidates and cut down on yard signs. This photograph of the little pup urges Williamsburg residents to vote for "Cowdrey for Board of Public Affairs." (Photograph courtesy of Tim and Windy Ferree.)

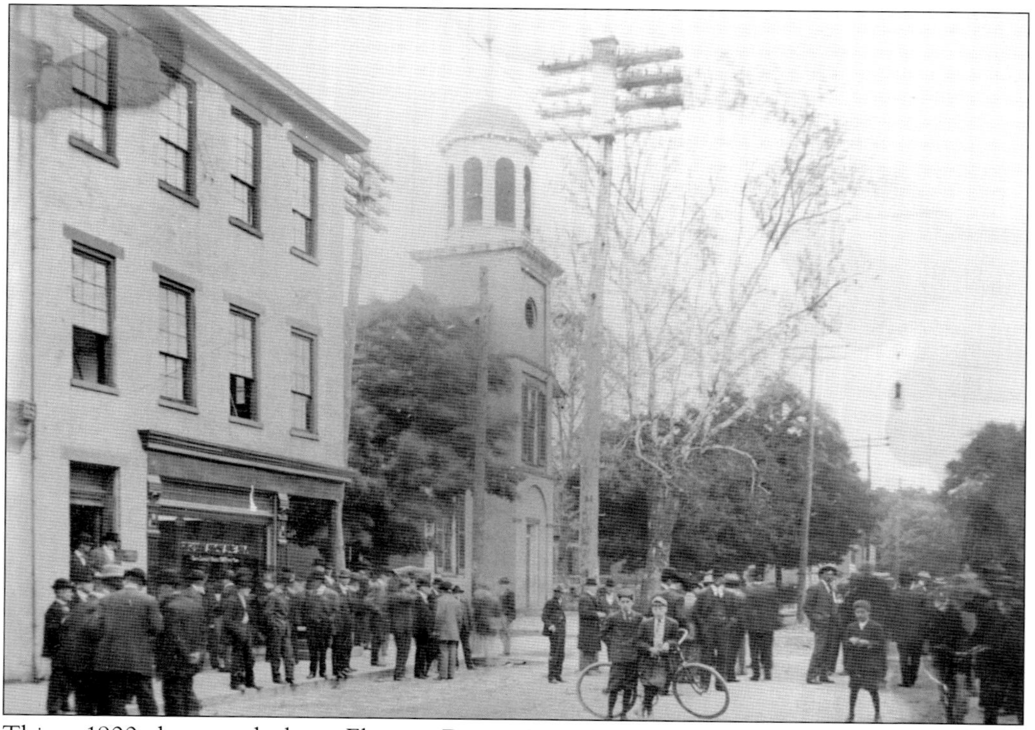

This c. 1900 photograph shows Election Day on Main Street in Batavia. (Photograph from the Sharp Collection, courtesy of the Clermont County Library.)

Six

Social Outings and Activities

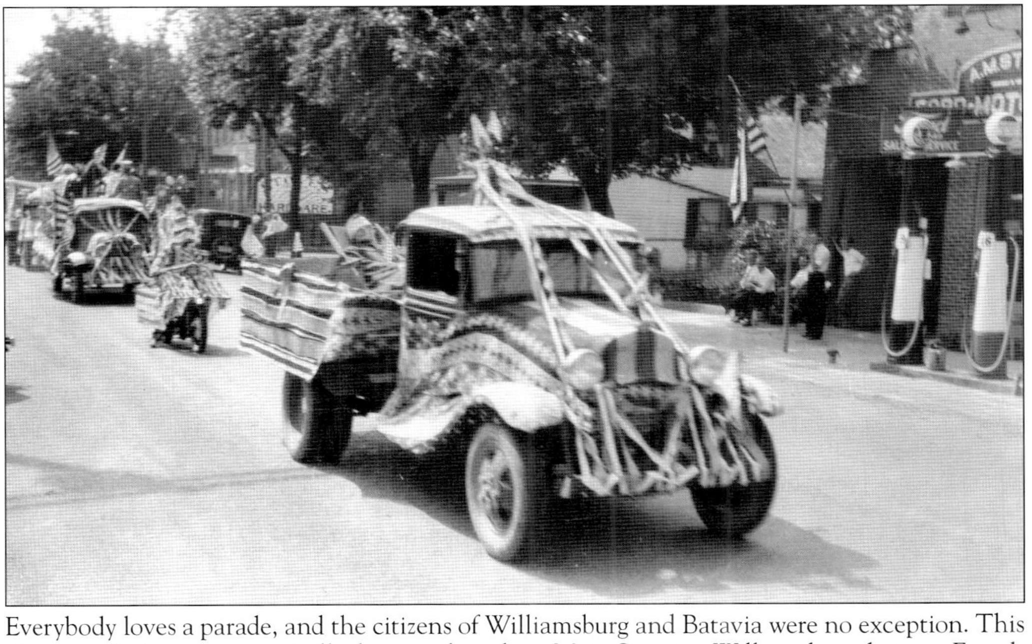

Everybody loves a parade, and the citizens of Williamsburg and Batavia were no exception. This photograph shows a patriotically decorated truck on Main Street in Williamsburg during a Fourth of July parade in the 1920s. (Photograph courtesy of Tim and Windy Ferree.)

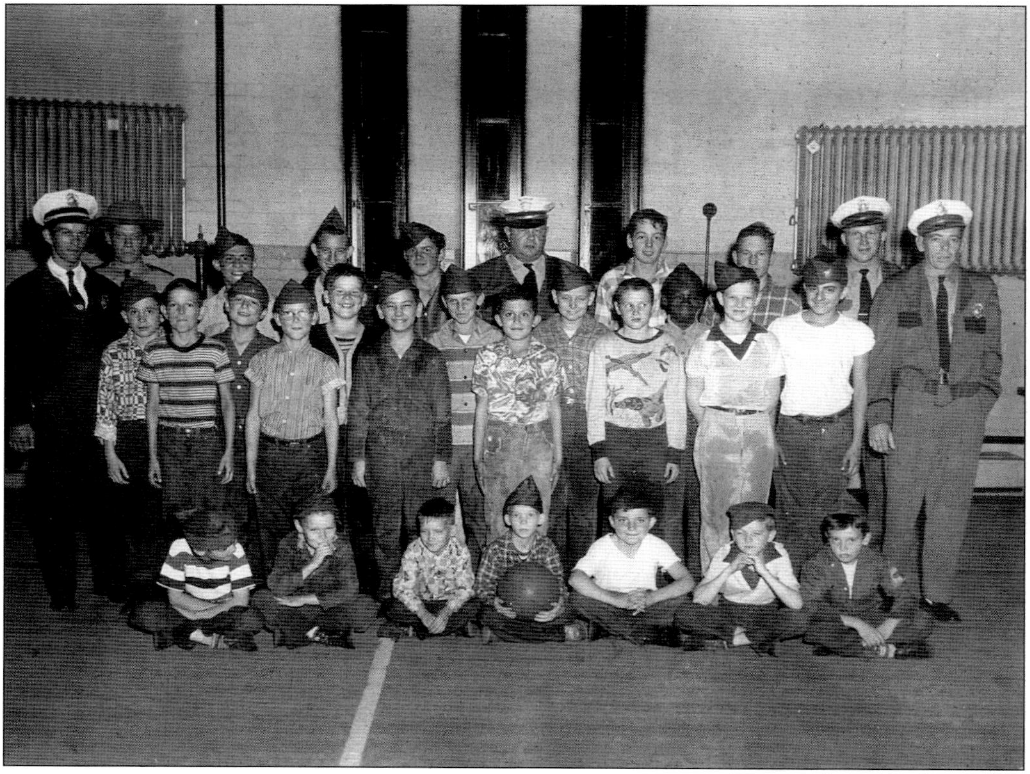

In the 1950s, Batavia's police department started a youth program to help keep village kids out of trouble. This is one of their group photographs. (Photograph courtesy of Steve Shinkle.)

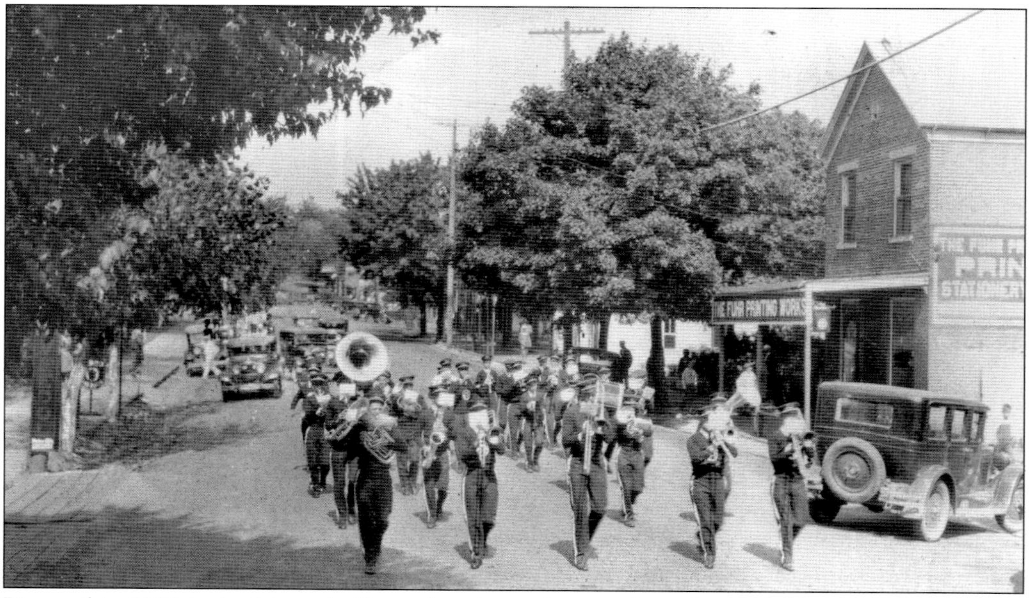

Pictured in 1933 is the Masonic House band marching in from Springfield, Ohio. (Photograph courtesy of Tim and Windy Ferree.)

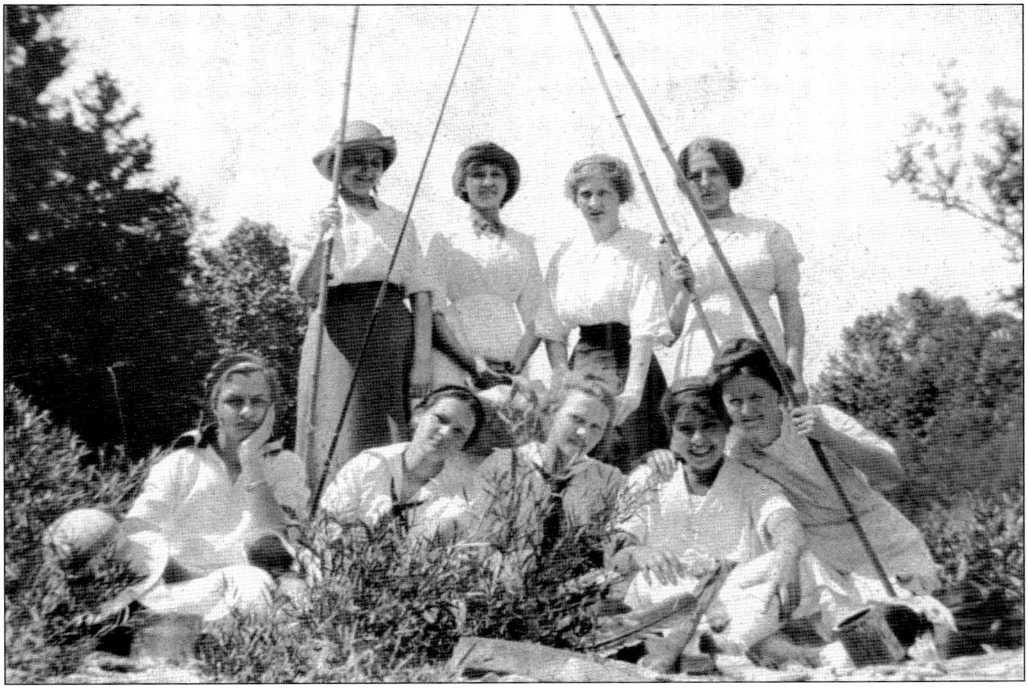

Edith Fuhr (second from right in back row) and several friends enjoy a day of fishing. Edith married Ralph Fuhr, one of Williamsburg's leading citizens in the beginning of the 20th century. (Photograph courtesy of Tim and Windy Ferree.)

The Clermont County Fair was a highlight for farmers and town residents every summer. This program announced the day's activities, including a hog calling contest followed by a 10:00 a.m. baseball game between Williamsburg and Owensville.

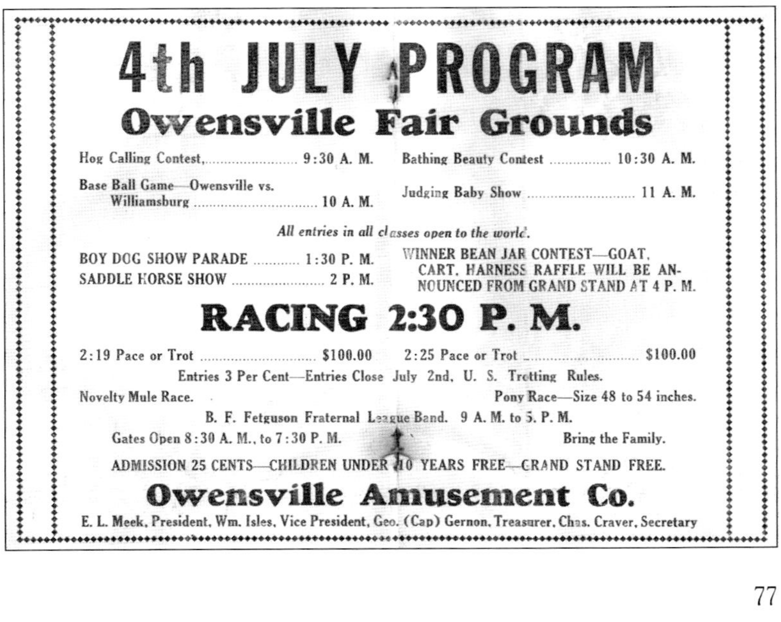

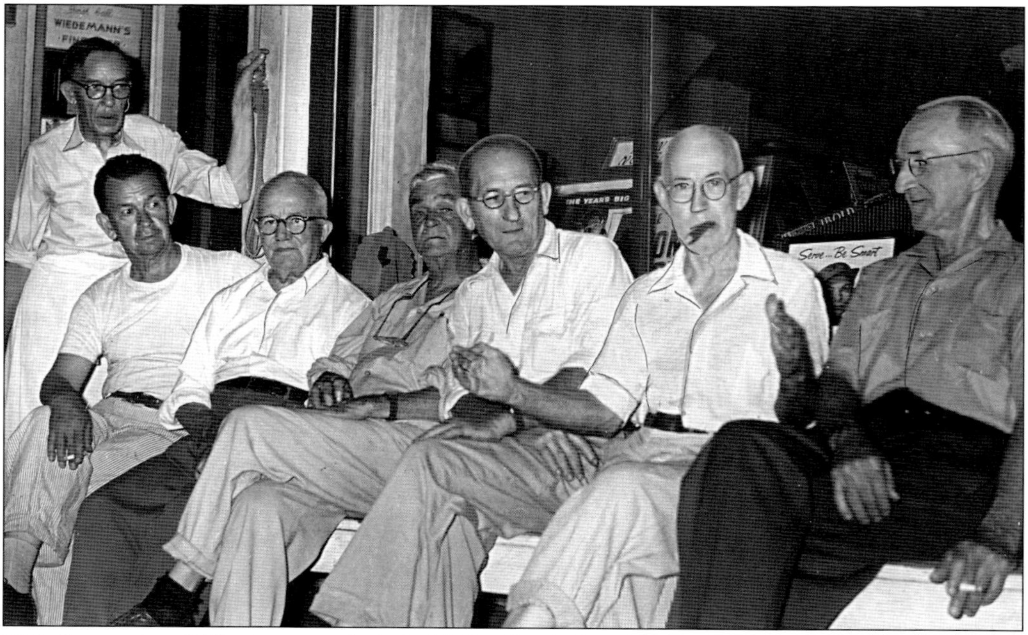

This September 1957 photograph (titled "The Liar's Bench") shows, from left to right, Batavia residents C.O. Rice, C.L. Slade, W.L. Grace, William W. Keen, J.B. Warner, N.B. Dennison, and Charles Daughery. They regularly gathered on the town's Main Street to share stories and news. (Photograph from the Sharp Collection, courtesy of the Clermont County Library.)

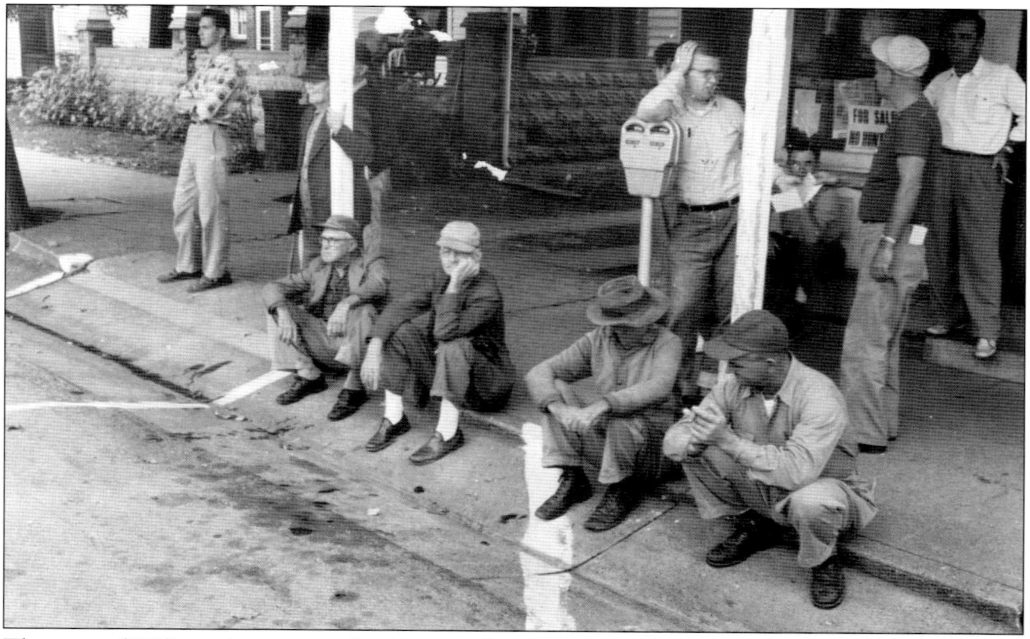

The men of Williamsburg seemed to like watching others working to put in the town's water lines in this early photograph. In 1962, work started on a $90,000 sewer system. E.A. Taylor and Son Company of New Lexington, Ohio, installed 65,000 feet of cast iron pipe. (Photograph courtesy of Tim and Windy Ferree.)

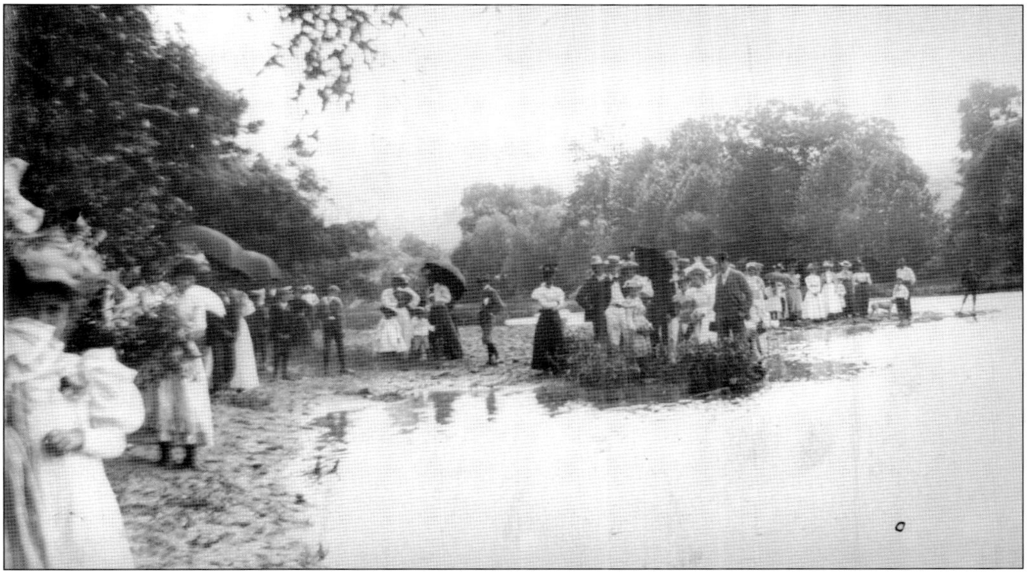

In 1928, the Cincinnati Rotary Club bought the property from the Cincinnati, Georgetown, and Portsmouth Railroad and began operating Camp Allyn for handicapped children. This same site was the earlier location of the Clermont County Fair (1857–1863) and Civil War Camps Lucas and Scott (1861). (Photograph courtesy of Tim and Windy Ferree.)

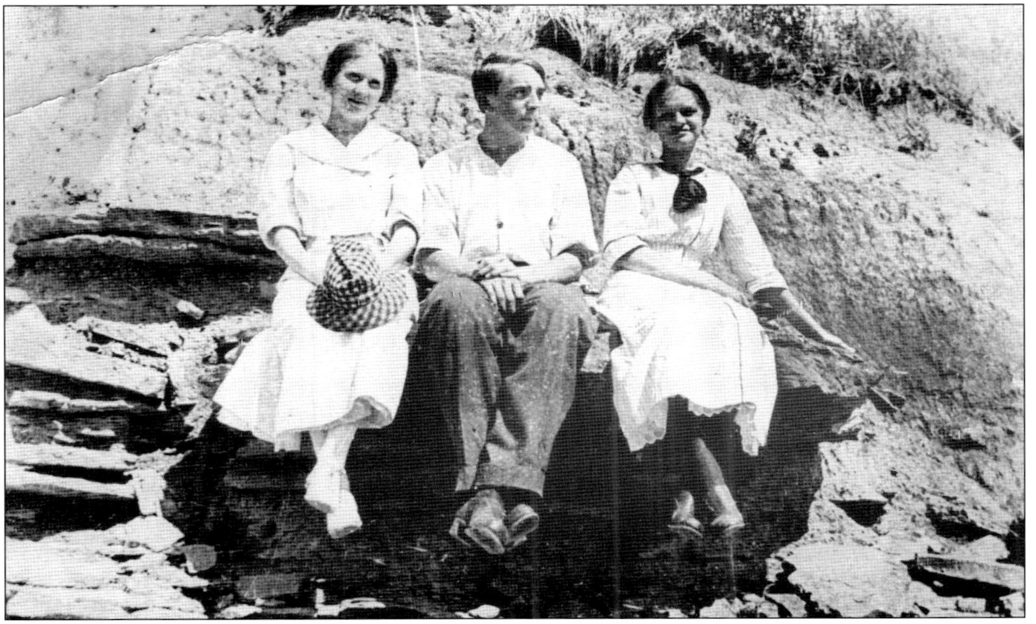

Williamsburg residents Edith and Ralph Fuhr (left and right) enjoy some sun on the East Fork of the Little Miami with an unidentified guest. (Photograph courtesy of Tim and Windy Ferree.)

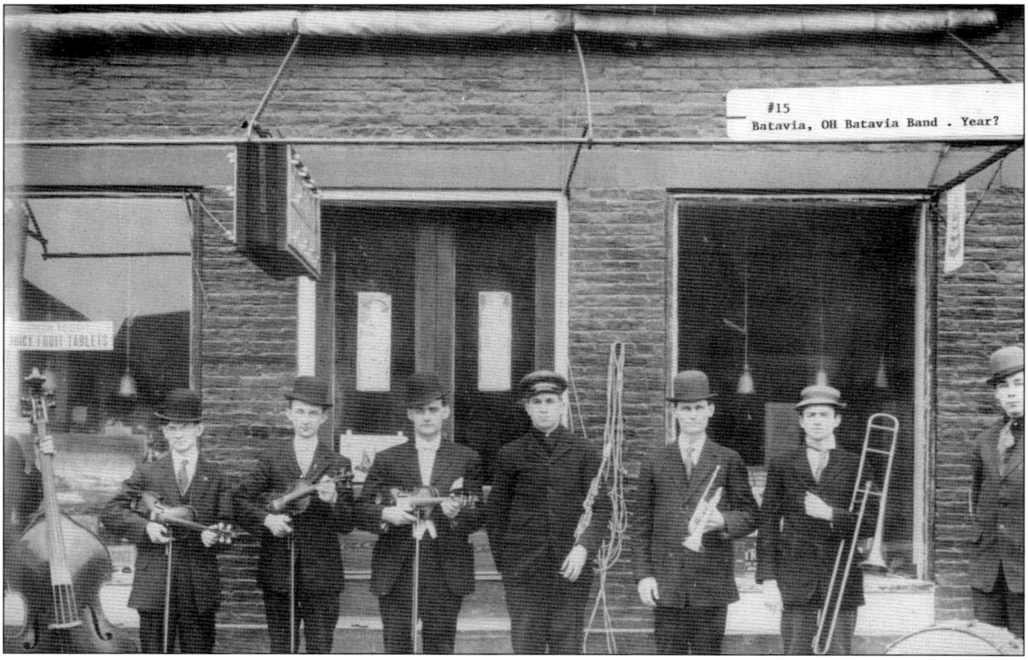

Town bands enjoyed popularity up until the 1930s. They would play weekly concerts and sometimes performed on street corners to entertain those strolling by. This photograph shows the Batavia Town Band. (Photograph from the Sharp Collection, courtesy of the Clermont County Library.)

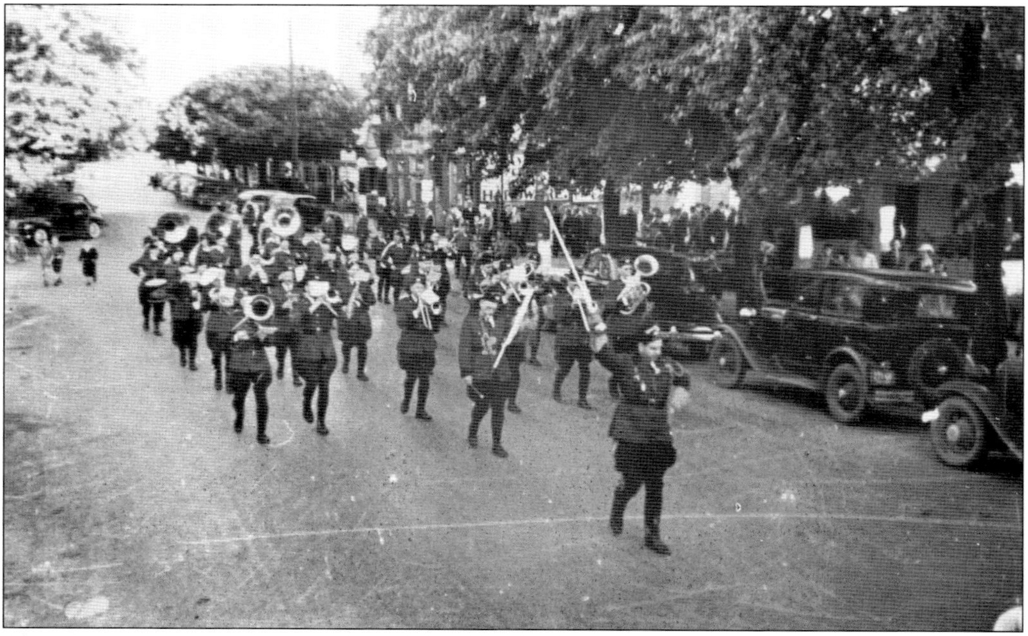

This photograph shows the Williamsburg Town Band marching down Main Street in one of the town's many parades. Dr. J.P. Allen, a physician in Williamsburg, also enjoyed being a bandleader directing the Methodist Church band and the community band. (Photograph courtesy of Tim and Windy Ferree.)

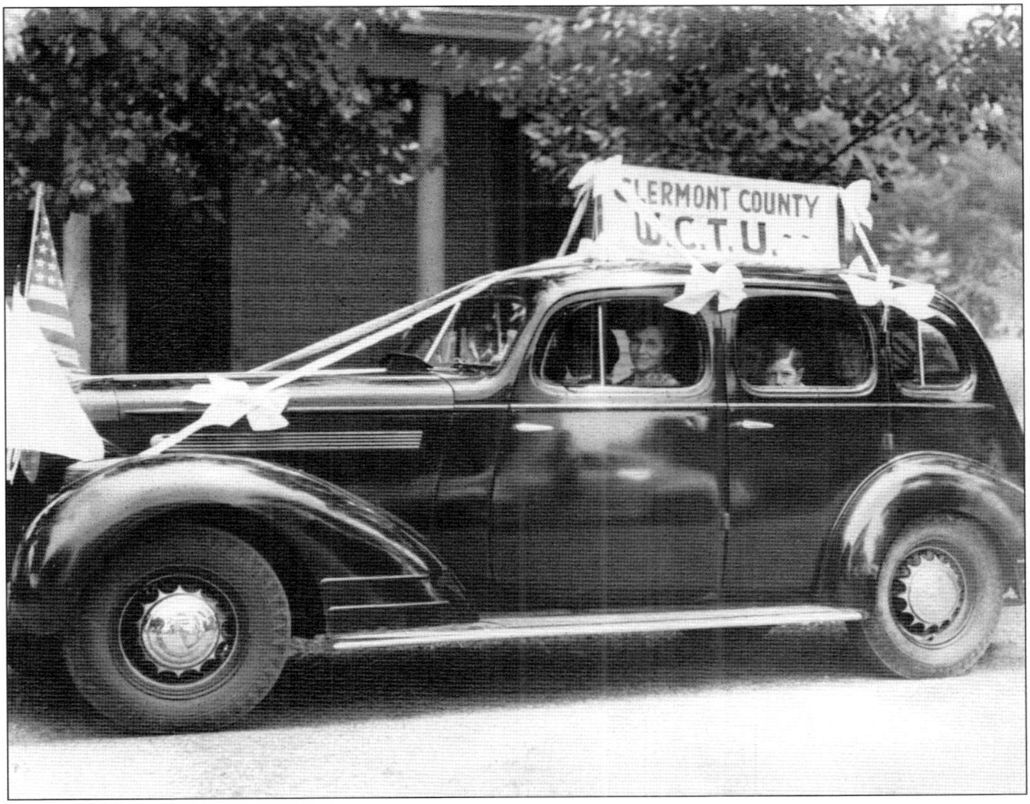

Everybody's favorite piano teacher in Williamsburg was Hazel Grimm, shown here driving a car in one of the town parades. Hazel taught piano from the 1920s until the 1960s at the home of her father, Frank Marshall, at 125 South Second Street. (Photograph courtesy of Tim and Windy Ferree.)

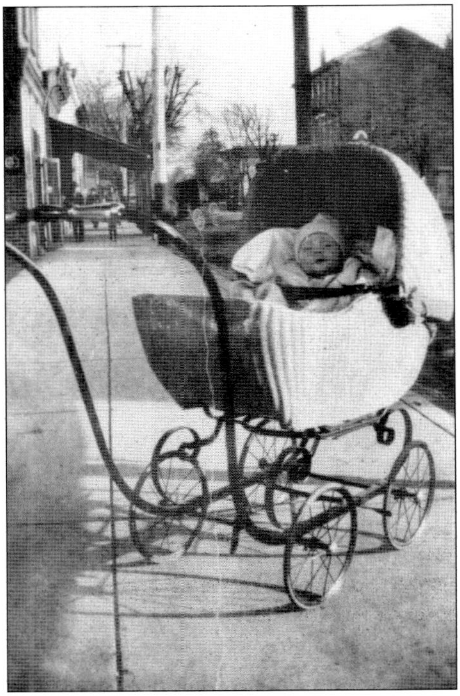

This unidentified toddler is bundled up and ready for a stroll down Main Street in Williamsburg. "Good sidewalks were the pride of a prosperous town," wrote assistant editor Rosanna Hoberg in her weekly column for the *Clermont Sun*. "We walked everywhere. Up the hill toward Williamsburg we could always count on Aunt Tillie (who lived at the top of the hill), to give us fresh baked bread and churned butter with a glass of cold root beer." (Photograph courtesy of Tim and Windy Ferree.)

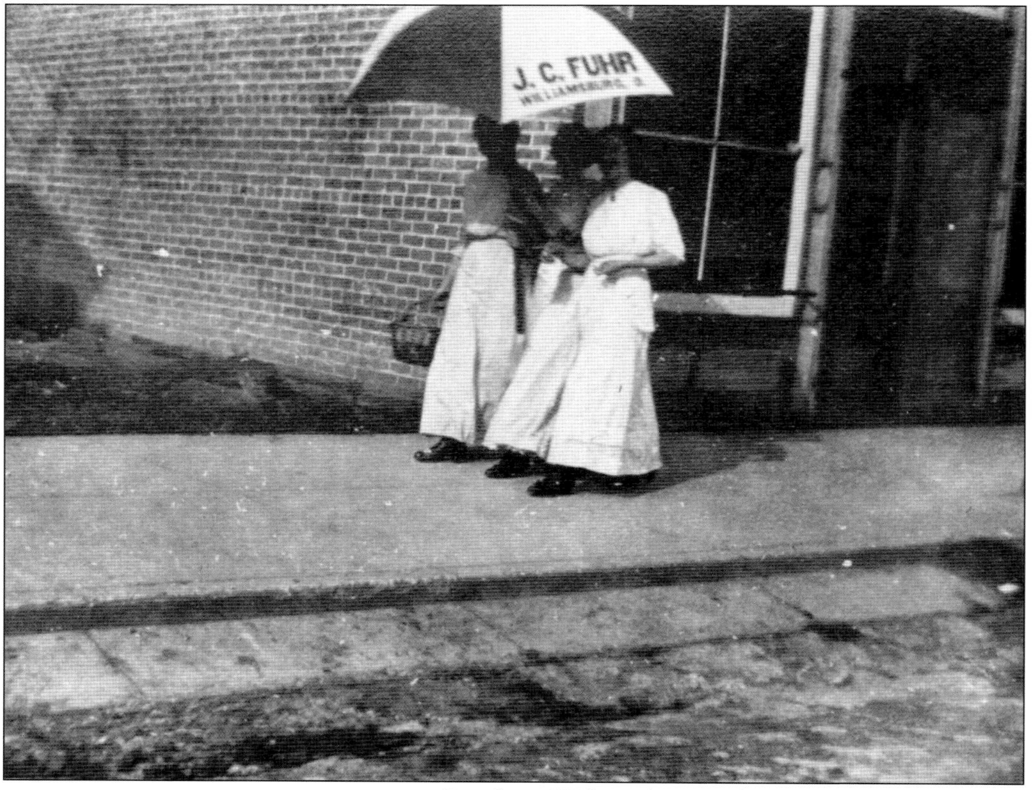

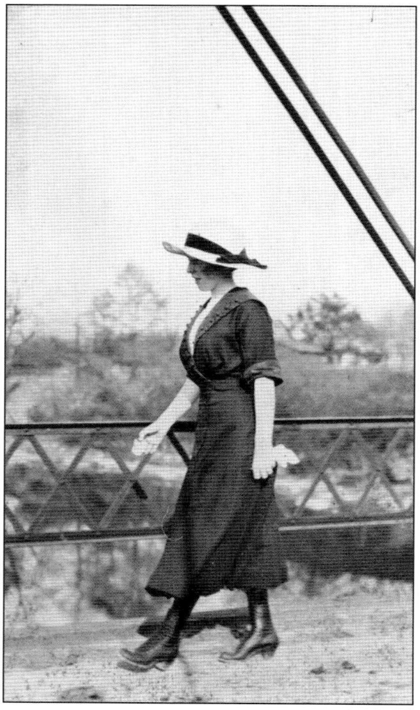

People in Williamsburg and Batavia walked to town to conduct business, shop, or visit with family and friends, and only hitched up the horse and buggy when the distance proved too far. Three young women are pictured walking along Main Street under an umbrella that protected them from the sun and served as a clever advertisement for the J.C. Fuhr store located on Williamsburg's Main Street. (Photograph courtesy of Tim and Windy Ferree.)

This photograph from the Fuhr family estate shows an unidentified young lady walking over the iron bridge that crossed over the East Fork of the Little Miami River in Williamsburg. After church services, many people would go for a walk with family and friends. (Photograph courtesy of Tim and Windy Ferree.)

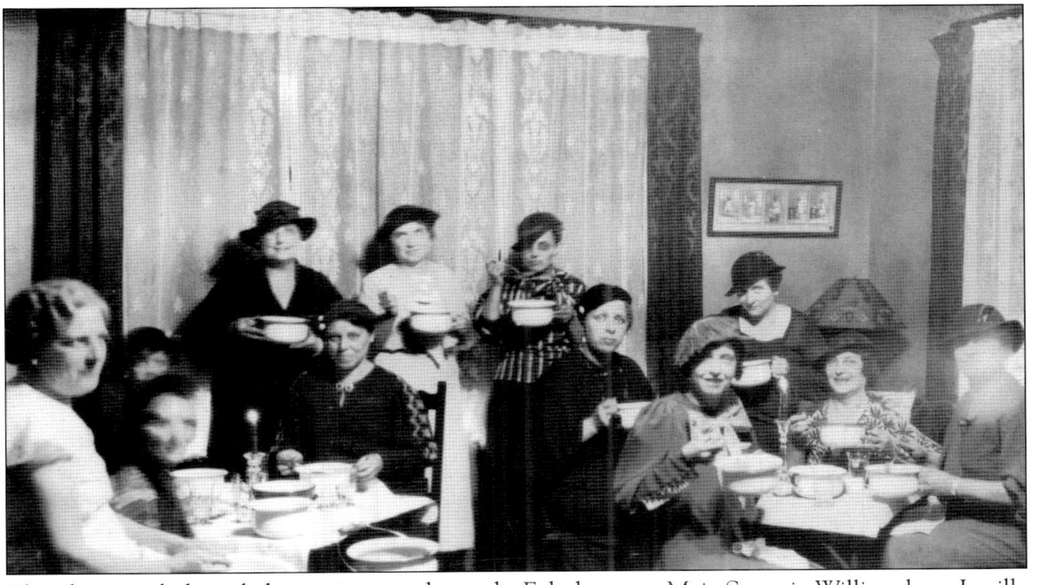

This photograph shows ladies getting together at the Fuhr home on Main Street in Williamsburg. Lucille Fuhr is seated at the table third from left. (Photograph courtesy of Tim and Windy Ferree.)

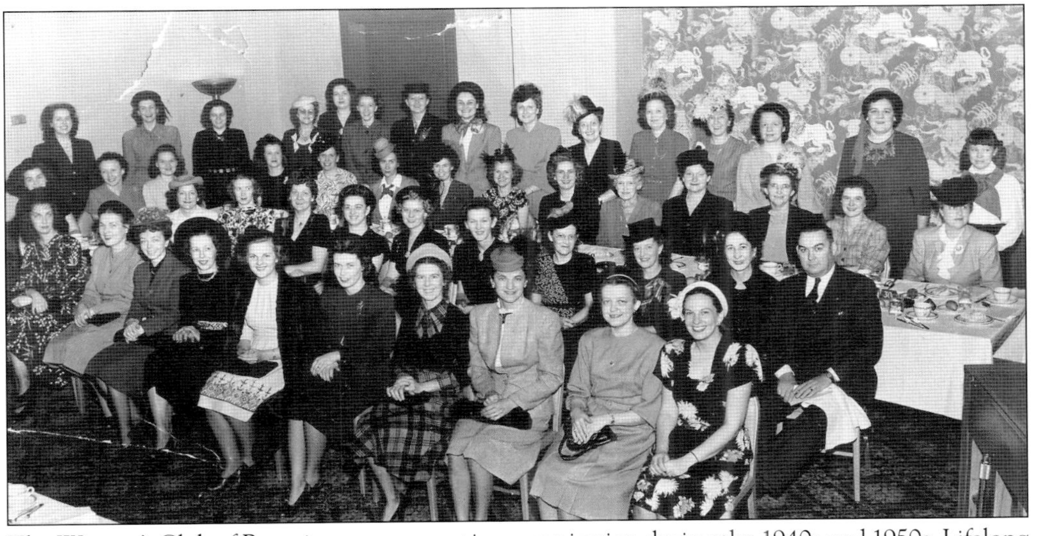

The Women's Club of Batavia was a very active organization during the 1940s and 1950s. Lifelong Batavia resident and town historian Rosanna Hoberg is seated at the far right in the front row. The only man in the room seated behind Rosanna is believed to be the program speaker. (Photograph courtesy of Molly Cribbet.)

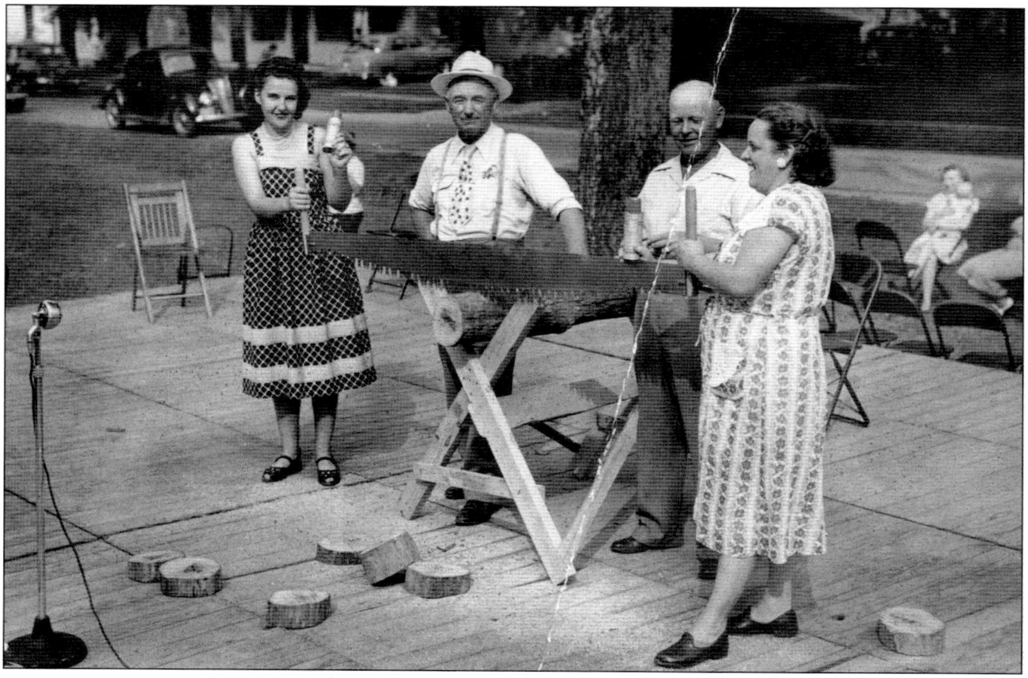

Competitions of all kinds were part of Williamsburg's community celebrations. In these photographs, women race to saw through a large log on Main Street. (Photographs courtesy of Tim and Windy Ferree.)

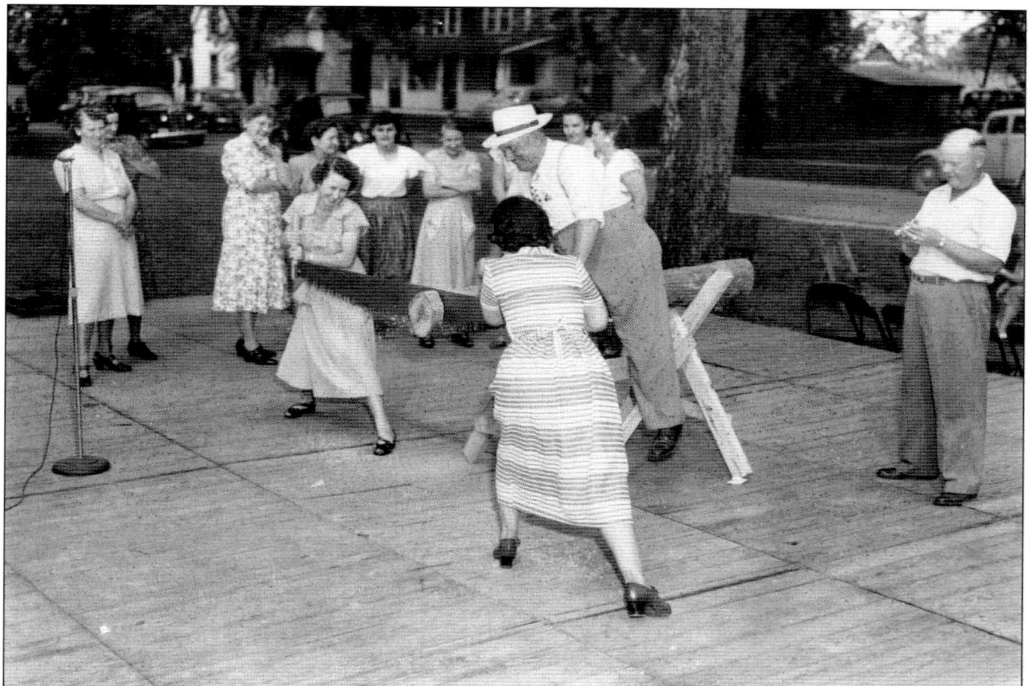

Seven

Town Sports

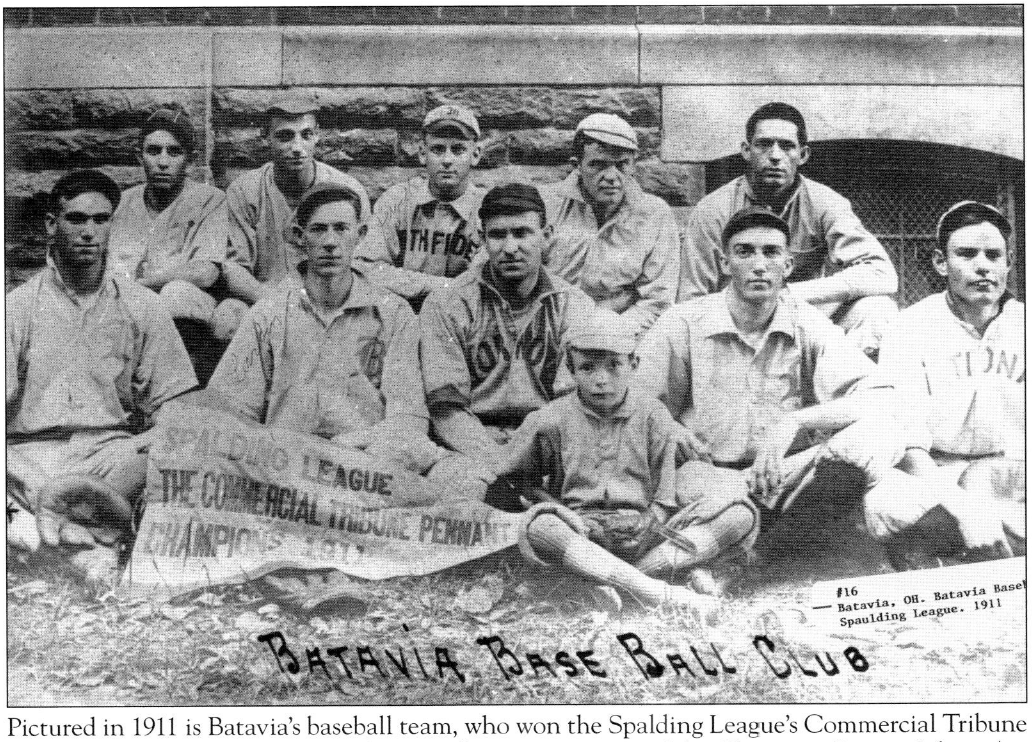

Pictured in 1911 is Batavia's baseball team, who won the Spalding League's Commercial Tribune pennant. (Photograph from the Sharp Collection, courtesy of the Clermont County Library.)

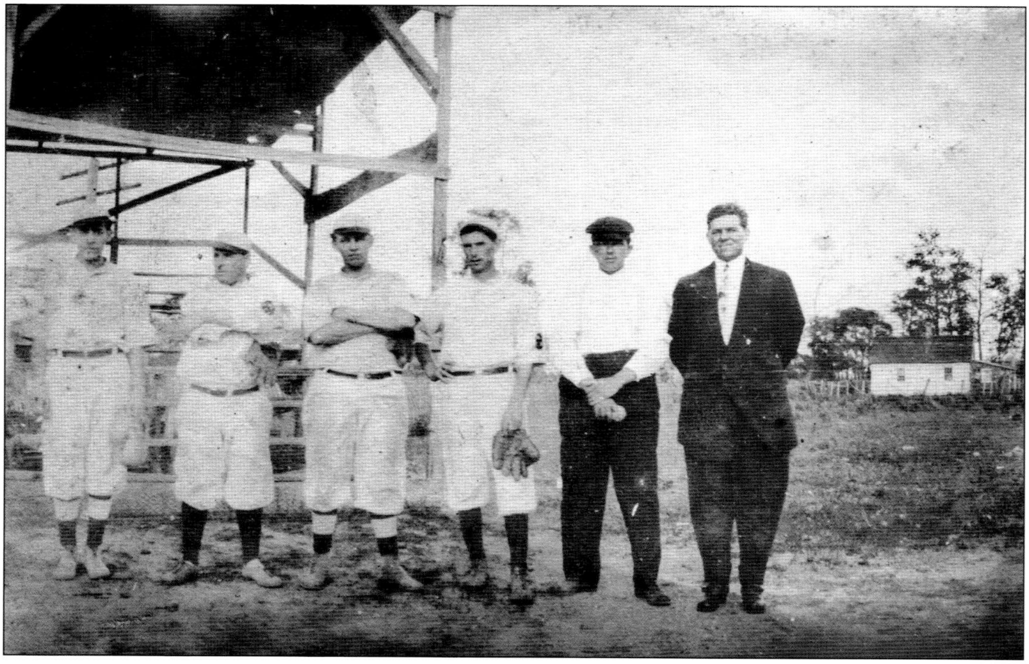

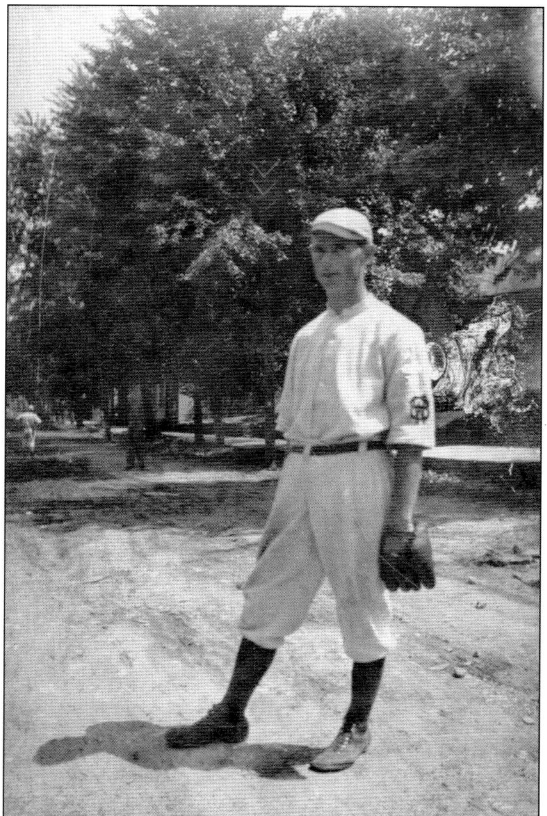

Baseball was a popular sport with small town teams like Williamsburg and Batavia, who vied against each other for pennants. Players on early 1900s Williamsburg teams included Lawrence White, Stanley Frazier, Bob McAfee, Walter Rose, George Barnes, Hugh Davidson, Roy Peterson, and Charley Deuchman. (Photograph courtesy of Tim and Windy Ferree.)

An unidentified pitcher gets ready to throw for the 1919 Williamsburg team. (Photograph courtesy of Tim and Windy Ferree.)

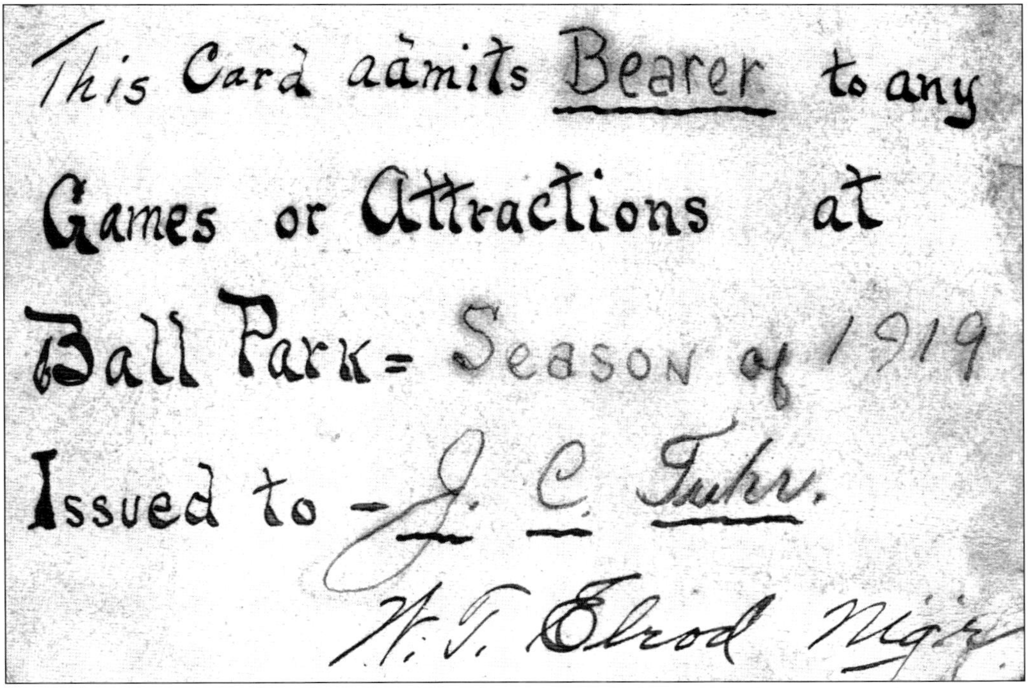

This Card admits Bearer to any Games or Attractions at Ball Park = Season of 1919
Issued to — J. C. Fuhr.
W. T. Elrod Mgr.

J.C. Fuhr received this handwritten ticket that admitted him to all the games and attractions during the 1919 Williamsburg season. (Photograph courtesy of Tim and Windy Ferree.)

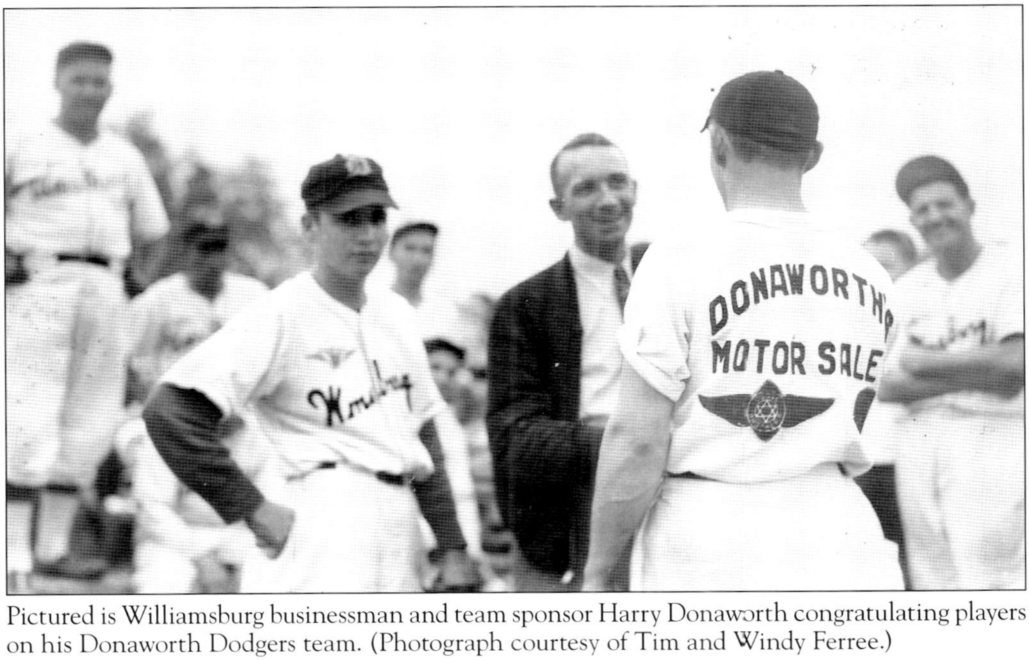

Pictured is Williamsburg businessman and team sponsor Harry Donaworth congratulating players on his Donaworth Dodgers team. (Photograph courtesy of Tim and Windy Ferree.)

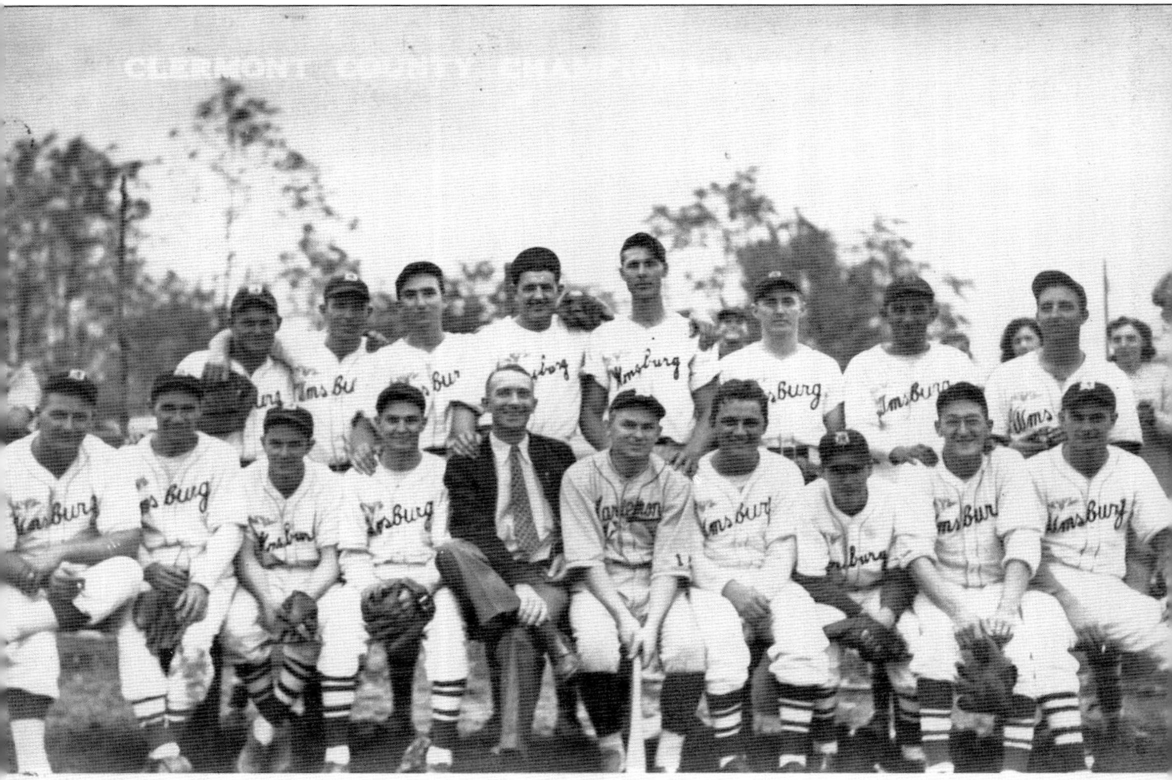

DONAWORTH'S DODGERS

Donaworth's Dodgers, Clermont County 1941 Championship Team, Reading from left to right in the front row: Jess Storer; Ed. Schebasta; Albert Craig; Kenneth Duchemin, Coach; Harry B. Donaworth, Owner; Henry Andres, Manager; Jim Hamilton, Assistant Manager and Coach; Harry Donaworth Jr., Utility; Ollie Grimm, Pitcher; and (Mack) Wilkins, Pitcher. Standing and in the back row from left to right: John Schebasta; Harry Vaught Jr.; Jim Vearil; (Mickie) Meranda; (Bud) Woods; Eldon Kirkpatrick; Harvie Hance and Virgil Malott, Catcher. © 41 TIMES

Williamsburg's Donaworth's Dodgers baseball team won the Clermont County championship in 1941. Team members from left to right are (first row) Jess Storer, Ed Schebasta, Albert Craig, Kenneth Duchemin (coach), Harry B. Donaworth (owner), Henry Andres (manager), Jim Hamilton (assistant manager and coach), Harry B. Donaworth Jr. (utility), Ollie Grimm (pitcher), and Mack Wilkins (pitcher); (second row) John Schebasta, Harry Vaught Jr., Jim Vearil, Mickey Meranda, Bud Woods, Eldon Kirkpatrick, Harvie Hance, and Virgil Malott (catcher). (Photograph courtesy of Tim and Windy Ferree.)

Eight

Organizations and Activities

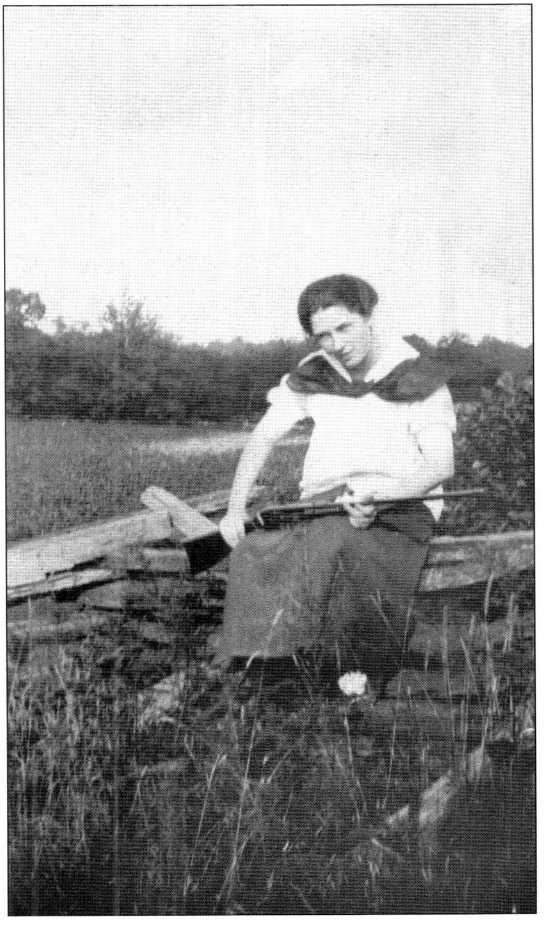

An unidentified young woman in Williamsburg gives new meaning to the phrase, "sitting shotgun." (Photograph courtesy of Tim and Windy Ferree.)

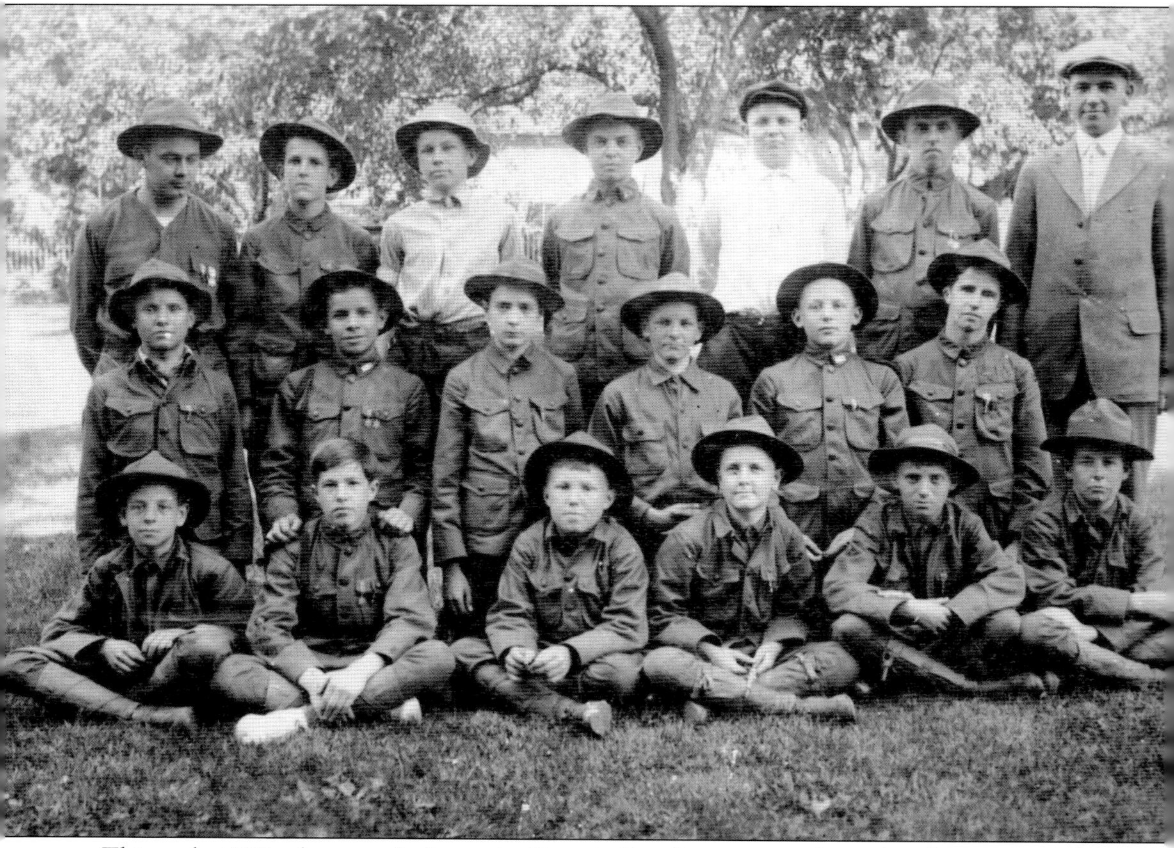

This early 1900s photograph shows the Batavia Boy Scout troop. Area churches sponsored the scouts and allowed their spaces to be used for meetings and special events. (Photograph courtesy of Lou Moore.)

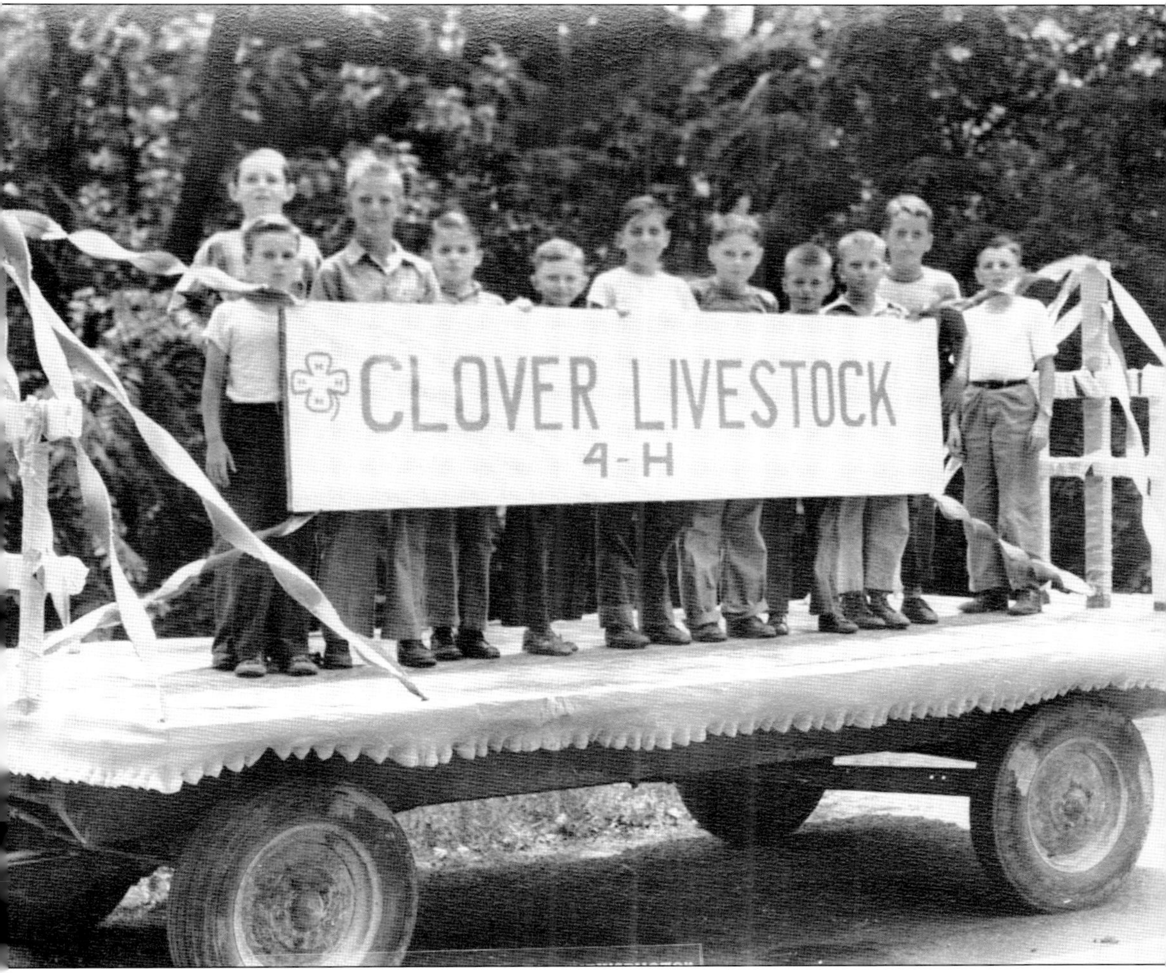

Clermont County 4-H participants made a float to represent their club during a 1940s Williamsburg parade. The official 4-H emblem, which is still used today, is represented in this photograph as a green four-leaf clover with a white "H" on each leaf standing for head, heart, hands, and health. As of 2011, there were 45 active 4-H Clubs in Clermont County and over 1,000 children and young adults involved in the program. (Photograph courtesy of Tim and Windy Ferree.)

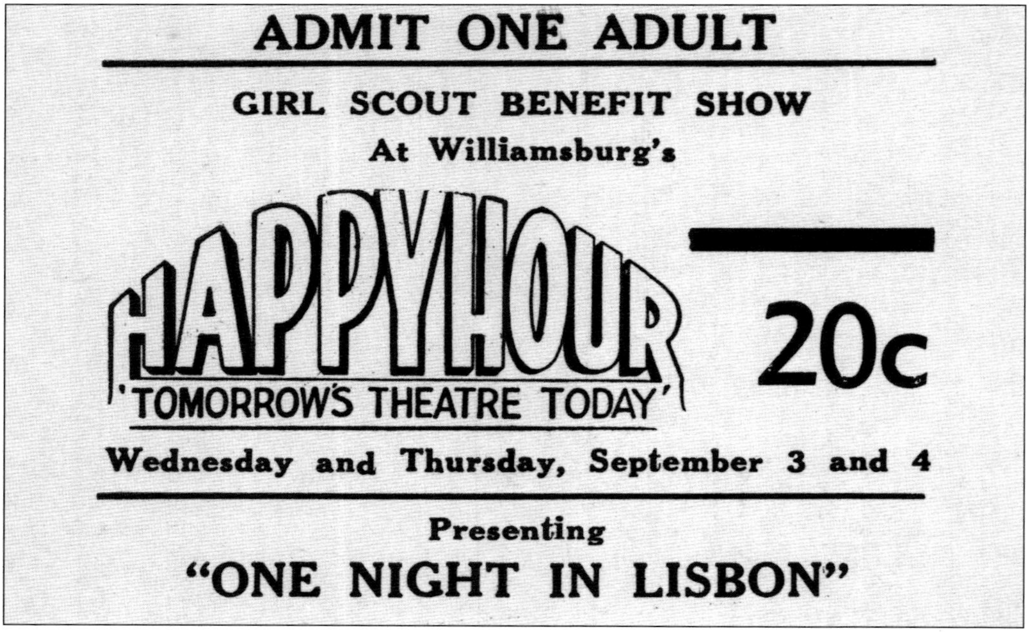

ADMIT ONE ADULT

GIRL SCOUT BENEFIT SHOW

At Williamsburg's

HAPPY HOUR

'TOMORROW'S THEATRE TODAY'

20c

Wednesday and Thursday, September 3 and 4

Presenting

"ONE NIGHT IN LISBON"

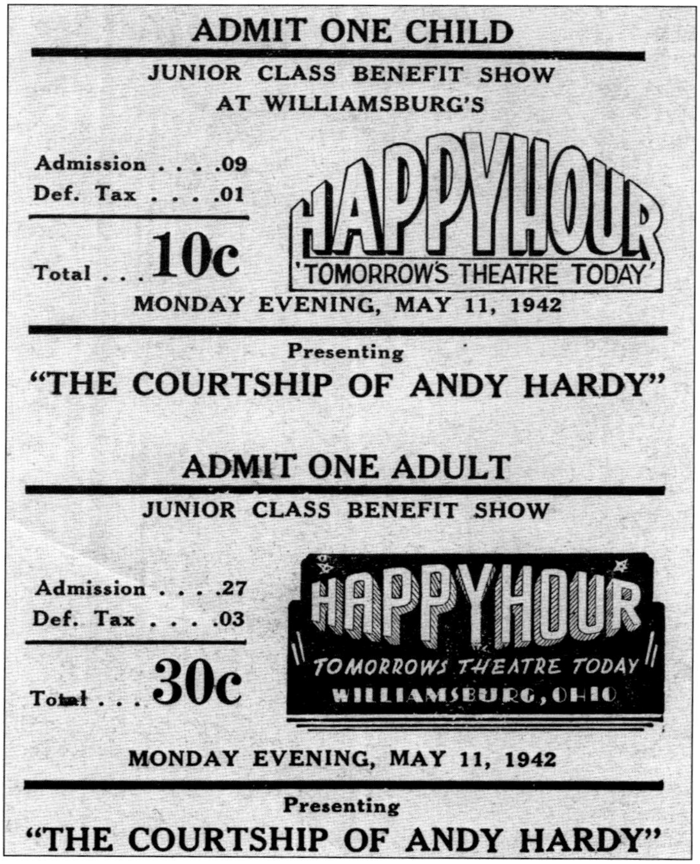

ADMIT ONE CHILD

JUNIOR CLASS BENEFIT SHOW

AT WILLIAMSBURG'S

Admission 09
Def. Tax 01

Total . . . 10c

HAPPY HOUR

'TOMORROW'S THEATRE TODAY'

MONDAY EVENING, MAY 11, 1942

Presenting

"THE COURTSHIP OF ANDY HARDY"

ADMIT ONE ADULT

JUNIOR CLASS BENEFIT SHOW

Admission 27
Def. Tax 03

Total . . . 30c

HAPPY HOUR

TOMORROWS THEATRE TODAY

WILLIAMSBURG, OHIO

MONDAY EVENING, MAY 11, 1942

Presenting

"THE COURTSHIP OF ANDY HARDY"

In the late 1930s, Jerry Jackson opened the Jackson Theatre in Williamsburg, and 20 years later built the Happy Hour Theatre on north Third Street. At a 1942 benefit show, children paid 10¢ and adults paid 30¢ to see movies like *The Courtship of Andy Hardy* at the place Jackson called "Tomorrow's Theatre Today." (Photographs courtesy of Hazel Arnold.)

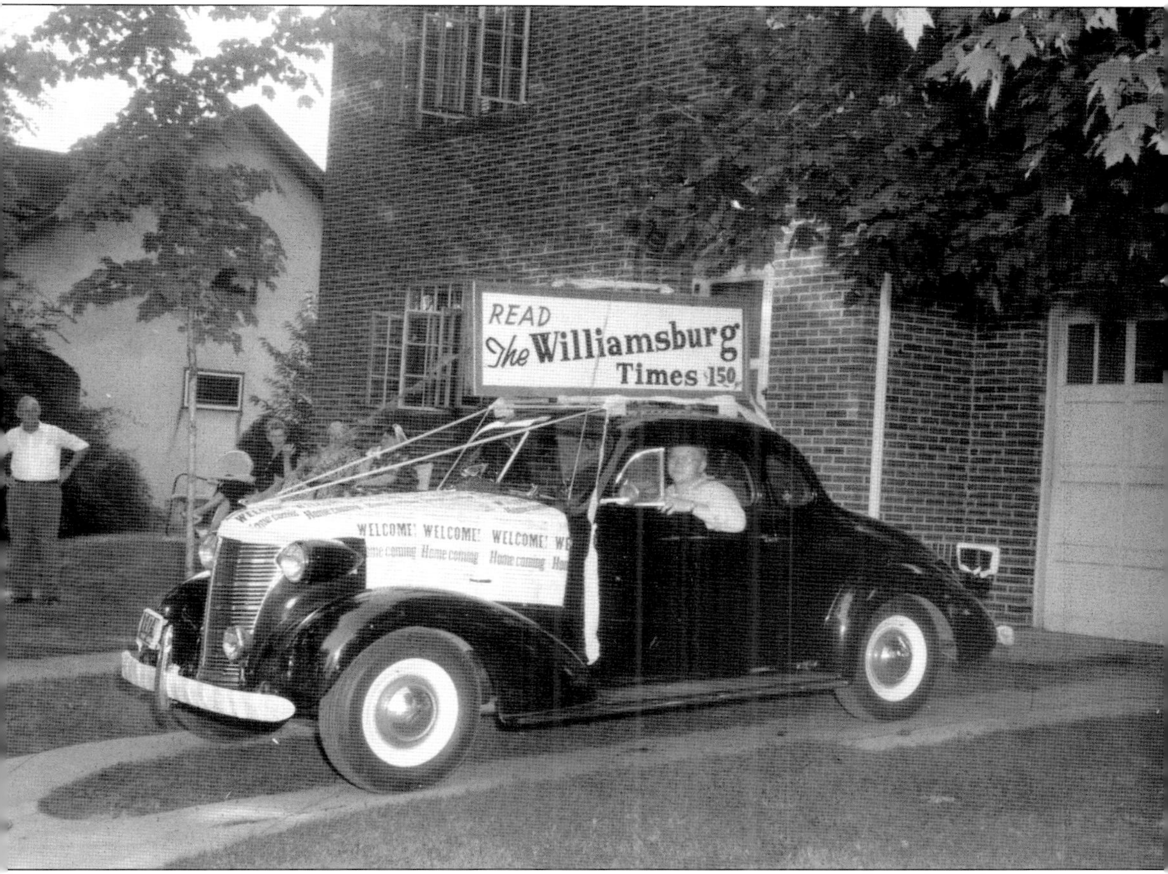

Williamsburg Times editor Ralph Fuhr decorated his car for the 1954 parade. (Photograph courtesy of Tim and Windy Ferree.)

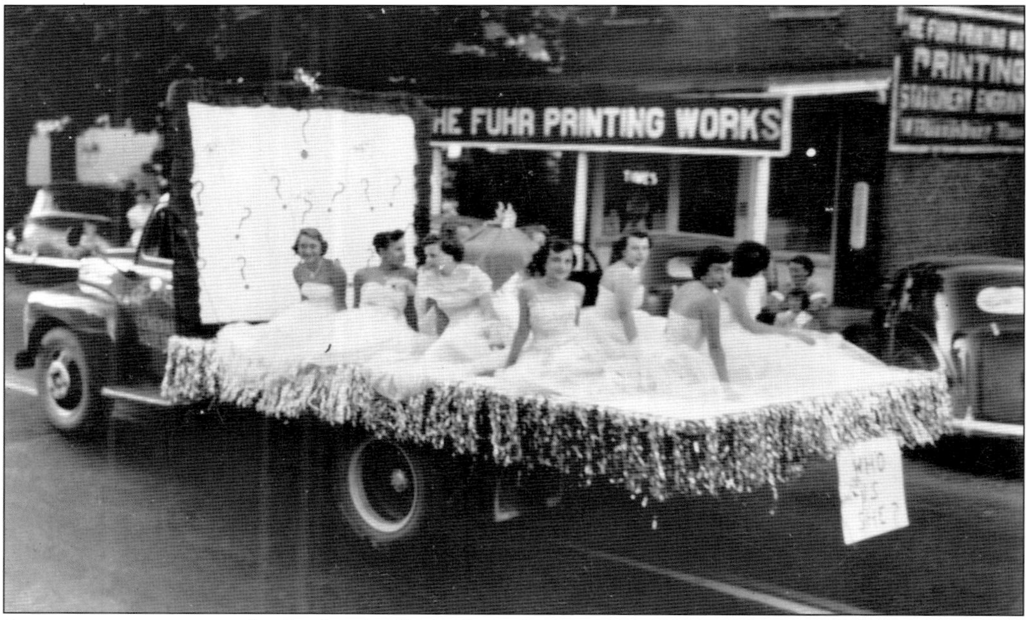

Beauty queens grace the back of a flatbed trailer in an early 1950s parade in Williamsburg. (Photograph courtesy of Tim and Windy Ferree.)

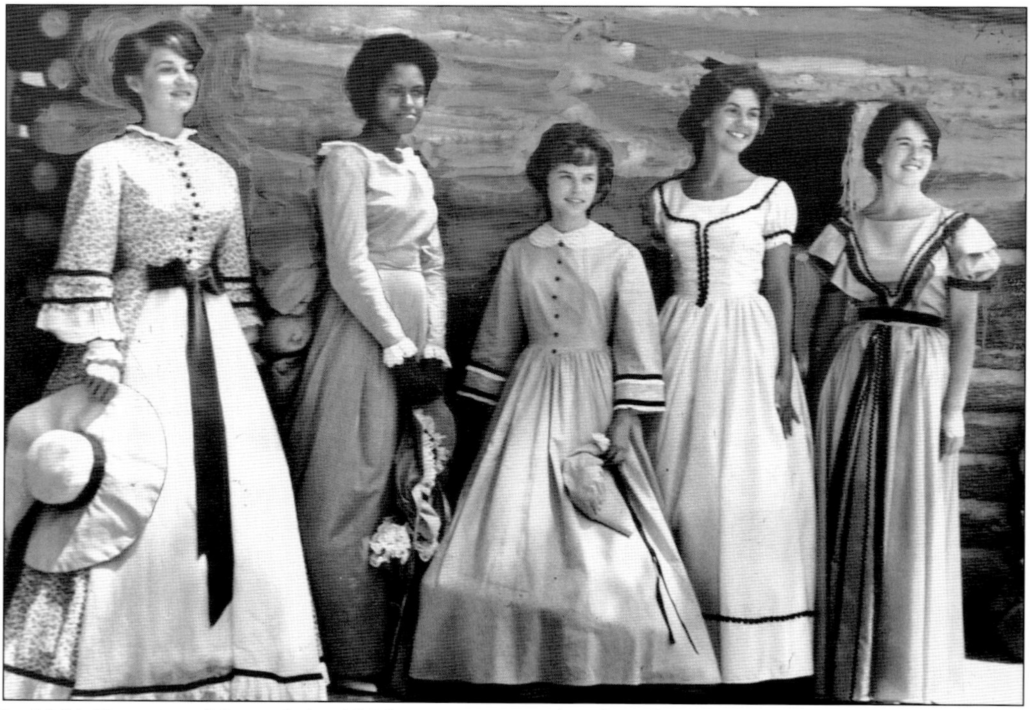

In 1964, Batavia celebrated the 150th anniversary of its founding. Sesquicentennial celebrations included the crowning of Queen Susan Lewis (far right), and her court (left to right) Pam Bitzer, Sue Hamilton, Sandy Rapp, and Shirley Singleton. (Photograph courtesy of the Clermont County Historical Society.)

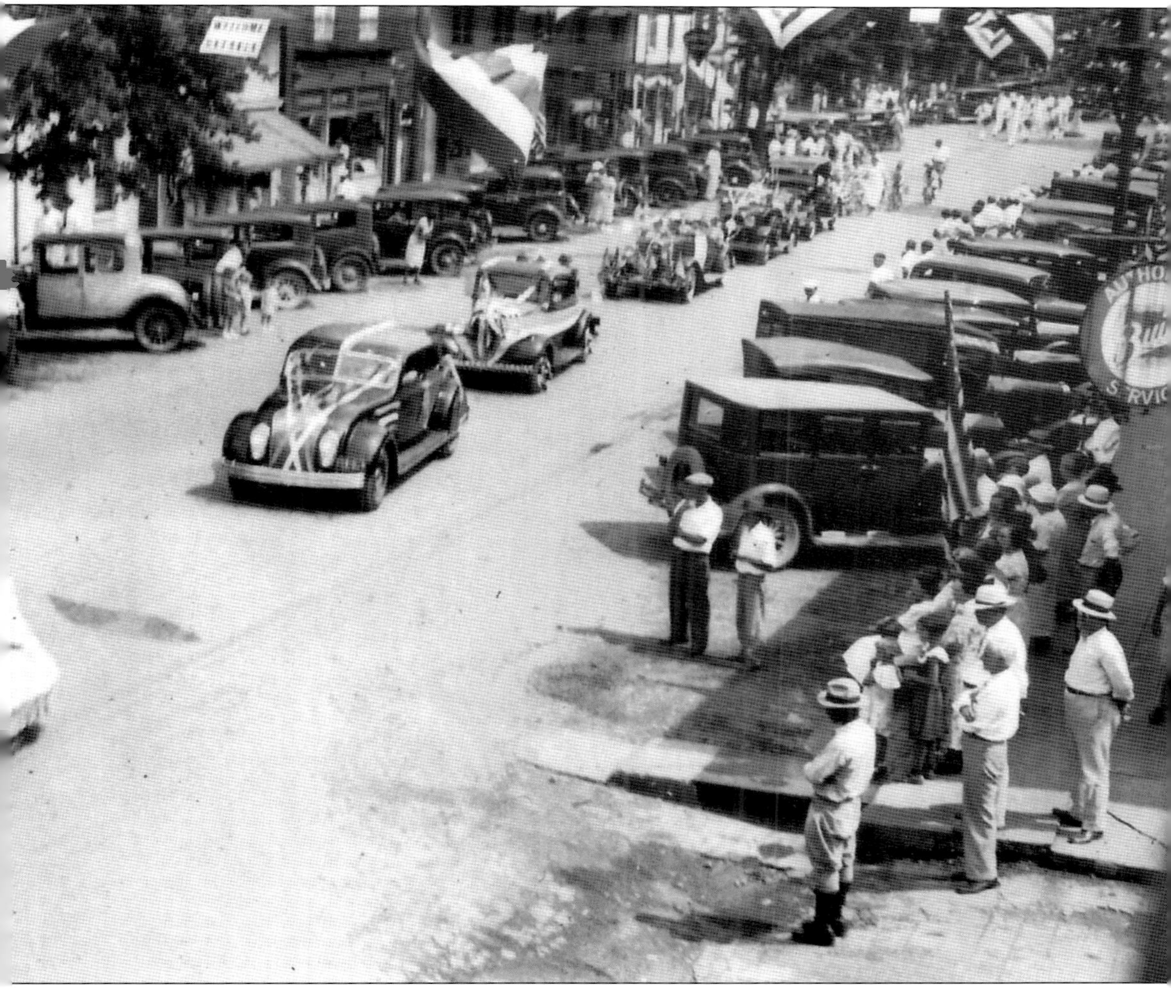

Batavia pulled out all the stops to celebrate its centennial from August 5 to 8, 1914. Celebrations included a reunion at the old sycamore tree in front of the courthouse, a militant suffragette parade by the ladies, a spinning contest, and a big automobile parade. A band concert was held every evening, and old time hymn singing and a sermon concluded the celebrations on Sunday. (Photograph courtesy of Steve Shinkle.)

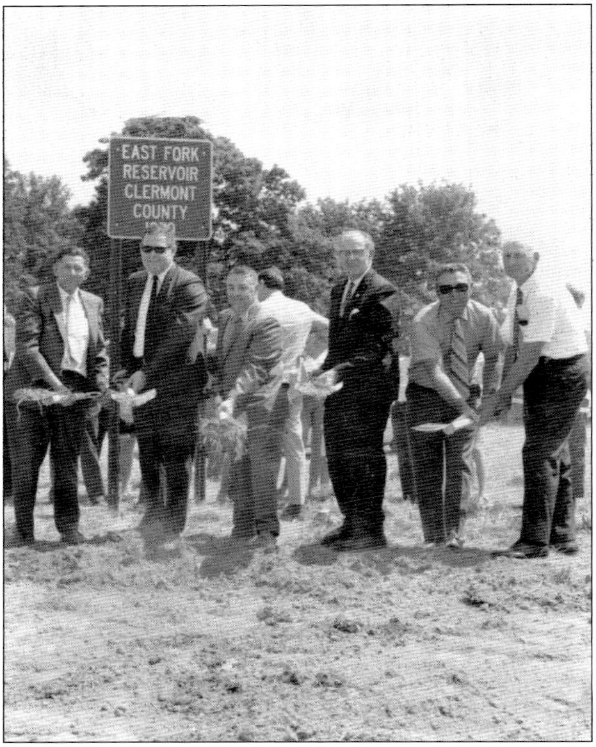

Designed, built, and operated by the Louisville District of the US Army Corps of Engineers, ground was broken for construction on the East Fork Lake project in May 1970. Construction was complete in 1978. East Fork Lake State Park, one of Ohio's largest, consists of 4,870 acres surrounding the William H. Harsha Lake. The park offers camping, picnicking, swimming, boating, and 85 miles of trails. The park and lake are located in three townships: Williamsburg, Batavia, and Tate. (Photograph courtesy of Lou Moore.)

In 1996, a 172-foot high water intake tower was installed on the north shore of the William H. Harsha Lake. Ten million gallons of water are drawn from the lake daily and pumped to a water treatment plant that provides drinking water to a large area of Clermont County. (Photograph courtesy of the Clermont County Historical Society.)

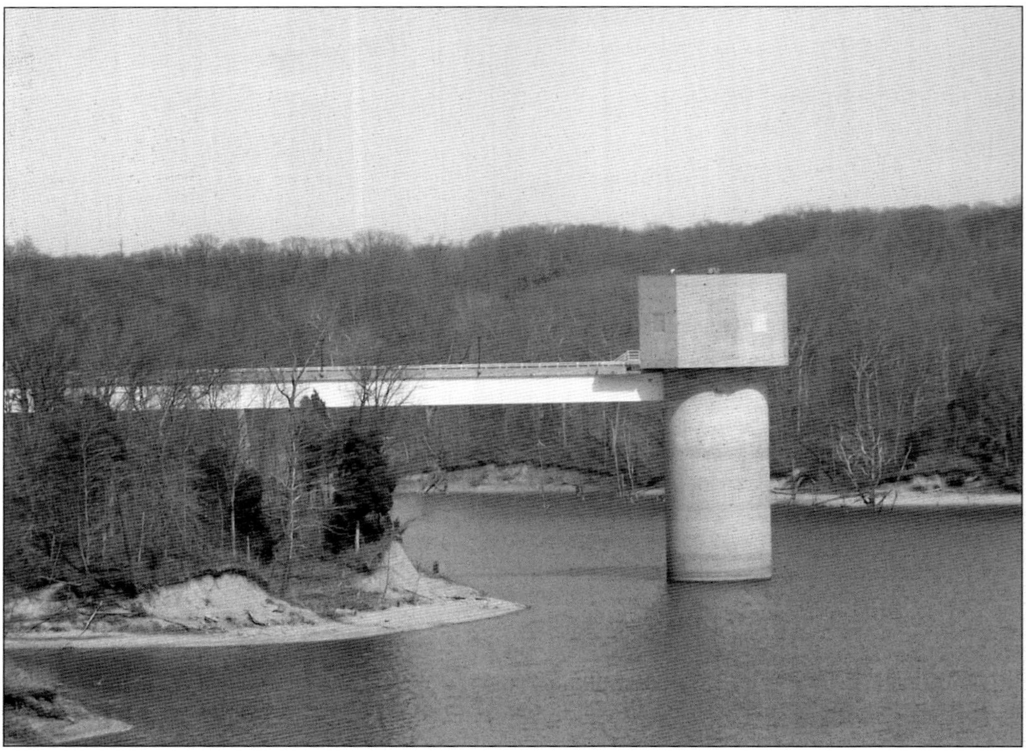

Nine

Schools and Churches

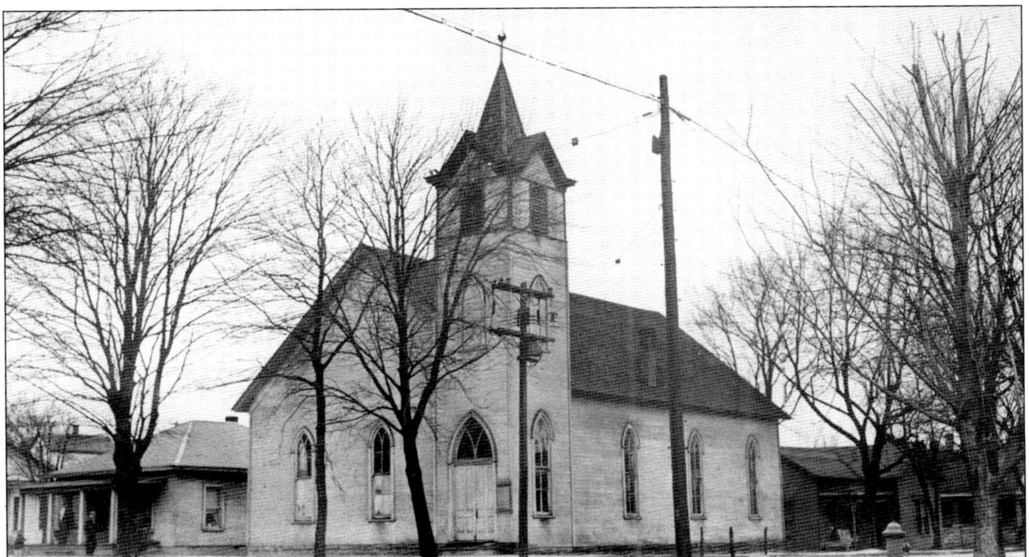

The Williamsburg United Brethren Church later became the Cumberland Presbyterian Church on the corner of Gay and Fourth Streets. In the 1950s, it was a Baptist church and then the Pentecostal church. Today, it is a private residence.

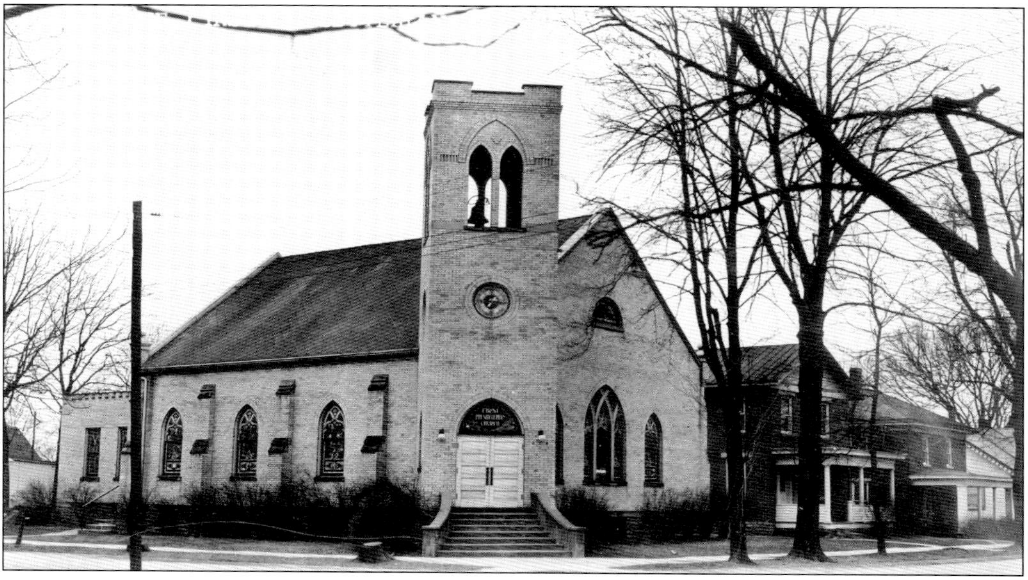

In 1806, the first Presbyterian sermon was preached in Williamsburg, and in 1808, the church was officially organized by the Rev. Dr. Hodge (or Hoge) and met for more than 20 years at the old courthouse. The church building in this photograph was finished in 1912, and still stands at the corner of Second and Gay Streets. It was constructed by local architects and builders and boasted stunning stained glass windows imported from Germany. The steeple contains the bell from the 1845 church, which was located on Front Street on land donated by William Lytle Jr. (Photograph courtesy of Hazel Arnold.)

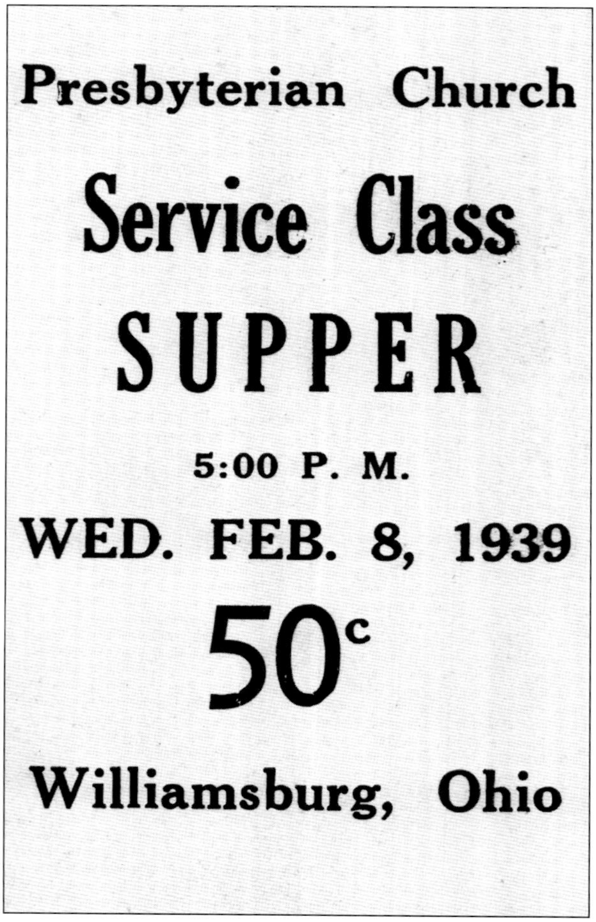

The Williamsburg Presbyterian Church sponsored a community supper in 1939, and the price was a modest 50¢. (Photograph courtesy of Hazel Arnold.)

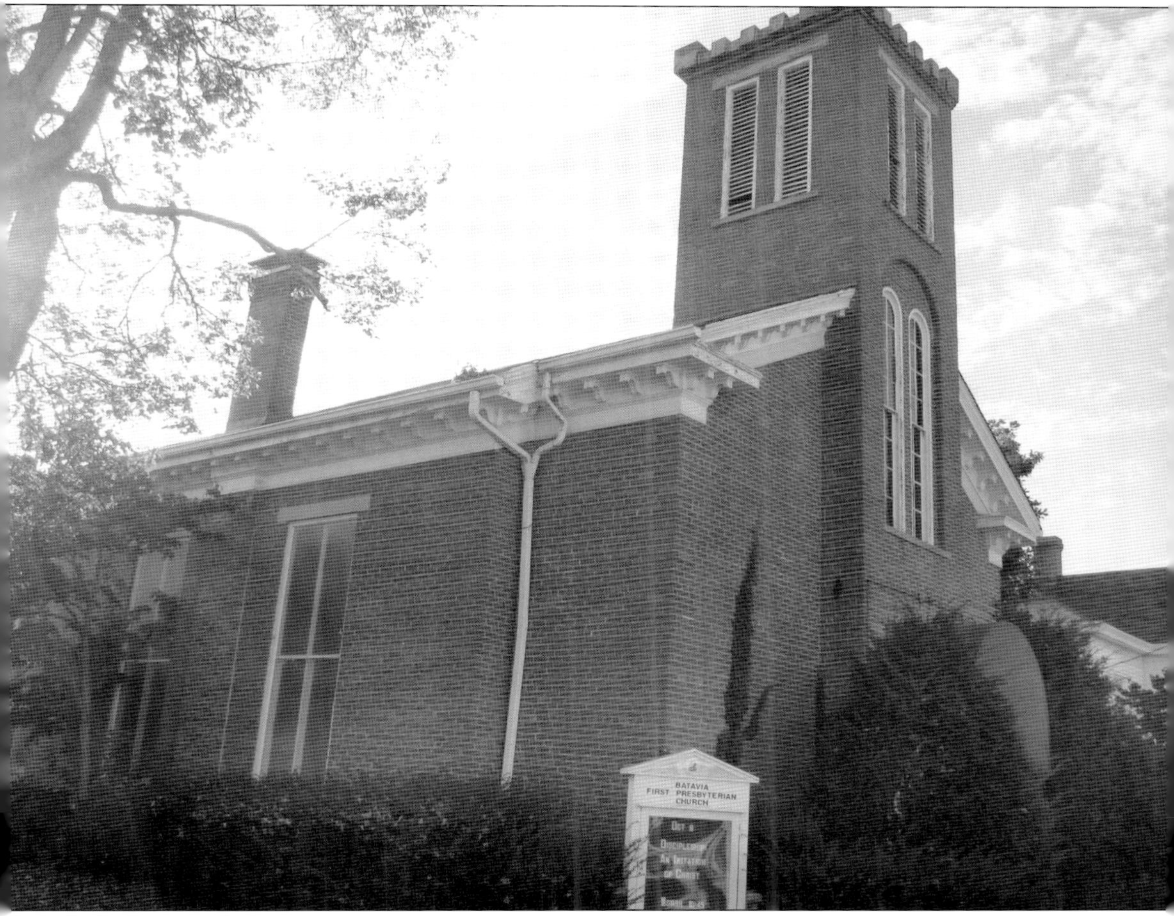

Meetings that were held in the courthouse by ministers occasionally sent by the Presbytery awakened so much interest that a society was formed on December 19, 1829. A frame meetinghouse was begun in 1830, and at the end of the first year, there were 30 members. Henry Ward Beecher, brother of Harriet Beecher Stowe, the author of *Uncle Tom's Cabin*, occasionally spoke from the pulpit here in pre–Civil War days. In December 1859, the old church was sold for $200 and a new church building (pictured) was begun. The cornerstone was laid in April 1860. (Author photograph.)

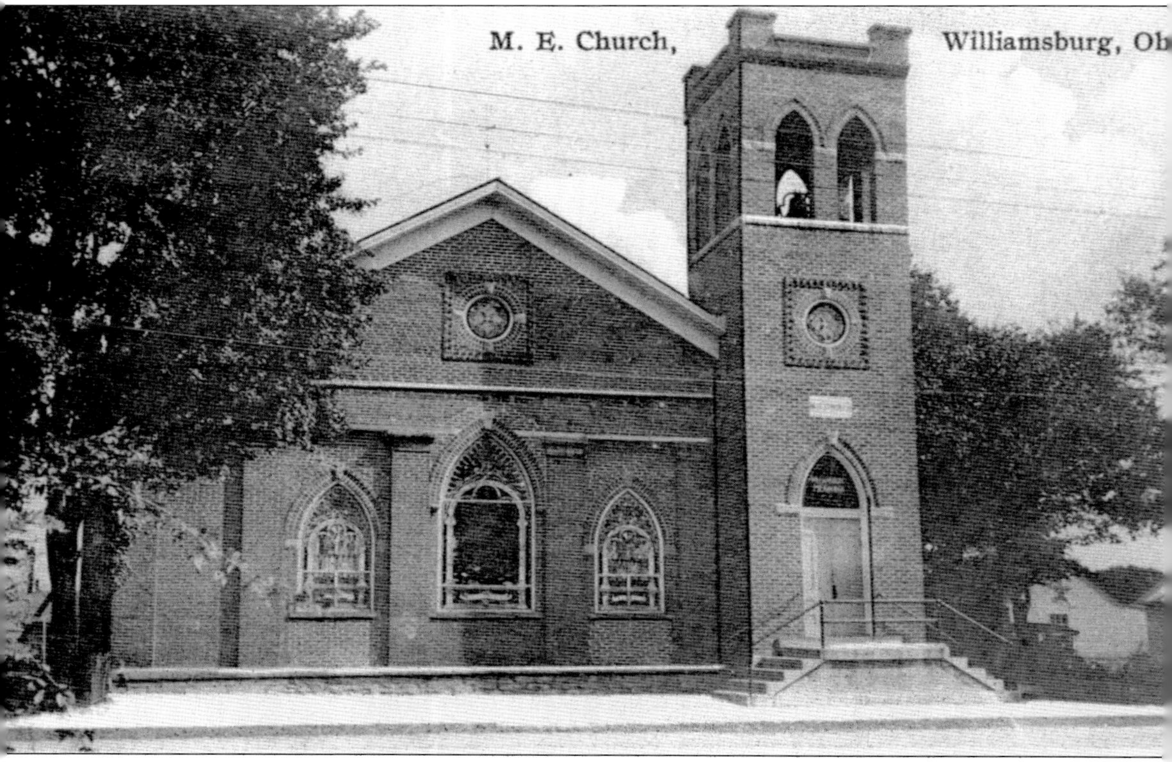

The Methodist faith has been in Williamsburg almost since the founding of the town. Meeting first in homes and then in the courthouse, early church members chose two in-town lots, and a church and manse were built and consecrated in 1845. The church in this photograph is on Gay Street and shows the addition built in the early 1900s. (Photograph courtesy of Tim and Windy Ferree.)

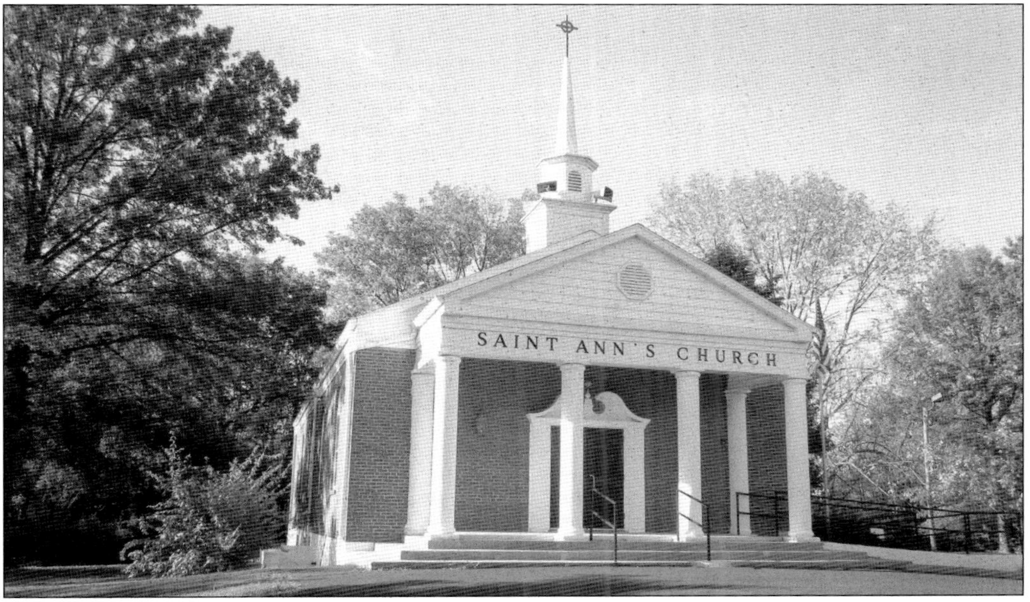

The Green Gables, a log cabin roadside diner on Fifth Street in Williamsburg, was purchased by the archdiocese of Cincinnati in 1947 and renovated into Saint Ann's Catholic Church. Groundbreaking on a new, larger church took place in August 1958. In June 1959, Archbishop Karl J. Alter dedicated the present church building. (Author photograph.)

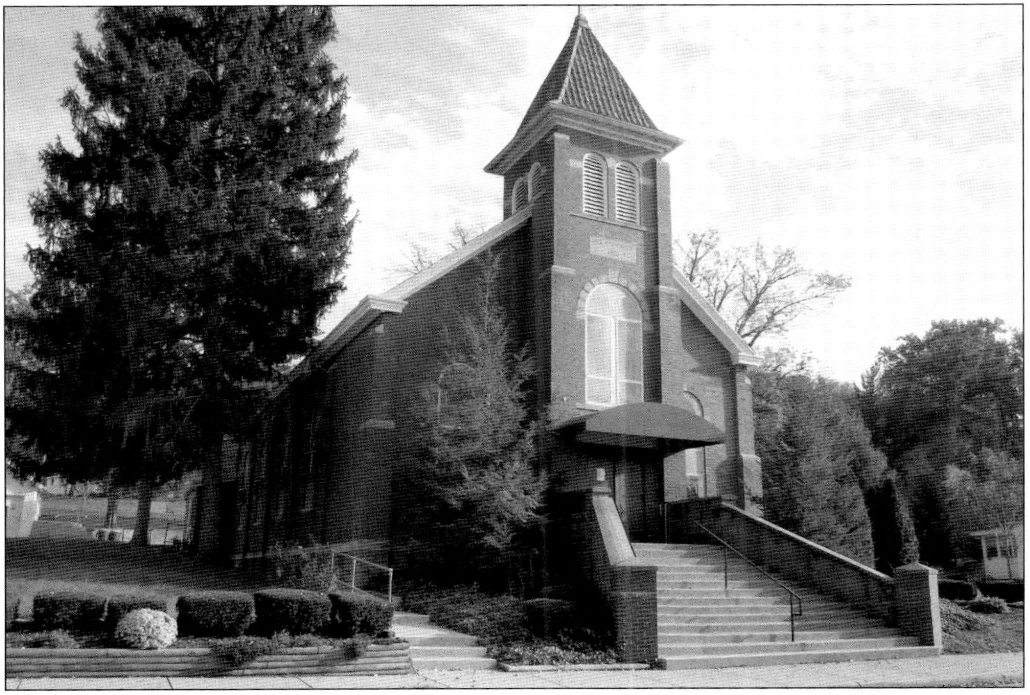

Holy Trinity Church at 6th and Wood Streets in Batavia has been serving the Catholic community there for over 100 years. Since 1990, Holy Trinity has shared a pastor with Saint Ann's in Williamsburg. (Author photograph.)

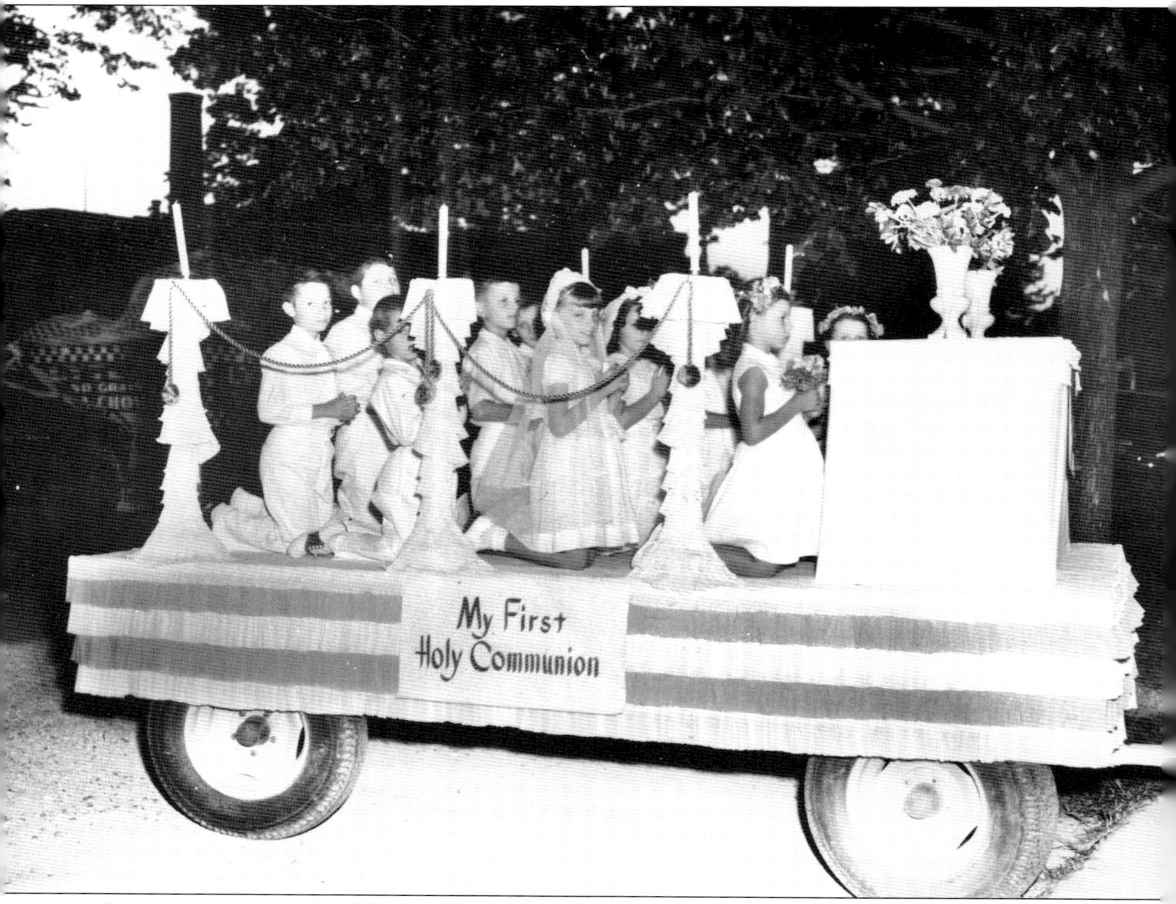

Saint Ann's Catholic Church entered a "First Communion" float in one of Williamsburg's community parades, as seen in this early 1950s photograph. Nothing was written about how long the children had to stay on their knees. (Photograph courtesy of Tim and Windy Ferree.)

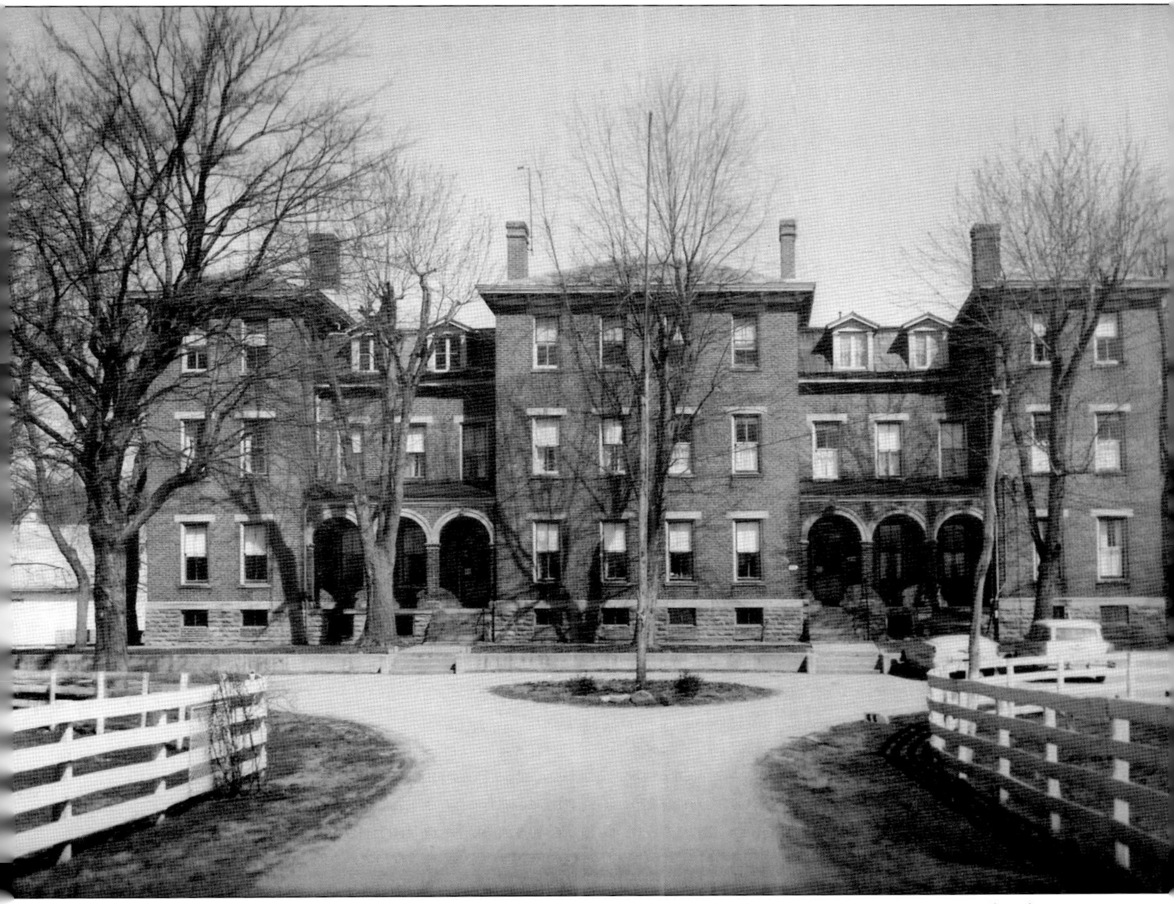

Clermont County Infirmary on State Route 222 just outside of downtown Batavia was built in 1883 but removed in 2002 to make room for the new municipal courthouse. For over 100 years, the infirmary served the sick, homeless, elderly, and orphans of the county. (Photograph courtesy of the Clermont County Historical Society.)

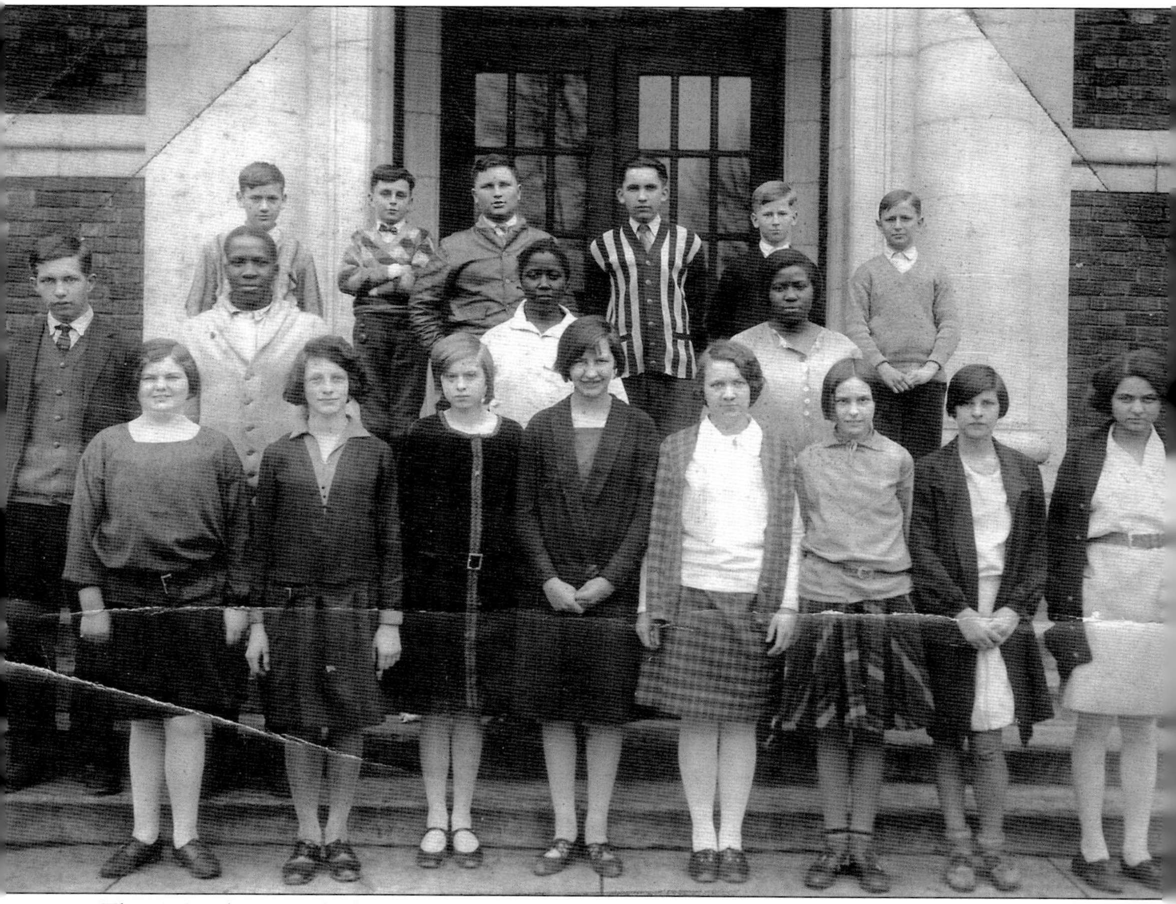

This 1929 photograph shows the graduating eighth grade class from Batavia Elementary School. Included are Sue Speidel Garner, Ruth Grace Haglage, Almeda Hughes, Walter Acomb, Marjorie Murphy Hughes, Rosanna Rice Hoberg, Margaret Kenner Tolin, Fanny Carroll Kennedy, Jim Henderson, Jim Hall, Mamie Hice, Kate Hall, Charles Seibert, Donald Lytle, Bill Coyle, John Hugo, Cecil Hines, and Harley Hauck. (Photograph courtesy of Molly Cribbet.)

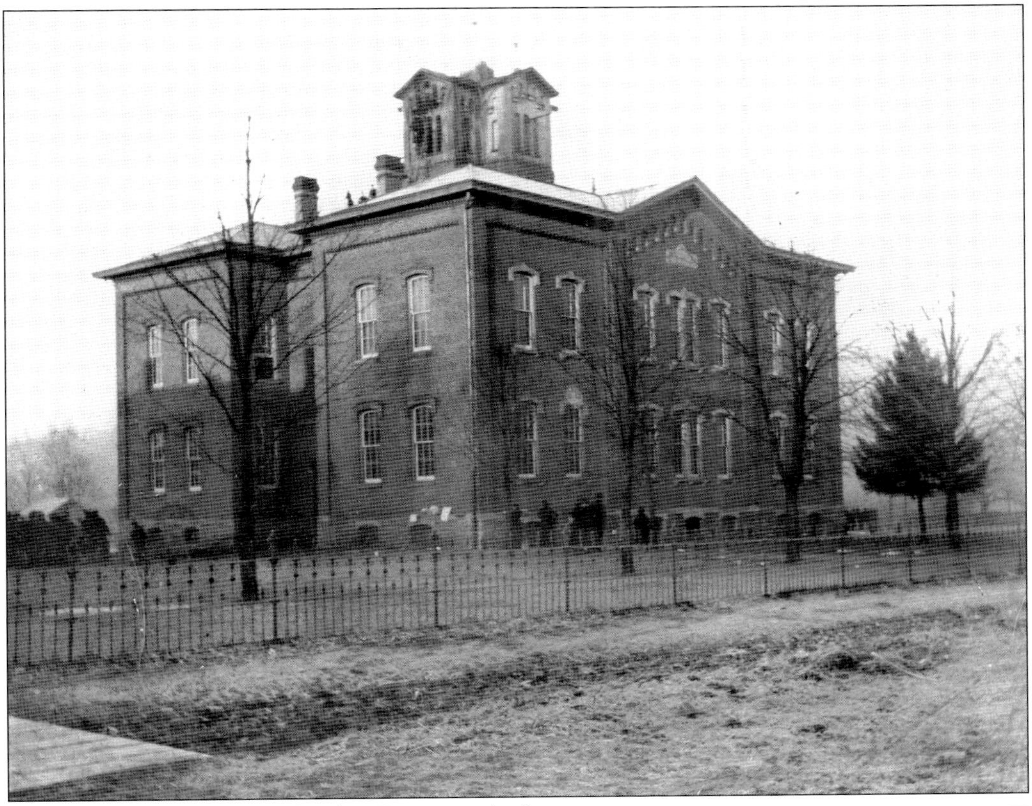

Pictured is the first high school in Batavia, which was built in 1872 at the cost of $18,800. The square-shaped building rested on a limestone foundation and was trimmed with Ohio River stone. It stood two stories high and was topped with a slate roof and a center belfry containing a 700-pound bell. It had six large recitation rooms and a lecture hall. (Photograph courtesy of Molly Cribbet.)

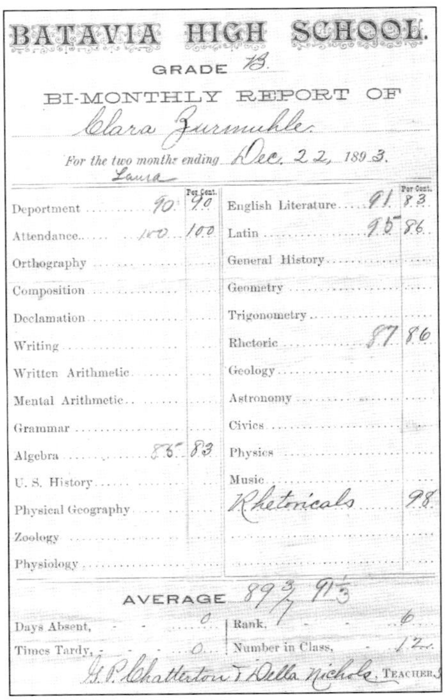

BATAVIA HIGH SCHOOL.

GRADE B.

BI-MONTHLY REPORT OF

Clara Zurmuhle.

For the two months ending Dec. 22, 1893.

Laura

		Per Cent.			Per Cent.
Deportment	90	90	English Literature	91	83
Attendance	100	100	Latin	95	86
Orthography			General History		
Composition			Geometry		
Declamation			Trigonometry		
Writing			Rhetoric	87	86
Written Arithmetic			Geology		
Mental Arithmetic			Astronomy		
Grammar			Civics		
Algebra	85	83	Physics		
U. S. History			Music		
Physical Geography			Rhetoricals		98
Zoology					
Physiology					

AVERAGE 89 3/7 91 1/3

Days Absent,	0	Rank,	6
Times Tardy,	0	Number in Class,	12

G. P. Chatterton & Della Nichols, TEACHERS

In 1893, Batavia High School student Clara Zurmuhle studied algebra, English literature, rhetoric, and Latin, earning a "B" average for her two months of study. (Photograph courtesy of Steve Shinkle.)

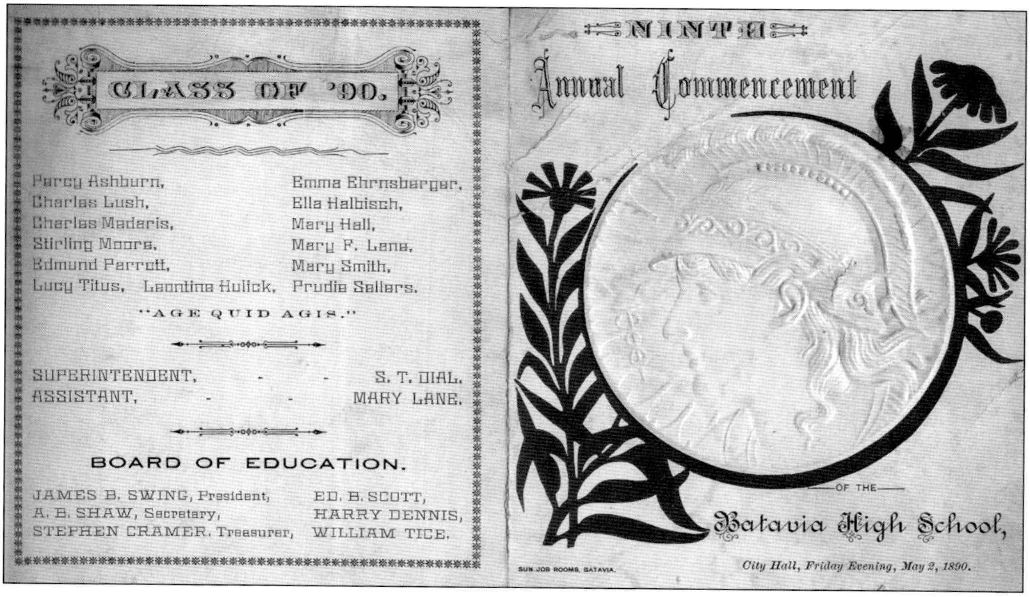

CLASS OF '90.

Percy Ashburn,
Charles Lush,
Charles Madaris,
Stirling Moore,
Edmund Parrott,
Lucy Titus,
Leontine Hulick,
Emma Ehrnsberger,
Ella Halbisch,
Mary Hall,
Mary F. Lane,
Mary Smith,
Prudie Sellers.

"AGE QUID AGIS."

SUPERINTENDENT, - - S. T. DIAL.
ASSISTANT, - - MARY LANE.

BOARD OF EDUCATION.

JAMES B. SWING, President,
A. B. SHAW, Secretary,
STEPHEN CRAMER, Treasurer,
ED. B. SCOTT,
HARRY DENNIS,
WILLIAM TICE.

NINTH
Annual Commencement
OF THE
Batavia High School,
City Hall, Friday Evening, May 2, 1890.

SUN JOB ROOMS, BATAVIA.

Batavia High School held its commencement ceremonies in the town hall on May 2, 1890. Thirteen students graduated and presented essays at the ceremony. Mary Hall's paper was titled, "A Grain of Wheat is Not Content to be a Germ," while valedictorian Edmund Parrott chose to look forward, speaking about what life would be like in the 20th century. (Photographs courtesy of Steve Shinkle.)

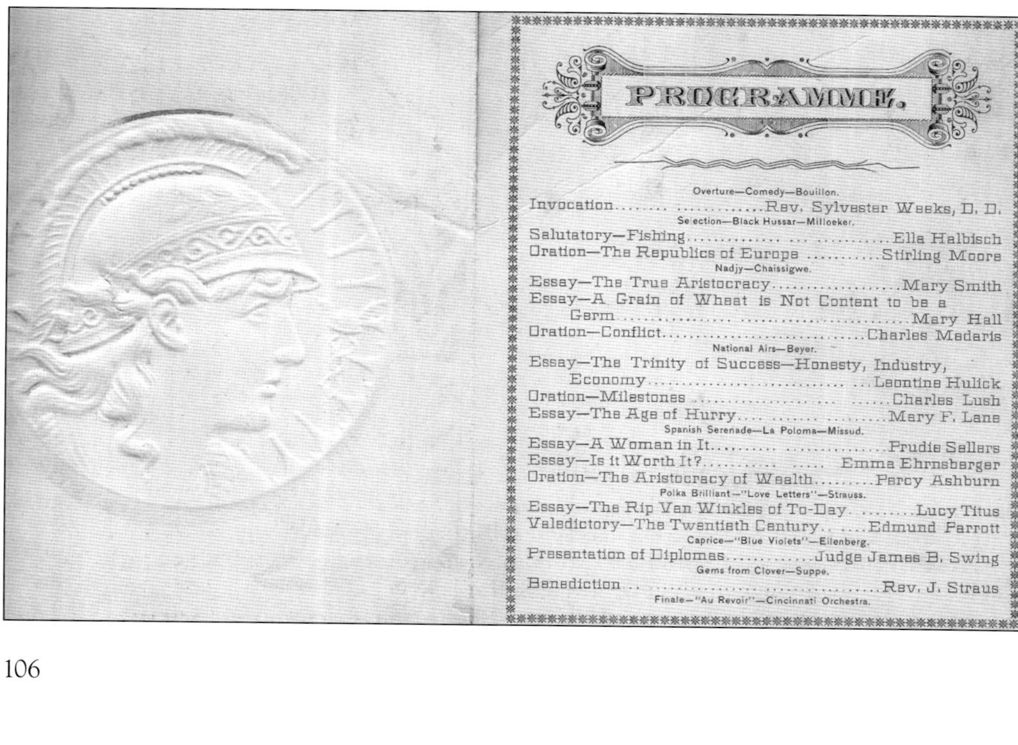

PROGRAMME.

Overture—Comedy—Bouillon.
Invocation.......................Rev. Sylvester Weeks, D. D.
Selection—Black Hussar—Milloeker.
Salutatory—Fishing.......................Ella Halbisch
Oration—The Republics of Europe ....Stirling Moore
Nadjy—Chaissigwe.
Essay—The True Aristocracy..................Mary Smith
Essay—A Grain of Wheat is Not Content to be a Germ.......................Mary Hall
Oration—Conflict.......................Charles Madaris
National Airs—Beyer.
Essay—The Trinity of Success—Honesty, Industry, Economy.......................Leontine Hulick
Oration—Milestones.......................Charles Lush
Essay—The Age of Hurry.......................Mary F. Lane
Spanish Serenade—La Poloma—Missud.
Essay—A Woman in It.......................Prudie Sellers
Essay—Is it Worth It?.......................Emma Ehrnsberger
Oration—The Aristocracy of Wealth.........Percy Ashburn
Polka Brilliant—"Love Letters"—Strauss.
Essay—The Rip Van Winkles of To-Day.........Lucy Titus
Valedictory—The Twentieth Century.........Edmund Parrott
Caprice—"Blue Violets"—Eilenberg.
Presentation of Diplomas............Judge James B. Swing
Gems from Clover—Suppe.
Benediction.......................Rev. J. Straus
Finale—"Au Revoir"—Cincinnati Orchestra.

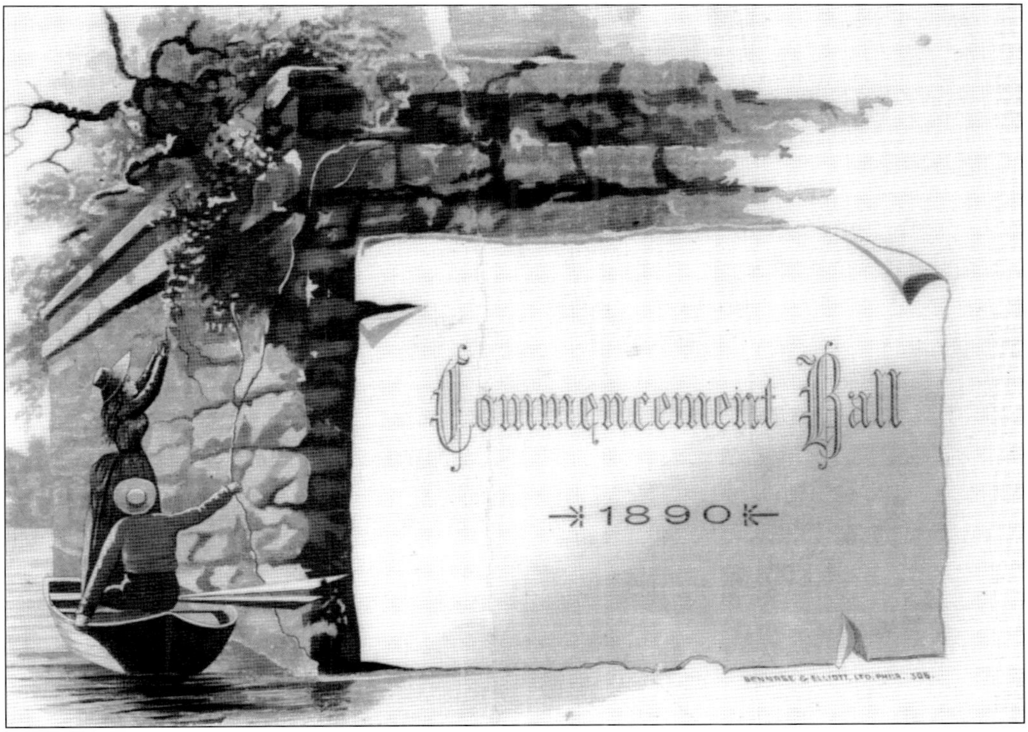

This invitation to the 1890 class dance for Batavia High School graduates is interesting, as it appears to contain several misspellings. (Photographs courtesy of Lou Moore.)

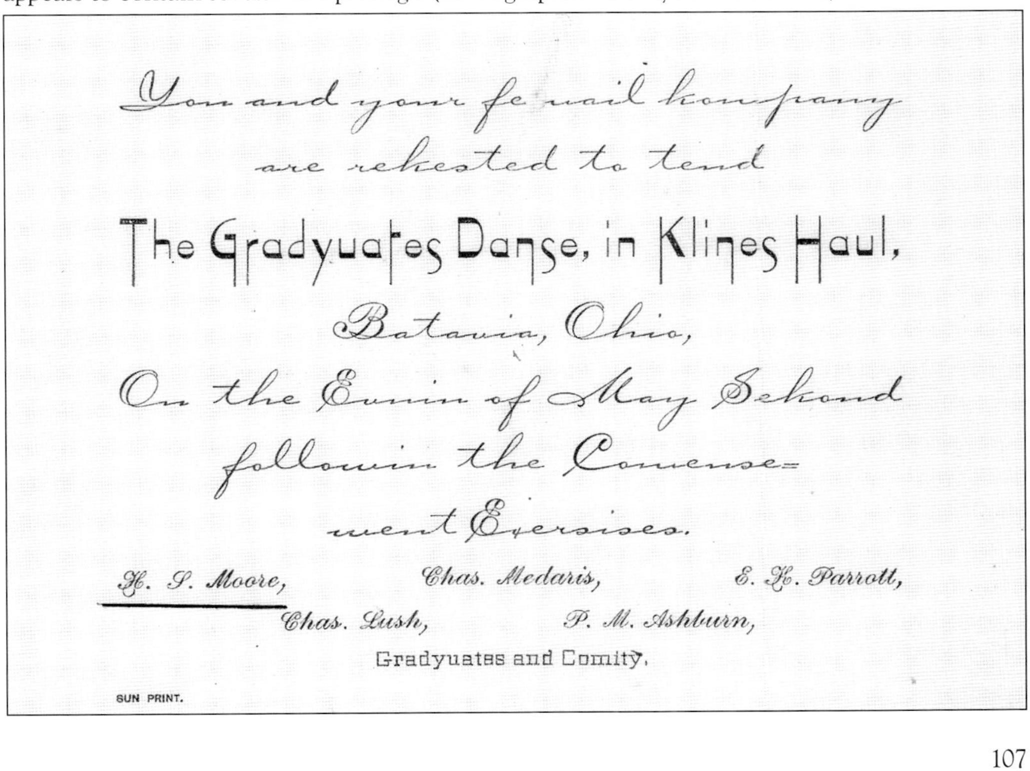

You and your fe mail konpany
are rekested to tend
The Gradyuates Danse, in Klines Haul,
Batavia, Ohio,
On the Evnin of May Sekond
followin the Conense=
ment Eversises.

H. S. Moore, Chas. Medaris, E. K. Parrott,
Chas. Lush, P. M. Ashburn,
Gradyuates and Comity.

SUN PRINT.

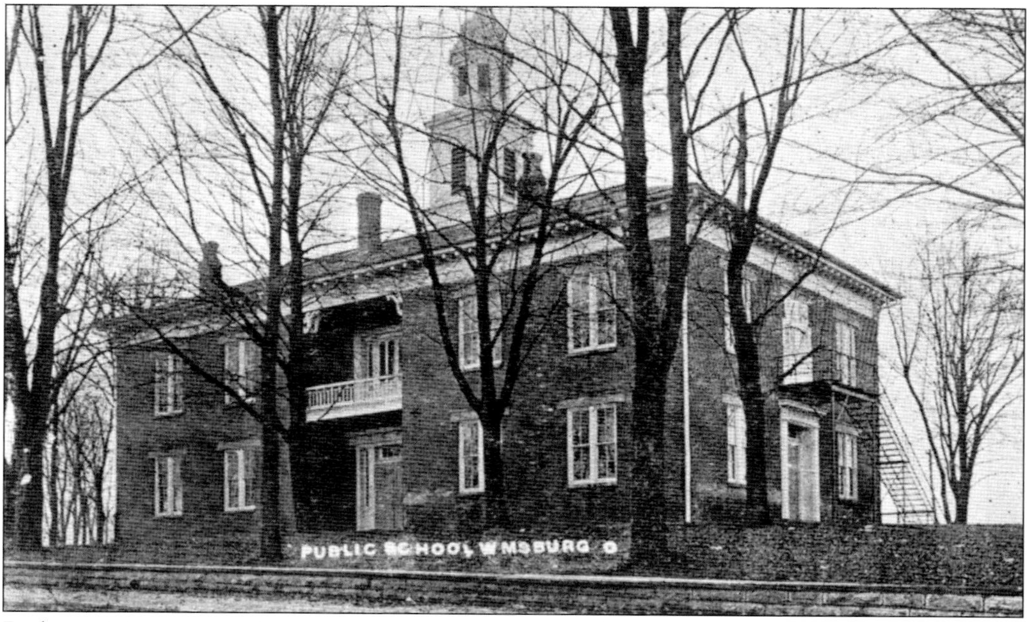

Built in 1860 on ground set aside by William Lytle for the town's public square, Williamsburg's two-story brick school contained eight rooms. It burned to the ground in 1922, but was replaced by a new school on the same site. (Postcard courtesy of Hazel Arnold.)

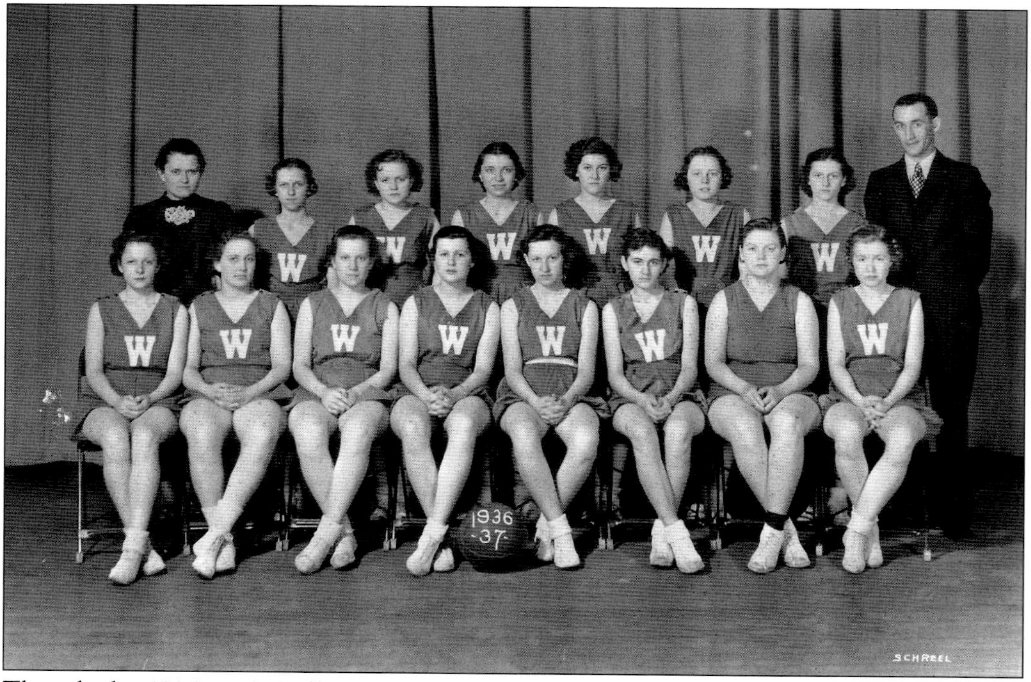

Though the 1936–1937 Williamsburg girls' basketball team shown in this photograph was unsuccessful in their bid for a championship, the Williamsburg boys' basketball team won the Clermont County Athletic Association trophy in 1936. (Photograph courtesy of Tim and Windy Ferree.)

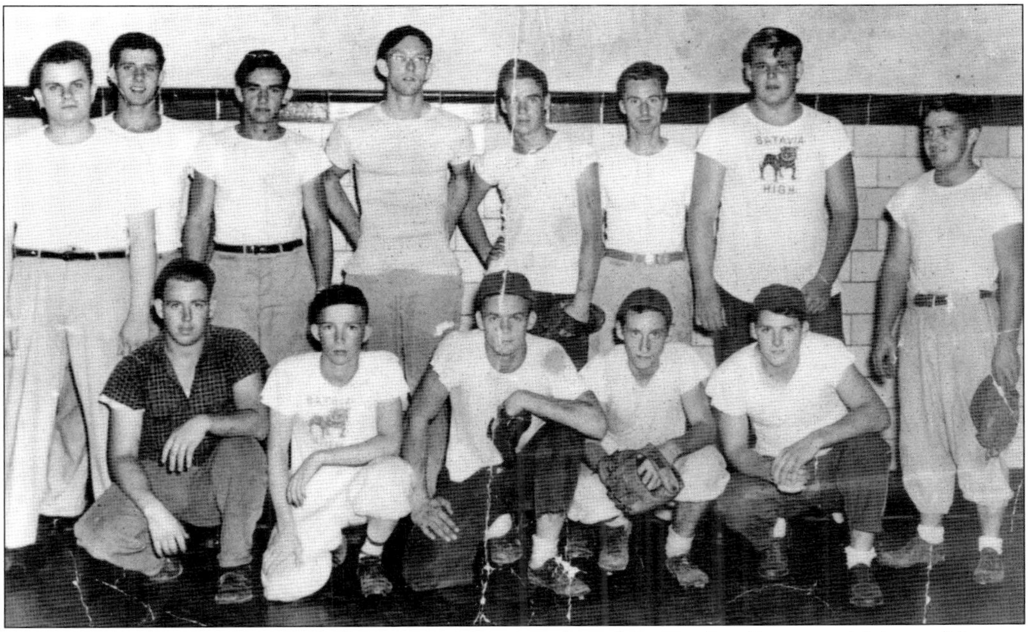

The 1930 Batavia boys' basketball team members are, from left to right, (front row) Moore, Mussey, Kinner, South, Andres, and Hugo; (second row) Weichering, Wolf, Moore, Hoberg, and Snyder. (Photograph courtesy of Steve Shinkle.)

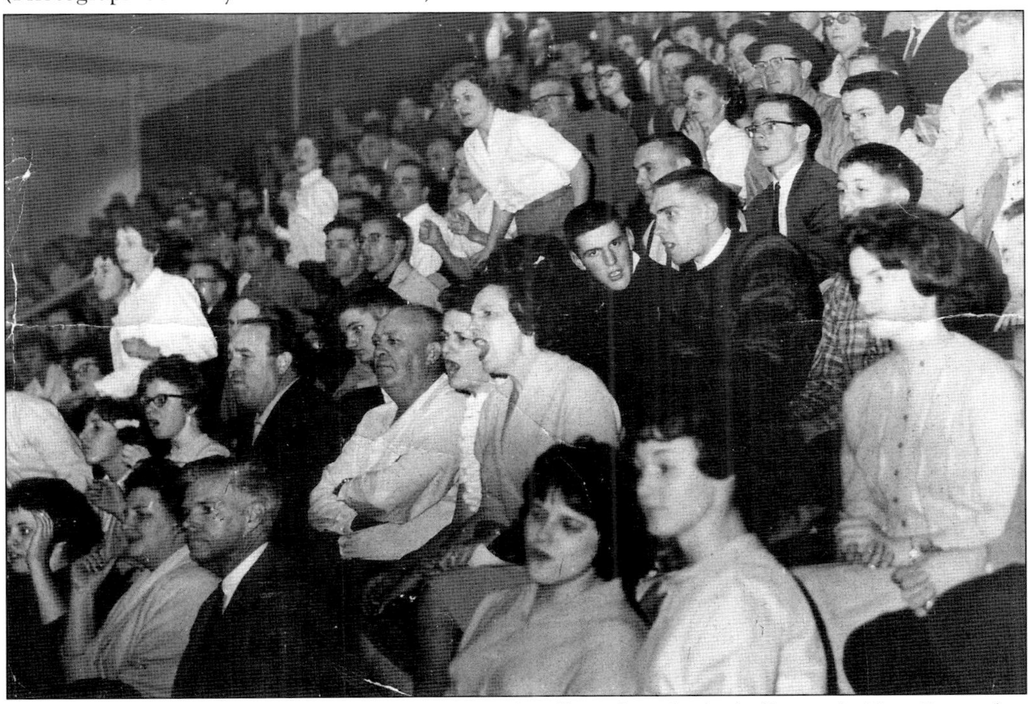

Spectators cheer their teams on at the Batavia and Williamsburg basketball game held on December 10, 1962. According to the back of the photograph, Williamsburg was beating rival Batavia 72-40 at the time the photograph was taken. (Photograph courtesy of Steve Shinkle.)

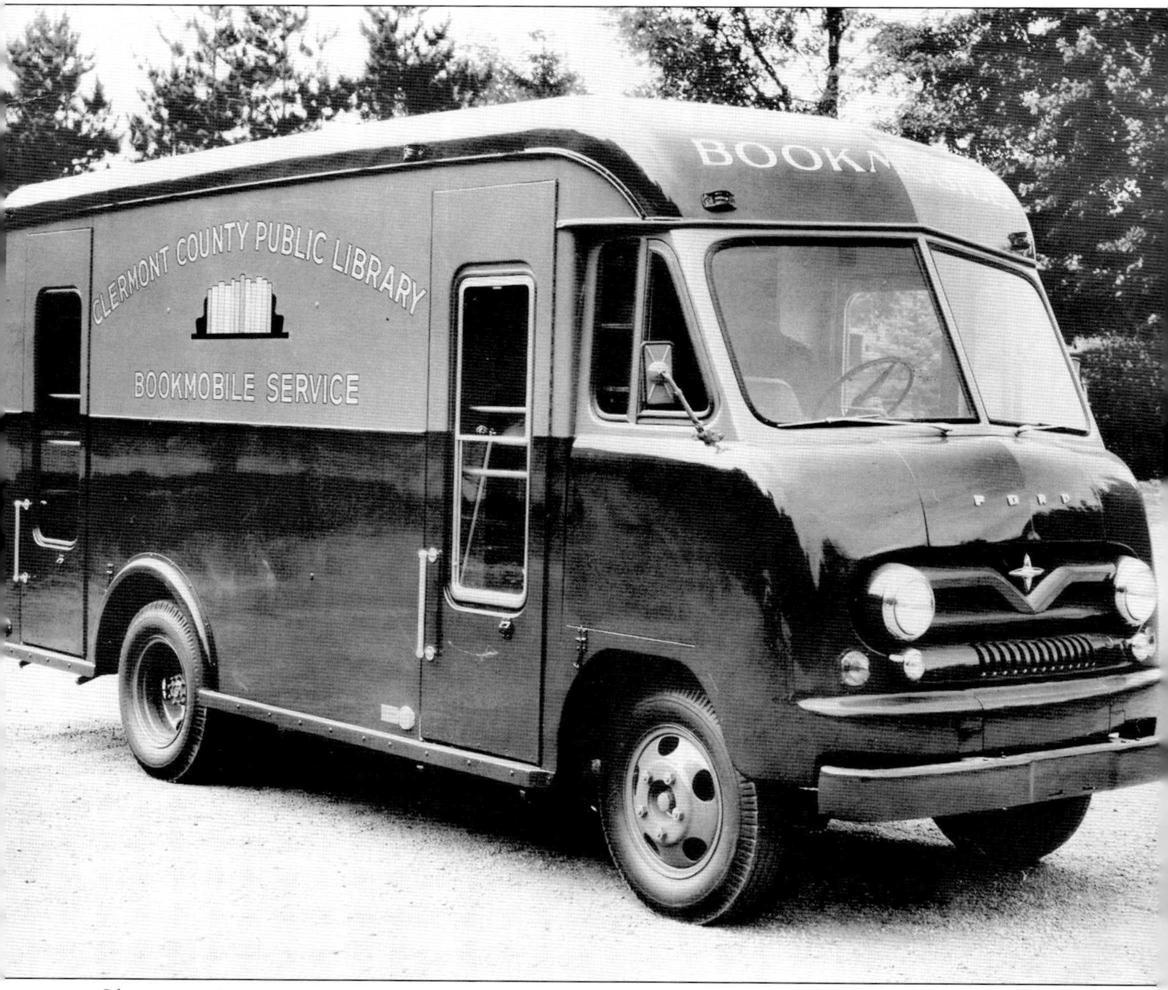

Clermont County was without a public library service until the summer of 1955, when Doris Wood was hired as the librarian and a bookmobile was ordered. Headquarters for the library was established in a storeroom rented from a local merchant. By the end of 1955, the bookmobile was travelling several days a week, serving 10 schools and 28 adult stops. A year later, the book collection was expanded and bookmobile routes increased. Finally, local contractor Harry Kahle offered to build a library building in Batavia big enough to house two bookmobiles and the Batavia branch library. Ground was broken and the library, named after Doris Wood, opened for business in December 1959. (Photograph from the Sharp Collection, courtesy of the Clermont County Library.)

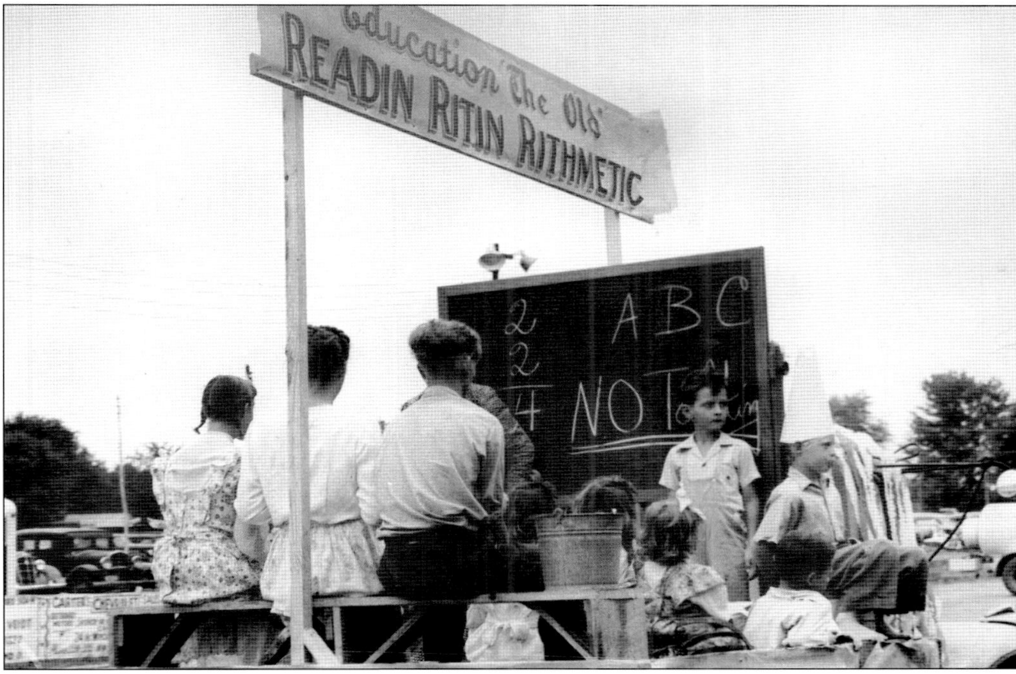

Passing a school levy in 1947 was of utmost importance to Williamsburg. Students, teachers, and parents took to the streets to show their support and convince voters to vote "yes" for the levy. (Photograph courtesy of Tim and Windy Ferree.)

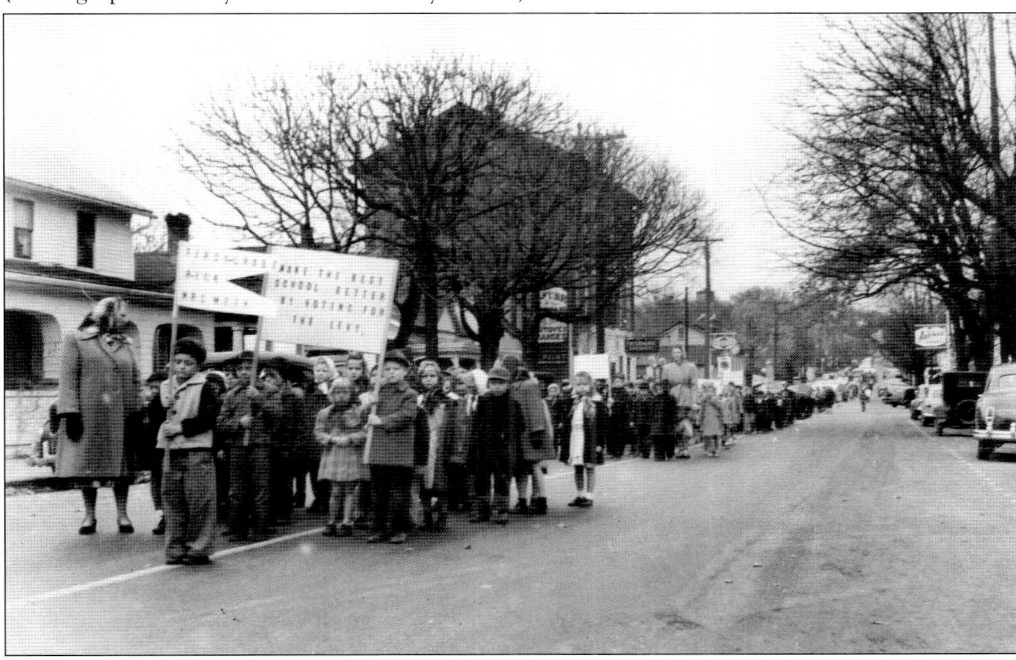

The Williamsburg School Board gathered support for passage of levies by staging parades and making door-to-door visits. In this photograph, teacher Mrs. Meek lined up her first grade students on Main Street to march in support of a 1940s school levy. (Photo courtesy of Tim and Windy Ferree)

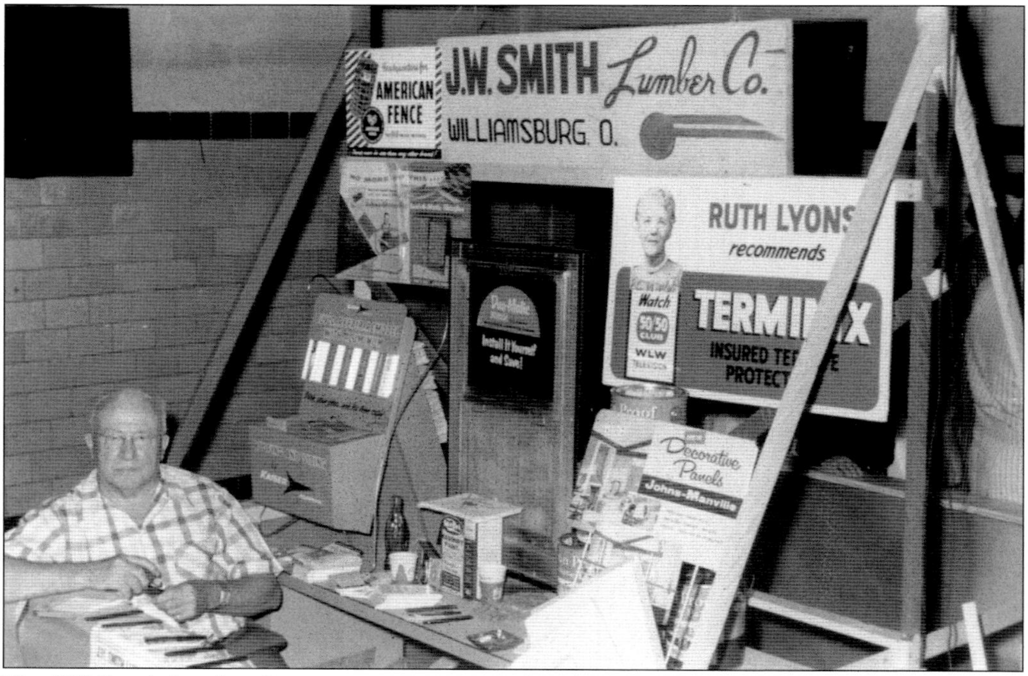

The J.W. Smith Lumber Company was represented at this booth at the Williamsburg High School career fair. (Photograph courtesy of Tim and Windy Ferree.)

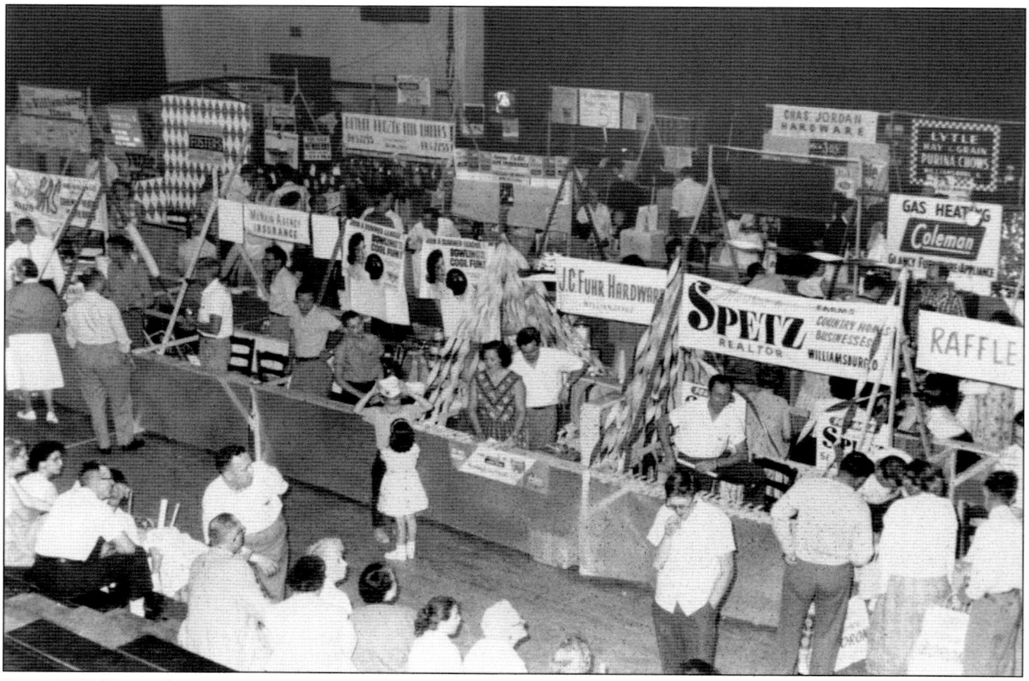

Local Williamsburg companies, such as the J.C. Fuhr Hardware Store, Lytle Hay and Grain, and Charles Jordan Hardware, set up booths to promote their business and job opportunities at the high school's career fair. (Photograph courtesy of Tim and Windy Ferree.)

Ten

GETTING AROUND TOWN

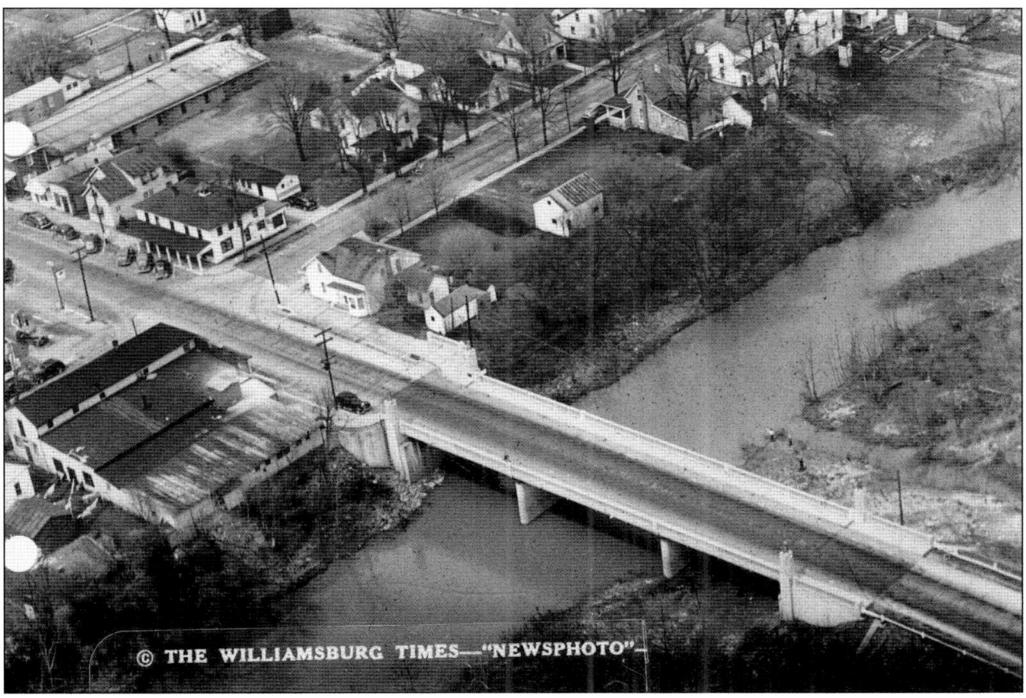

According to the May 8, 1936, bridge dedication issue of the *Williamsburg Times*, the new bridge shown in this 1947 aerial photograph contained over 120,000 pounds of reinforced steel bars, 200,000 pounds of structural steel, 12,000 sacks of cement, 2,500 tons of gravel, and 1,600 tons of sand. In order to construct the detour bridge and build the new one, 200 working days were required. John Hill of Ada, Ohio, was awarded the construction contract. Approximately 70 laborers were involved in the $64,972 project. (Photograph courtesy of Tim and Windy Ferree.)

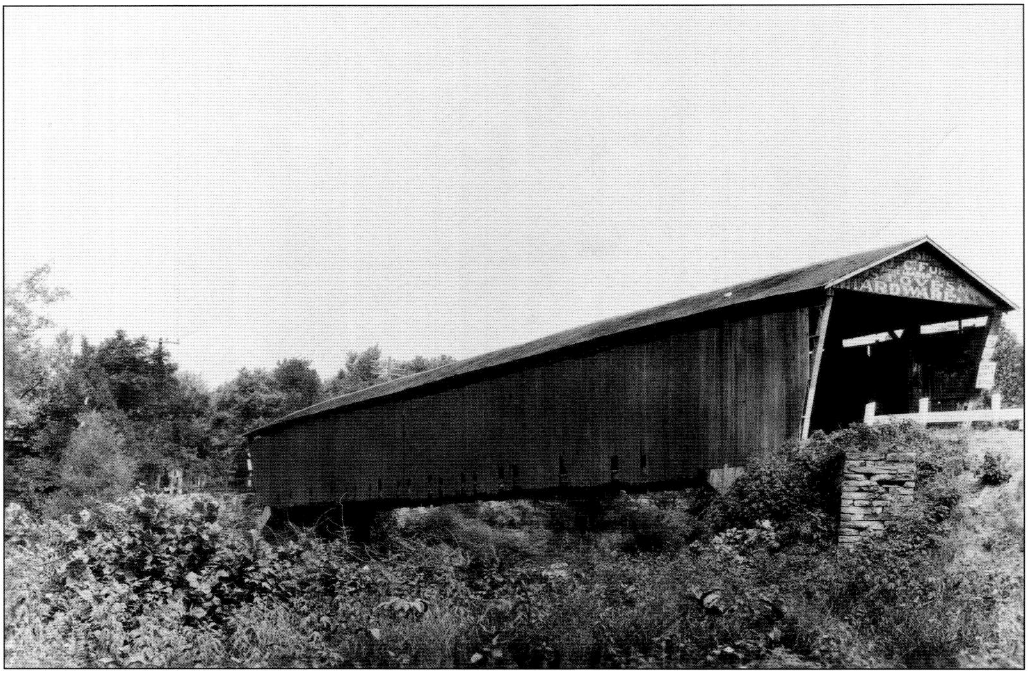

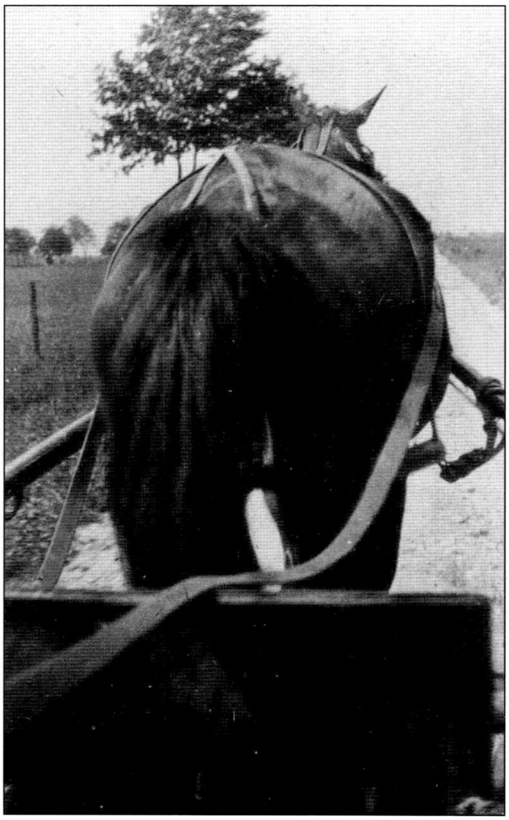

Williamsburg's beloved covered bridge crossing the East Fork of the Little Miami River was built from 1863 to 1864 and designed by George Felter, Peter Snell, and Isaac McAdams. It replaced a previous wood bridge that was burned by Confederate general John Morgan on his way out of Williamsburg on July 15, 1862. (Photograph courtesy of Tim and Windy Ferree.)

Folks in small towns like Batavia and Williamsburg walked nearly everywhere, except when the distance proved too great. Then, the buggy or wagon was hitched up to the family horse, as this view shows. (Photograph courtesy of Tim and Windy Ferree.)

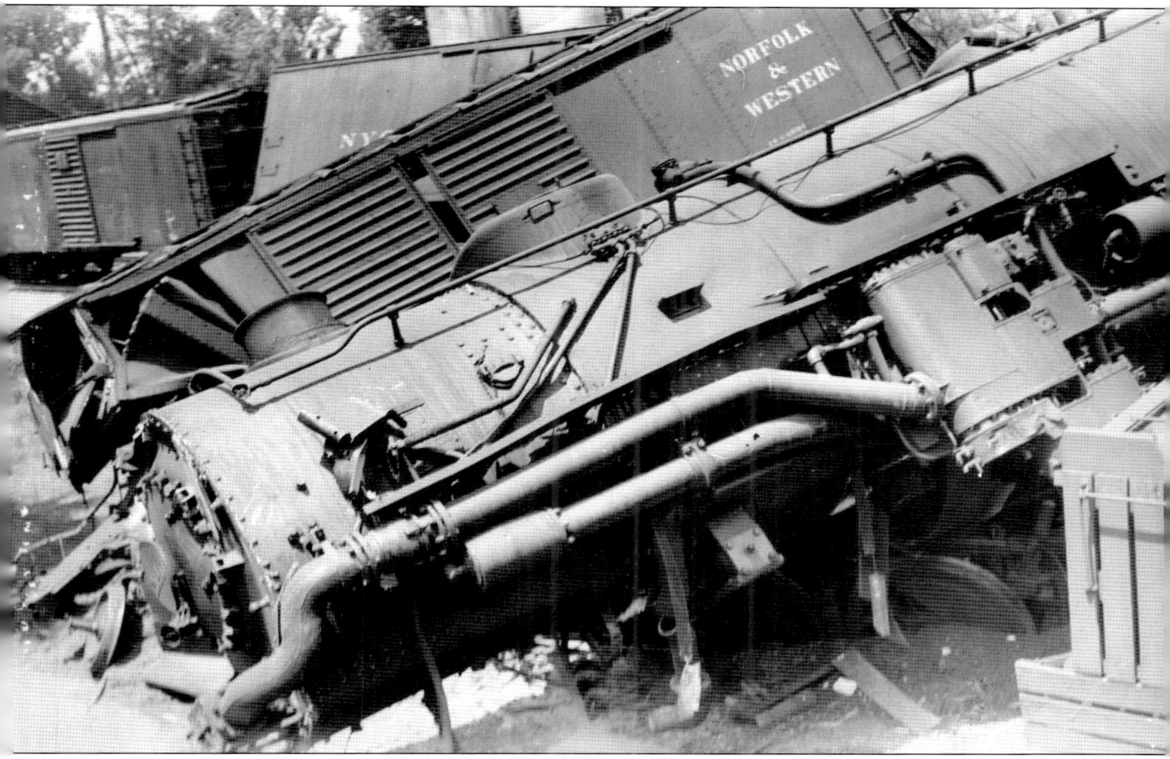

Train accidents happened all too frequently in the early days of rail travel. On October 17, 1884, the railroad bridge over the East Fork of the Little Miami River at Batavia gave way under a Norfolk & Western passenger train. The locomotive and cars fell into the river, killing the engineer and fireman and seriously injuring several passengers. One car remained precariously balanced on the edge of the bridge with 30 passengers inside. They all survived. This photograph taken in the 1920s shows another accident of a Norfolk & Western engine after it derailed near Second Street in Williamsburg. (Photograph courtesy of Tim and Windy Ferree.)

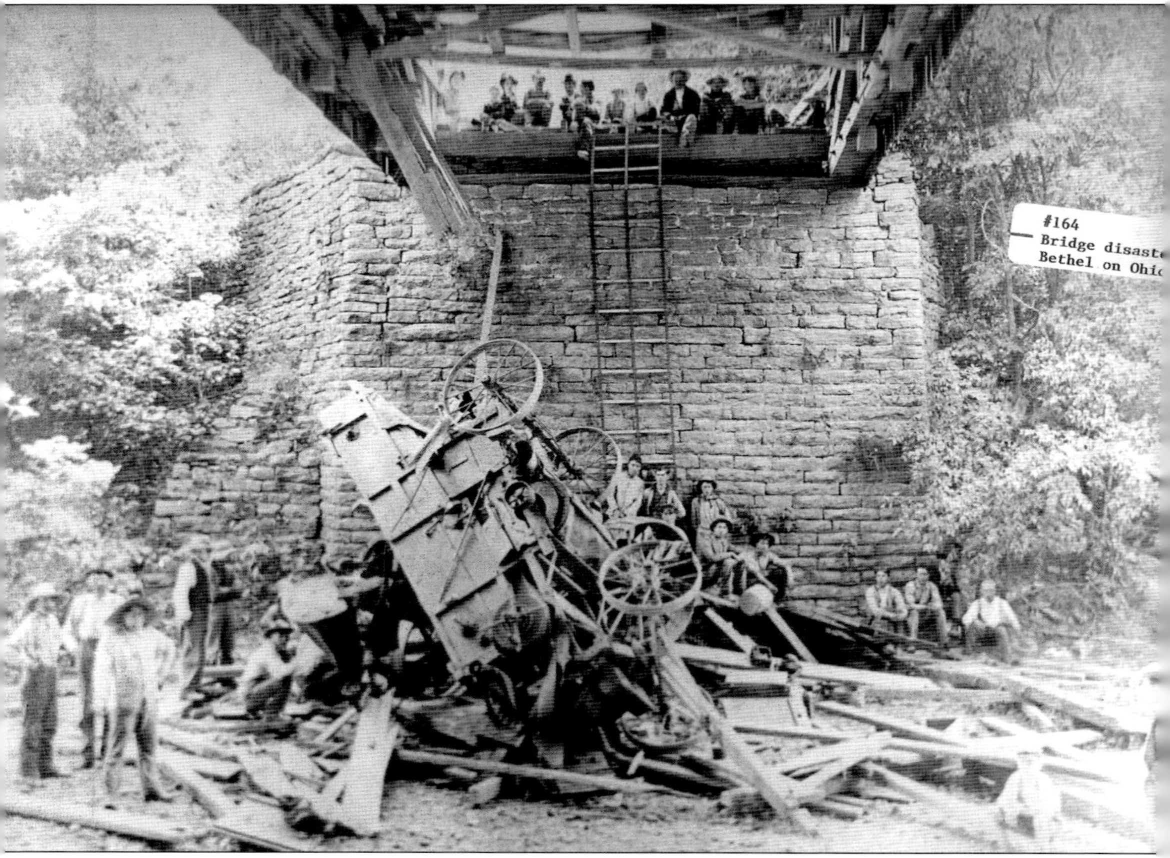

Up until the 1880s, most roads in Clermont County were made of dirt, making transportation very poor. Bridges and overpasses were notorious for causing serious accidents due to poor upkeep and wagons carrying loads too heavy for the wood supports. This was a serious bridge collapse near Batavia. (Photograph from the Sharpe Collection, courtesy of the Clermont County Library.)

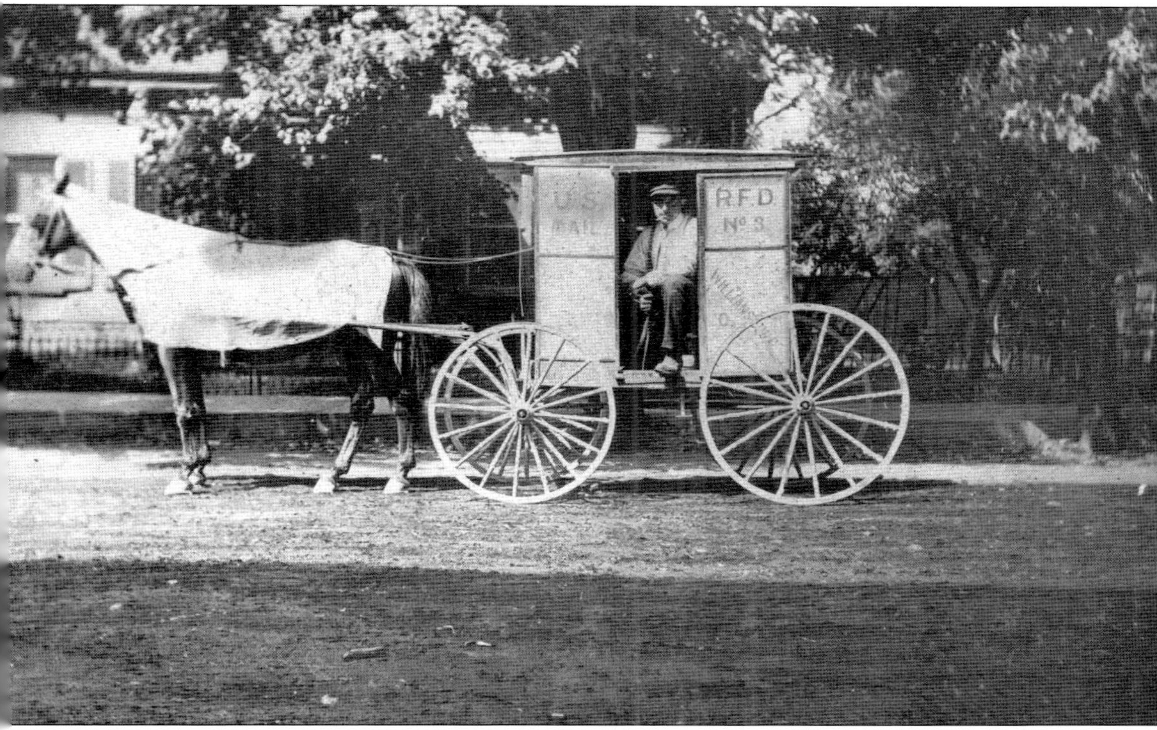

Williamsburg residents received their mail via an RFD mail carrier, like the one in this photograph, or they had to make daily trips to the Williamsburg post office. Early rural mail carriers rode horseback, walked, or used two and four-wheeled wagons. RFD began in 1896 when five mail carriers in Jefferson County, West Virginia, set out on their rounds on horseback. That was the first rural free delivery in US history. It wasn't until 1963 when council member Ralph Fuhr and postmaster Marvin Sprague developed a system in Williamsburg that allowed mail to be delivered to specifically numbered buildings. (Photograph courtesy of Tim and Windy Ferree.)

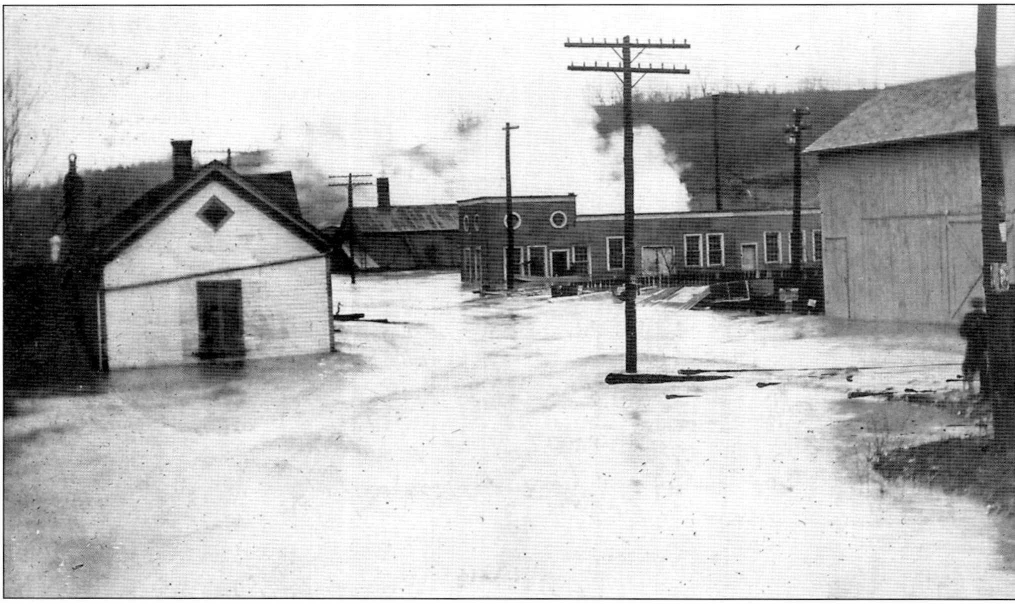

The March 1907 flood of the East Fork of the Little Miami River was devastating to Batavia. This view shows West Main Street and Davis Pike. Thanks to the 1970s East Fork dam project, there are no more devastating floods. (Photograph courtesy of Steve Shinkle.)

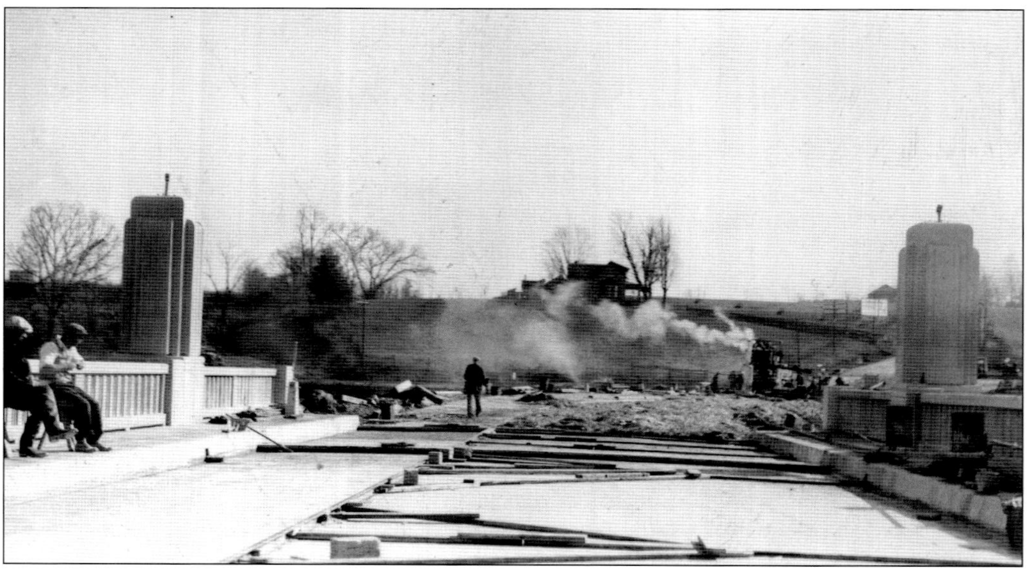

This postcard image shows the bridge spanning the East Fork of the Little Miami River at the entrance to Main Street in Batavia. (Photograph courtesy of Steve Shinkle.)

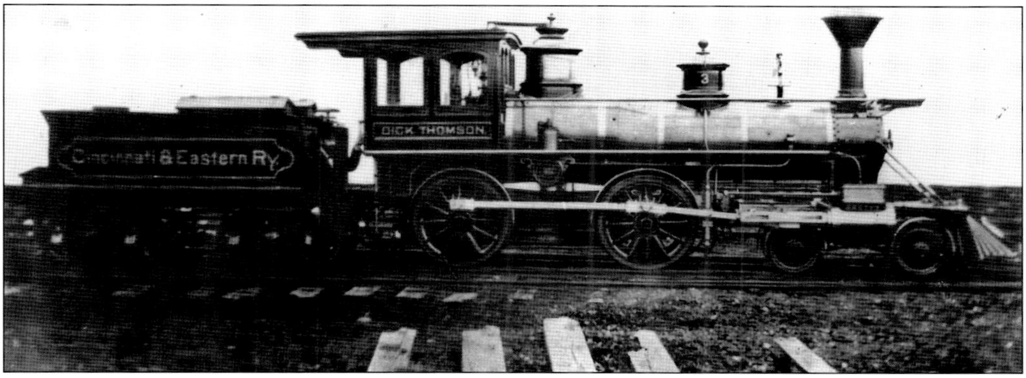

This 1877 photograph of the Cincinnati & Eastern (C&E) train "Dick Thomson" was taken by William Bissinger of Meadside, New York. This was the first passenger train to reach Batavia on the C&E Railroad. The train ran from Batavia to Winchester and then returned. It was named after Dick Thompson, who ran a general store in Winchester. Thompson and Milton Jamieson, a banker in Batavia, had each invested $15,000. The locomotive burned wood or coal. (Photograph courtesy of Steve Shinkle.)

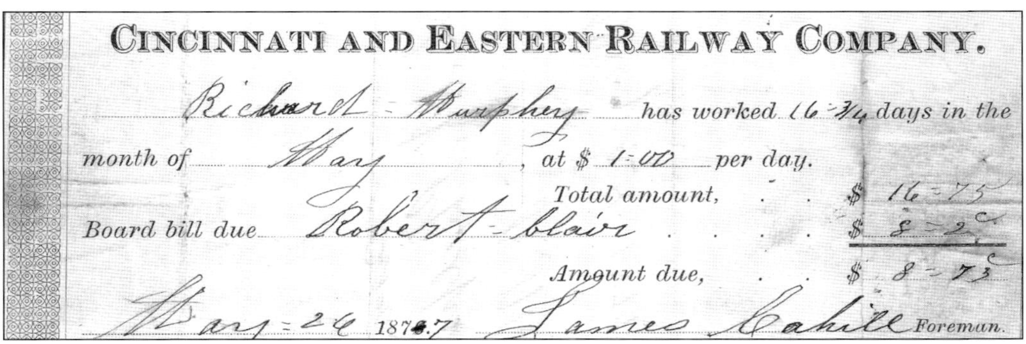

CINCINNATI AND EASTERN RAILWAY COMPANY.

Richard Murphey has worked 16 3/4 days in the month of May, at $ 1.00 per day.

Total amount, . . $ 16.75

Board bill due Robert Blair . . . $ 8.02

Amount due, . . $ 8.73

May 26 1877 James Cahill Foreman.

In 1877, Cincinnati & Eastern Railroad employee Richard Murphy worked for $1 a day. Board payment of $8.02 reduced his $16.75 earnings to $8.73 for 16-and-three-quarter days of labor. (Photograph courtesy of Steve Shinkle.)

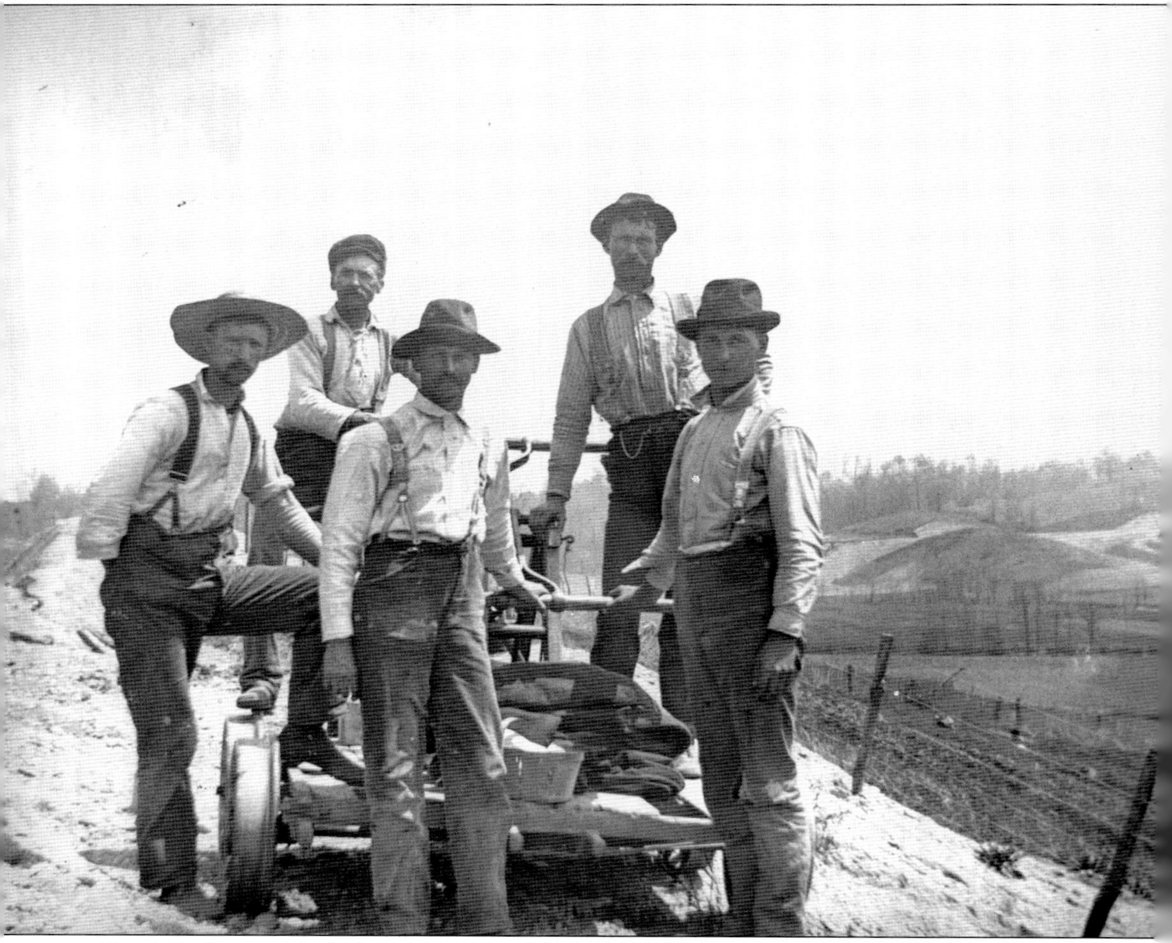

Workers for the Norfolk and Western (N&W) Railroad pause during their construction work. The N&W was a major carrier in the West Virginia coalfields. (Photograph from the Sharp Collection, courtesy of the Clermont County Library.)

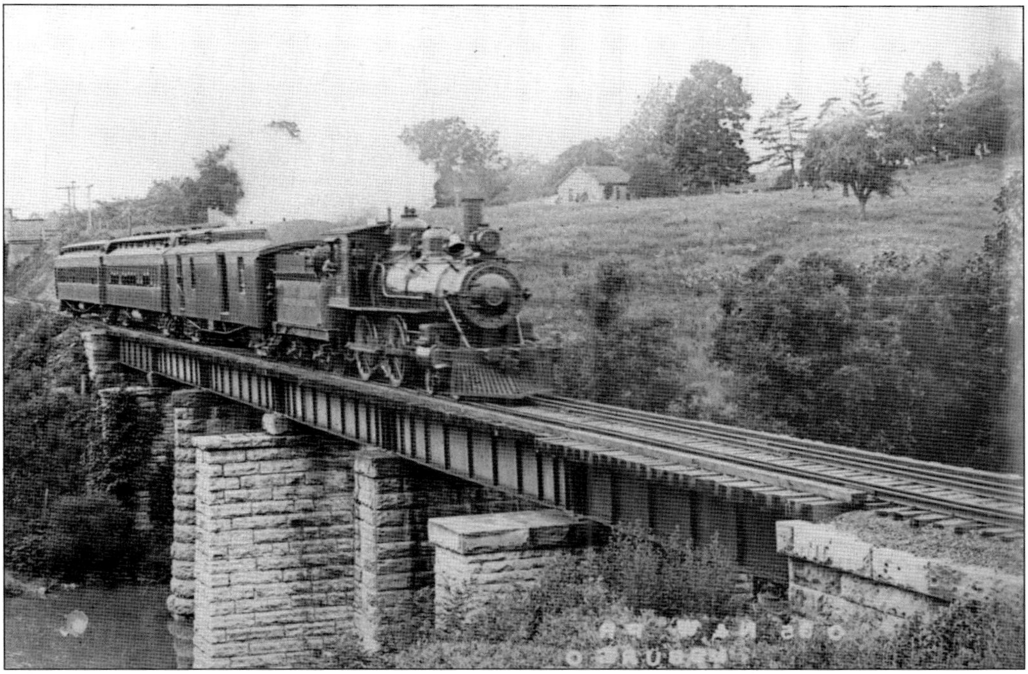

This 1912 photograph shows the Norfolk and Western train coming into Williamsburg at the De La Palma Road overpass. (Photograph from the Sharp Collection, courtesy of the Clermont County Library.)

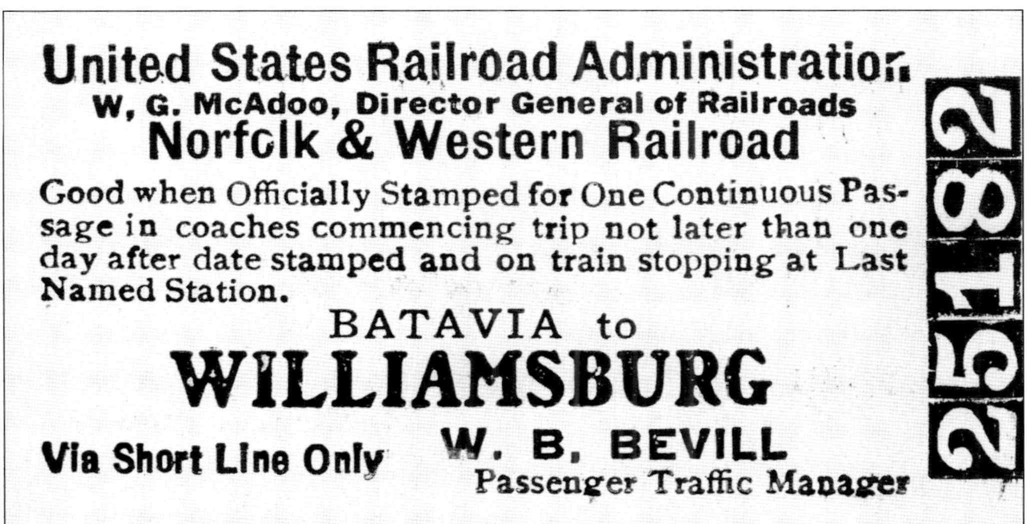

United States Railroad Administration
W, G. McAdoo, Director General of Railroads
Norfolk & Western Railroad
Good when Officially Stamped for One Continuous Passage in coaches commencing trip not later than one day after date stamped and on train stopping at Last Named Station.
BATAVIA to
WILLIAMSBURG
Via Short Line Only
W. B. BEVILL
Passenger Traffic Manager
25182

In 1919, coach fare tickets on the Norfolk & Western train were good for one continuous passage from Batavia to Williamsburg. (Photograph courtesy of Hazel Arnold.)

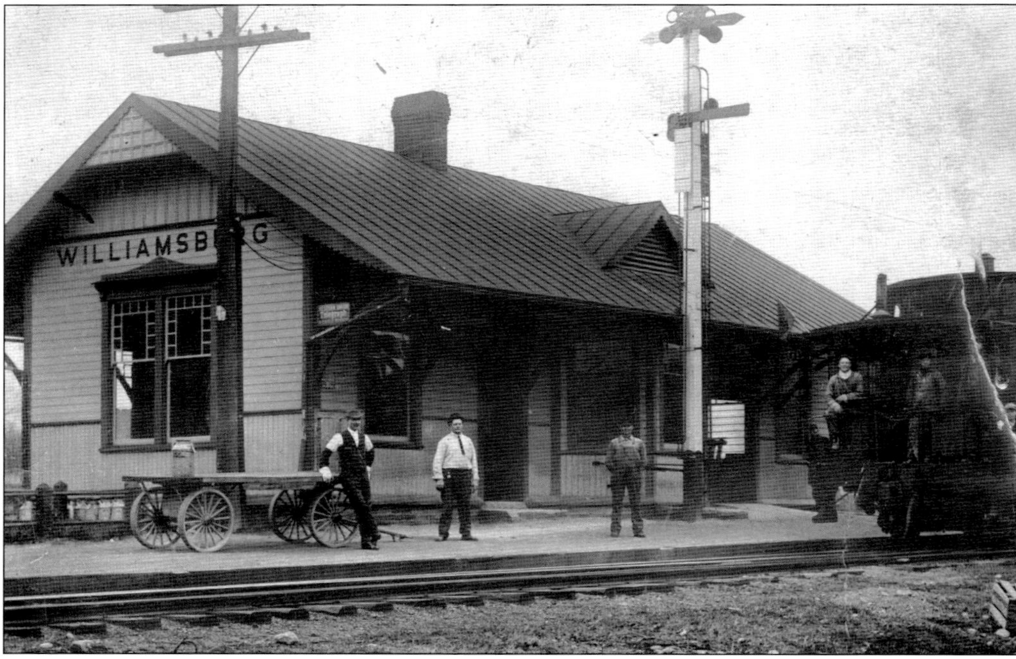

The Williamsburg train depot stood at the edge of town, as seen in this c. 1920 photograph. (Photograph courtesy of Hazel Arnold.)

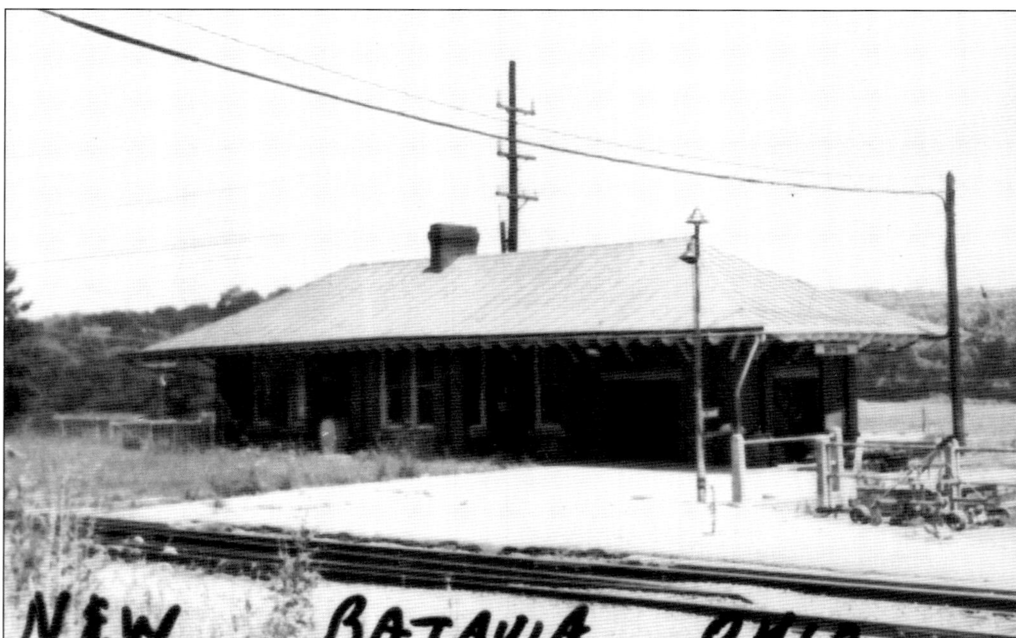

The last passenger train stopped at the Batavia depot in 1944. The depot, built in 1898, was torn down in 1989. (Photograph courtesy of Steve Shinkle.)

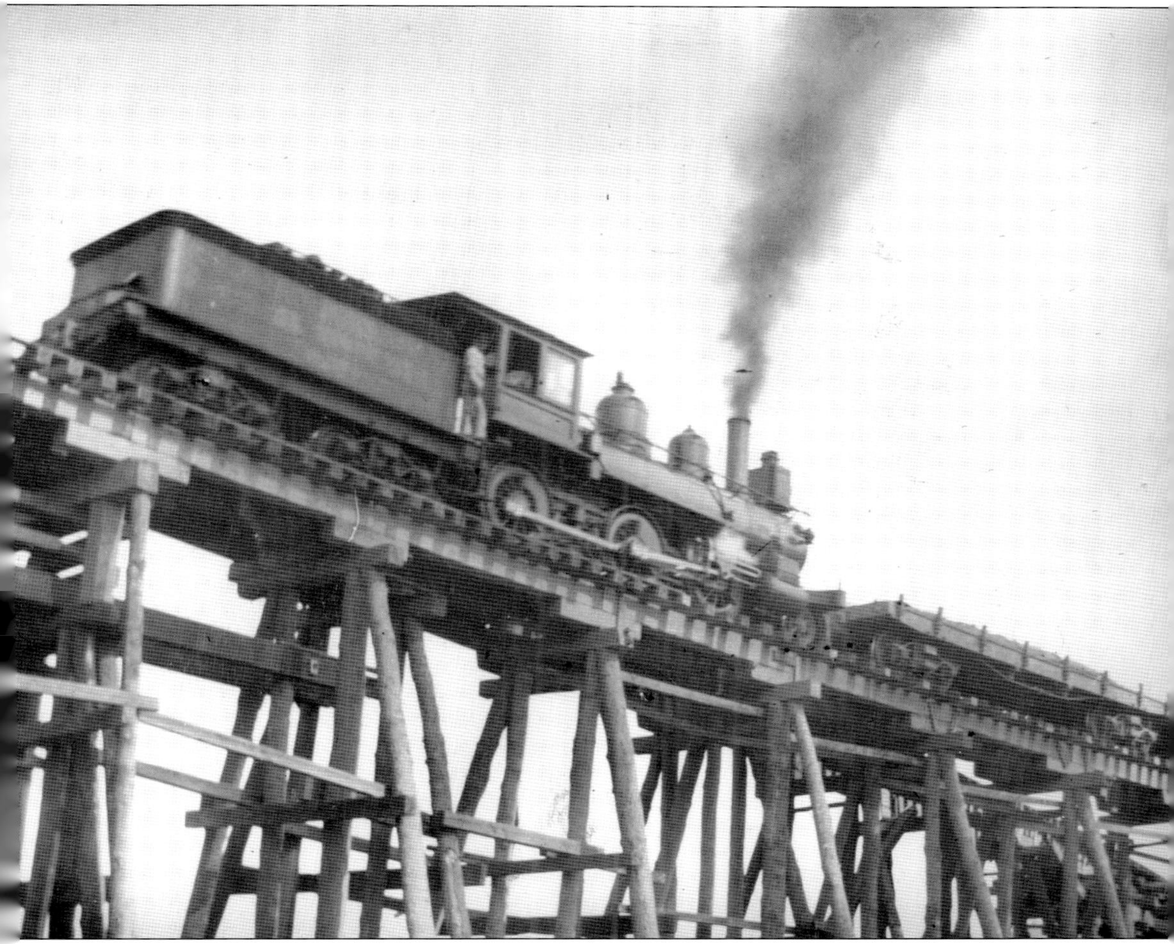

The narrow gauge track followed the East Fork of the Little Miami River and had to climb the hill out of Batavia. This steep grade and the curve of the track caused problems for years. C.P. Tracy, a railroad employee, said, "The Batavia hill had the worst grade and alignment of any section of the entire railroad, and stock cars loaded with tan bark had turned over on every rail length on the hill." The locomotives of the time couldn't pull more than six loaded cars up the hill at once. (Photograph from the Sharp Collection, courtesy of the Clermont County Library.)

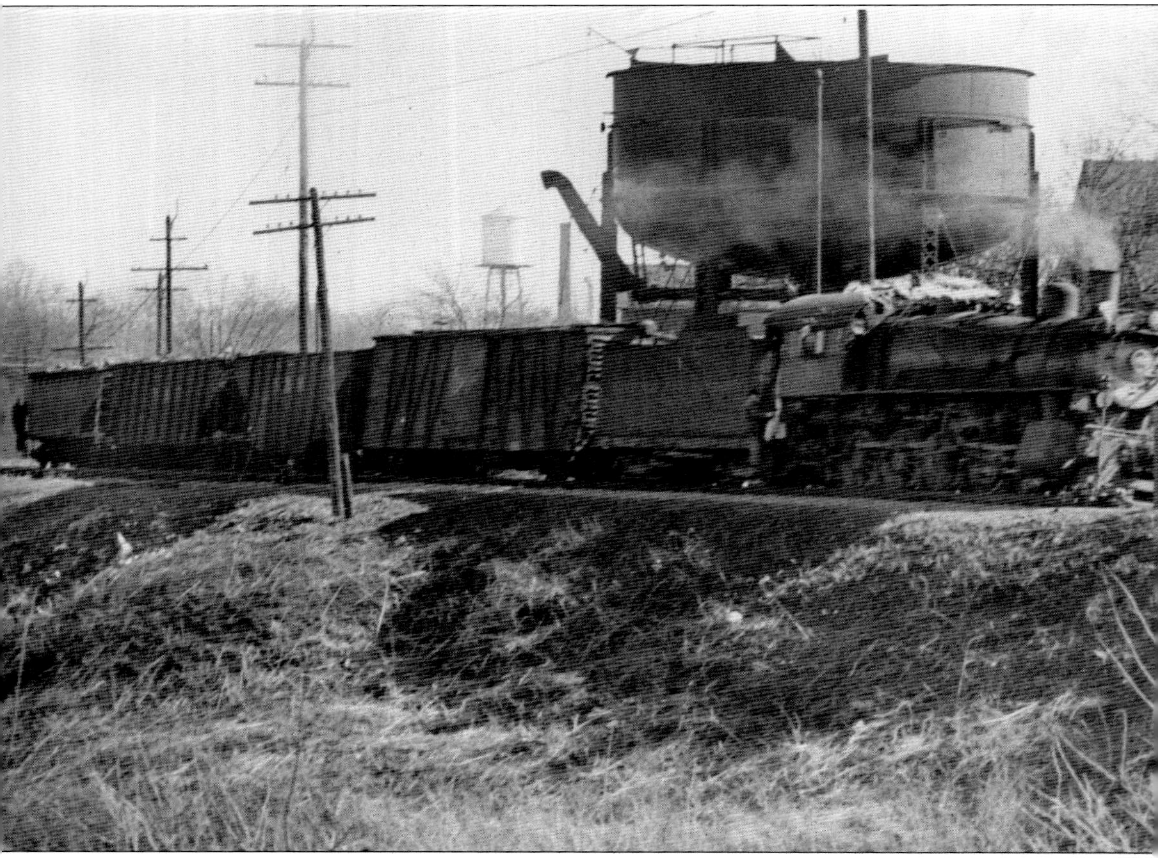

The Cincinnati, Georgetown, and Portsmouth Railroad (CG&P) operated in Batavia Township from 1876 to 1936. The CG&P constructed a 10-acre lake near Olive Branch to provide cooling water for the power plant, which provided electricity for the railroad and towns along the railroad right of way. (Photograph courtesy of Hazel Arnold.)

Eleven

Town Services

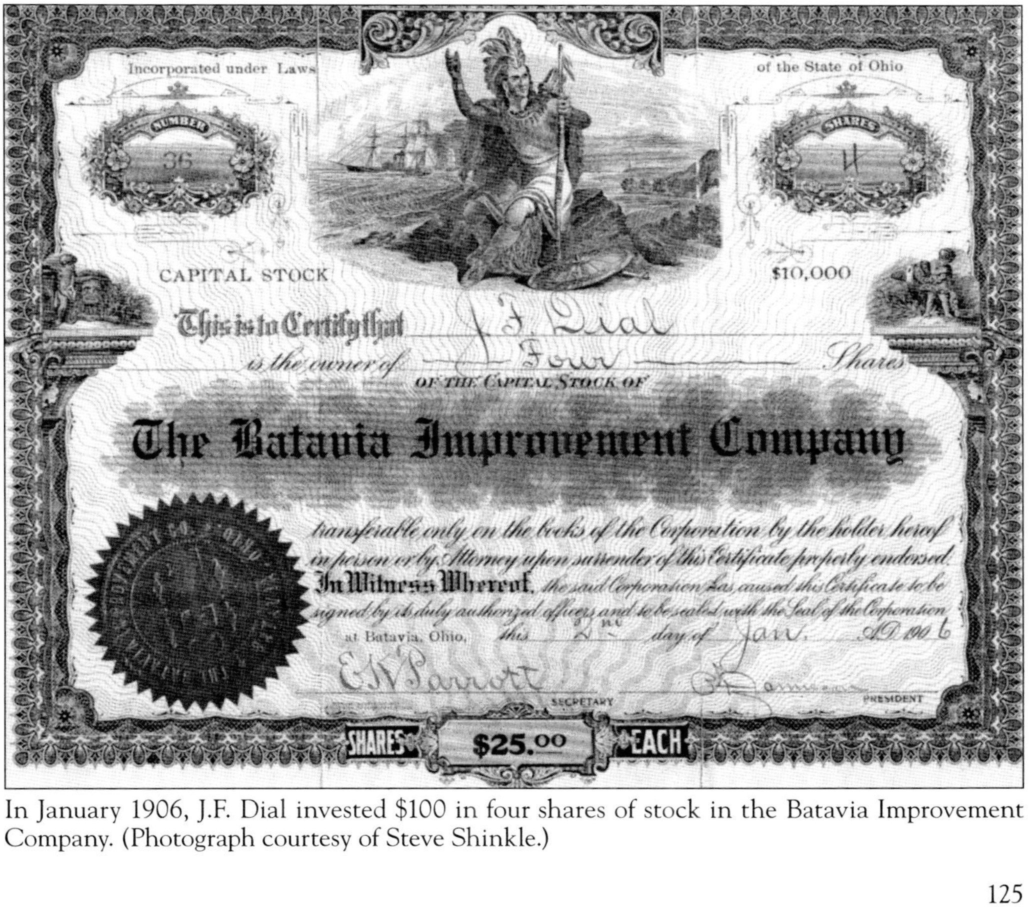

In January 1906, J.F. Dial invested $100 in four shares of stock in the Batavia Improvement Company. (Photograph courtesy of Steve Shinkle.)

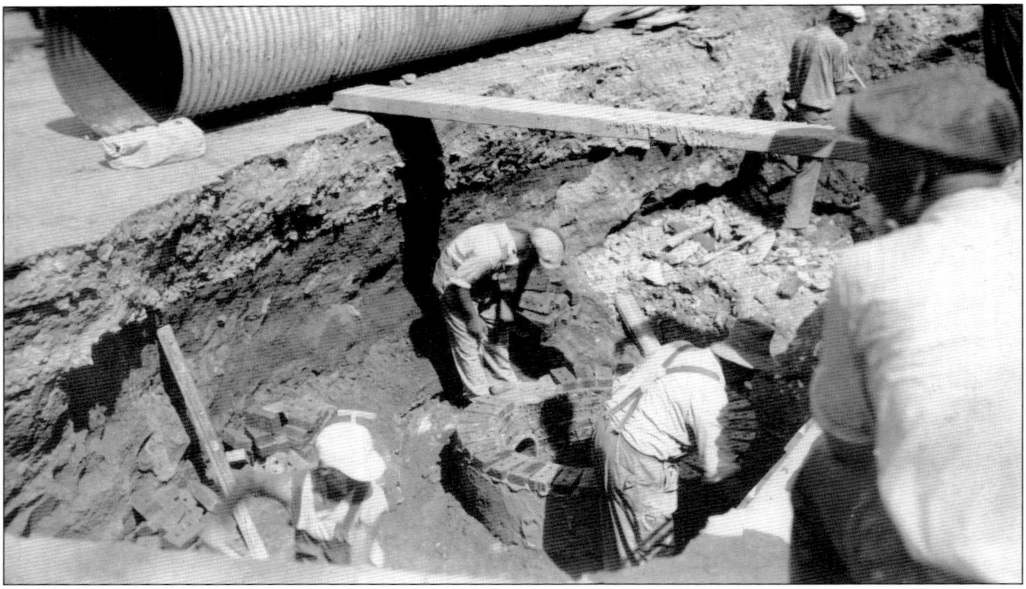

These are views of Williamsburg's Main Street in the early 1920s when the town installed water lines. (Both photographs courtesy of Tim and Windy Ferree.)

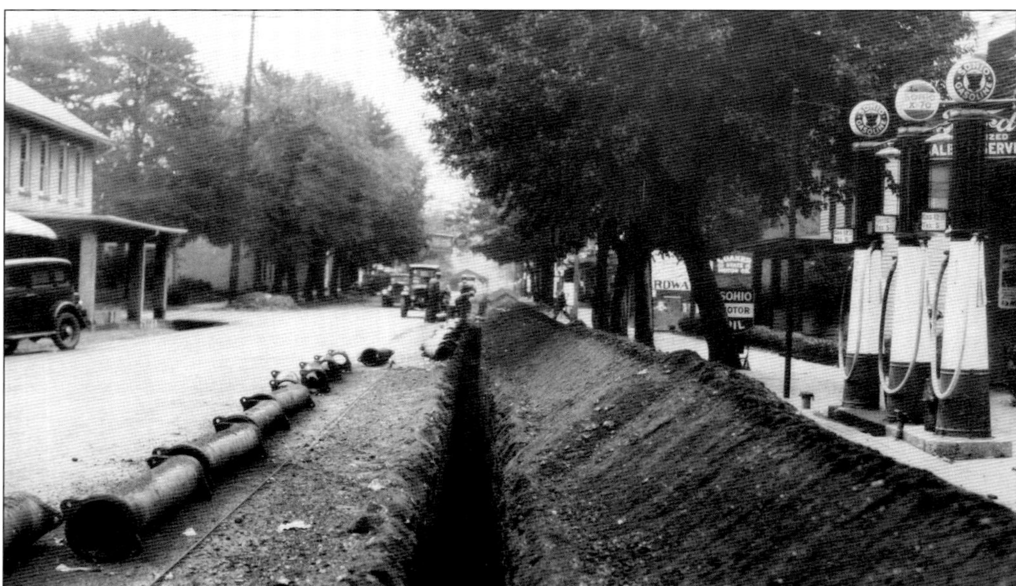

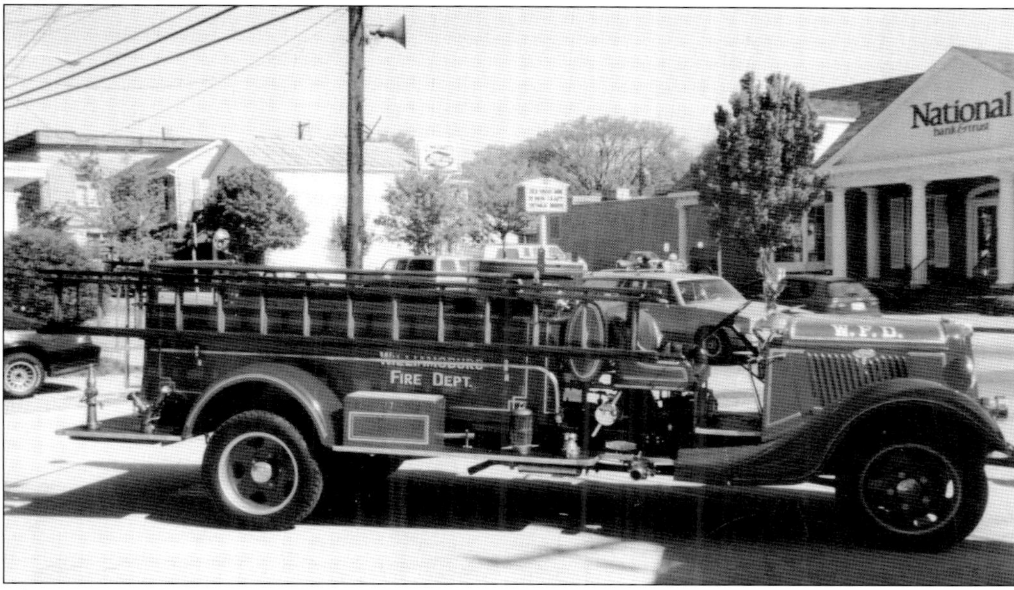

This 1935 Ford Seagrave fire truck served as the Williamsburg Fire Department's first pumper and was able to pump 500 gallons per minute. Though no longer in use, it is maintained by the department and kept at the fire station.

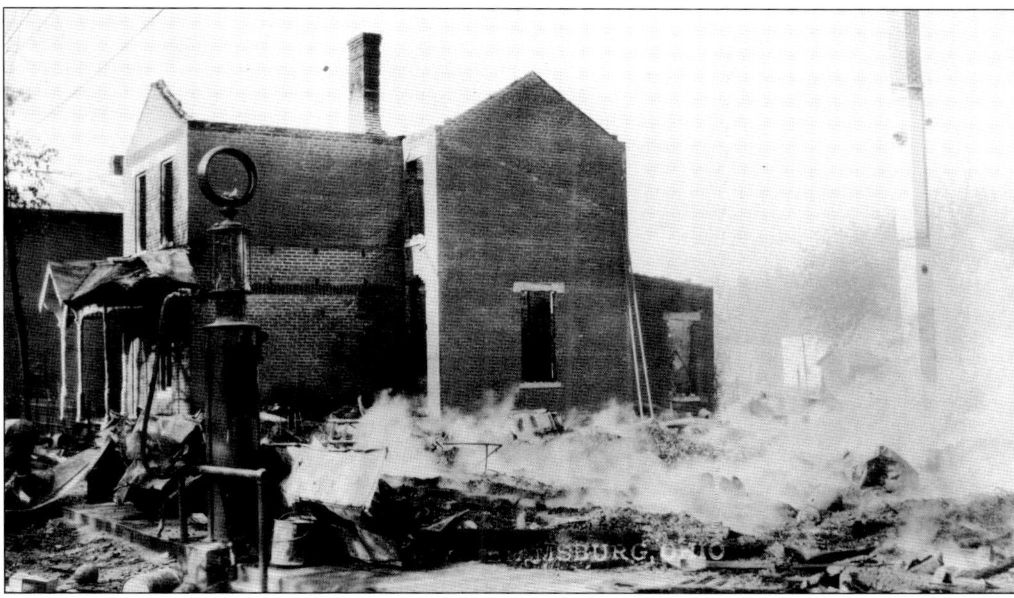

This photograph shows the aftermath of the Stamm's Garage fire. Before 1935, a "bucket law" was in effect that required men, women, and children to grab their buckets day or night and form a bucket brigade as soon as the fire alarm sounded. In 1935, the Village Council established the Williamsburg Fire Department. The department's first firemen were Chief Harry Stamm, Ernest Weeks, Charles Carpenter, Harold Chatterton, Julius Knauer, Charles Workman, Edwin Wise, William Hauck, Harley Kidd, William McManis, Clyde Wood, Victor Cowdrey and Nolan Adams. The department was enlarged and moved several times. It is presently located on North Main Street. (Photograph courtesy of the Williamsburg Fire Department.)